# JAGUAR

# JAGUAR

## AN ILLUSTRATED HISTORY

*Patrick Mennem*

The Crowood Press

First published in 1991 by
The Crowood Press Ltd
Ramsbury, Marlborough
Wiltshire SN8 2HR



British Library Cataloguing in Publication Data

Mennem, Patrick
Jaguar.
1. Cars. History
I. Title
629.2222

ISBN 85223 510 1

**Picture Credits**
The photographs in this book are reproduced courtesy of Jaguar Cars and The Motoring Picture Library, Beaulieu.

**Dedication**
I should like to dedicate this book to my wife Anne
and my three sons and daughter.

Typeset by Keyboard Services, Luton, Bedfordshire
Printed and bound in Great Britain by
BPCC Hazell Books, Aylesbury

# Contents

# Acknowledgements

The number of people from Jaguar, and the motor industry in general, who have helped me either directly or indirectly to produce this book, are too numerous to mention. In the forty years that I have been associated with the industry, and motor sport, conversations and observations from a hundred and one different people have helped.

But some must be specially mentioned for their unstinting and generous help, giving me their time when beseiged by other more pressing matters. In this regard, Sir John Egan, chief executive of BAA, and Bill Hayden, chairman and chief executive of Jaguar Cars, were exceptionally helpful, and I am greatly indebted to them.

David Boole, director of Communications and Public Affairs at Jaguar Cars is an old friend, and gave me hours of his time; Colin Cook, a manager on his staff, made everything on the history of the company available to me, and Roger Clinkscales and his assistant in Jaguar's photographic department were consistently helpful and patient.

Walter Hassan, and the late Harry Munday, were great sources of information over the years, but Walter put up with me on several visits to Warwickshire, and even wrote in great detail and in long hand historical pieces on the company and their engines. A truly magnificent effort for which I am eternally grateful.

R.E. (Bob) Berry, whom I have known since the 1950s, and who first demonstrated to me how a Jaguar could go, took great pains to share all the considerable knowledge he has on the company and its products. Robert Knight, formerly managing director of Jaguar Cars, was most helpful and informative.

There are many others such as Roger Putnam, director of sales and marketing, Jim Randle, director of vehicle and concept engineering, Keith Hopkins, who was managing director of Austin Morris in the BL days, and the staff of the Society of Motor Manufacturers and Traders.

Several have departed, and I shall have to wait to thank them personally.

# Foreword

It is difficult for me to read Pat Mennem's book without experiencing immense nostalgia and withdrawal symptoms from my job at Jaguar, which became an obsession for over ten years.

In his book Pat portrays the rich mosaic of Jaguar with its sense of family and history, its shoestring budgets, and its brilliance and ability to excite with beautiful cars and a rich racing pedigree.

When I first felt the pulse of Jaguar, I realized it had to be one of the best companies in the world or it could not exist at all; there was no place for mediocrity. Others could make cars to 'satisfy the accountant': Jaguar had to be a company that made cars that would excite its followers. Nothing less would do!

The enthusiasm that followed Jaguar's revival in the 1980s was felt all over the world – strong men wept in Australia when we won the great Bathhurst sports car race; in California, dealers fought over the franchise and divorced couples fought over which one would get the rare Sebring Red XJS; shareholders oversubscribed the privatization issue eight times over and sales in France doubled after we won Le Mans. However, Jaguar's heyday was in the 1950s, when Britain's car industry was world class and a specialist car company could hang on to the coat tails of the mighty volume car companies and their suppliers. But, by 1980, Britain's car industry had been eclipsed by many others, and my time at Jaguar was correctly described as a 'high-wire act', using our engineering inventiveness and marketing flair to balance out an uncompetitive industry base and uncompetitive inflation rates. Our formidable competitors in Germany and Japan could compete on terra firma.

Pat Mennem is a car industry 'groupie' and was an integral part of the Jaguar contingent that used to descend on Le Mans every year; he was unfailingly courteous, helpful and knowledgeable after attending all the previous Le Mans races for thirty years, but above all he was always optimistic. His book reflects this characteristic, as well as being a fine personal view of Jaguar's history.

I passed on the baton to Ford Motor Company, a world class company with immense technical resources; apparently, some of their executives have been dismayed by the size of the task that lies ahead of them. I can only say that if they try hard and learn to love Jaguar a little, as I did, I am sure that they can add lustre to the marque and bring as much reward to their shareholders and customers as we did in the 1980s.

Sir John Egan,
23 April 1991

## CHRONOLOGY OF THE JAGUAR COMPANY

| | | |
|---|---|---|
| **1901** | September | William Lyons, born Blackpool. |
| **1922** | September | Swallow Sidecar Company formed in Blackpool. |
| **1924** | September | William Lyons married Greta Brown in Blackpool. |
| **1927** | | First Austin Seven Swallow Produced. Swallow Sidecar and Coachbuilding Company formed. |
| **1928** | November | Move to Foleshill in Coventry. |
| **1931** | October | First SS1 car produced at £310. |
| **1935** | January | SS Cars Ltd becomes a public company. |
| | September | SS Jaguar saloon introduced at £385. |
| **1937** | September | SS Jaguar 100 3½-litre, first 100mph (161kph) Jaguar car. |
| **1938** | | Leaping Jaguar emblem appears for first time. |
| | September | SS Jaguar 100 fixed-head coupe produced, but never reached production. |
| **1939** | | 5000 cars produced for first time. |
| **1945** | September | SS name dropped. |
| **1948** | September | XK120 Super Sports announced with 3½-litre twin cam XK engine. |
| **1949** | June | Slightly modified XK120 reaches 132.5mph (213kph) at Jabbeke in Belgium. |
| | August | Jaguar XK120s come first and second at Silverstone. |
| **1950** | July | Ian Appleyard in XK120 wins Coupes des Alpes in Alpine Trial. |
| | September | First post war Tourist Trophy race won by twenty-years-old Stirling Moss in XK120. |
| **1951** | June | Peter Whitehead and Peter Walker win Le Mans 24-Hour Race in C-type Jaguar. |
| | September | Jaguar Mk VII introduced. |
| **1952** | | Move to Browns Lane factory. |
| **1953** | June | A.P.R. Rolt and Duncan Hamilton win Le Mans in C-type at over 100mph (161kph) average. |
| **1955** | January | Ronnie Adams wins Monte Carlo Rally in Jaguar Mk VII. |
| | June | Jaguar D-type wins Le Mans in year of disaster. |
| | September | Jaguar 2.4-litre compact car launched. First integral-bodied Jaguar. |
| **1956** | January | William Lyons knighted in New Year's Honours. |
| **1957** | February | Fire devastates Jaguar plant at Browns Lane. |
| | June | Jaguars 1st, 2nd, 3rd and 4th at Le Mans 24-Hour Race. |
| **1959** | October | Jaguar Mk II with either 2.4-litre, 3.4-litre or 3.8-litre engines. |
| **1960** | June | Jaguar buy Daimler. |
| **1961** | March | E-type launched at £2,097. |
| **1962** | September | Jaguar Mk X launched. |
| **1966** | July | British Motor Corporation–Jaguar merger. |
| **1967** | | Twin-cam version of V12 engine in XJ13 laps at 161.6mph (260kph) at MIRA test track. |
| **1969** | June | Jaguar XJ6 announced. |
| **1971** | April | 5.3-litre V12 engine introduced to E-type. |
| **1972** | July | XJ12 announced. |
| | September | Jaguar's jubilee celebrations. Sir William Lyons retires aged seventy-one. |
| | October | Jaguar Cars Ltd cease to exist as separate company. Part of British Leyland. |
| **1975** | September | XJS launched at Longbridge, Birmingham. |
| **1976** | March | Ill-fated competition debut of V12 coupes. |
| **1979** | September | Series III XJ6, coincides with paint shop troubles. |
| **1980** | April | John Egan joins Jaguar, aged forty. |
| **1983** | October | New AJ6 3.6-litre engine announced. New XJSC 3.6-litre also announced. Jaguar return to profit. |
| **1984** | August | Jaguar is privatized. |
| **1985** | February | Sir William Lyons dies aged eighty-three. |
| **1986** | January | John Egan knighted. |
| | October | Launch of the new XJ6, 3.6-litre. |
| **1988** | March | New XJS V12 convertible announced. |
| | June | Jaguar win Le Mans after thirty-one years. |
| | May | New engineering centre opened at Whitley. |
| | August | JaguarSport formed, with Tom Walkinshaw as managing director. |

| | | |
|---|---|---|
| **1989** | September | Jaguar 4-litre announced. |
| | November | Ford buy Jaguar for £1.6 billion. |
| **1990** | June | Jaguar win again at Le Mans. Sir John Egan retires. Bill Hayden becomes new chairman and chief executive. |
| | September | Jaguar 2.9-litre dropped and replaced by 24-valve 3.2-litre catalyst engine. Sports pack also offered on all models. |
| **1991** | April | Face-lifted XJS announced. |

# Introduction

In an industry where there is only room for giants it was inevitable that Jaguar would eventually have to surrender its independence. However, it fought more tenaciously and successfully than any other manufacturer, which is entirely in keeping with its history.

The name Jaguar is one of the twenty most recognizable names in the world. It conjures an image of silent power and graceful luxury that is universally admired, and it is still synonymous with a fifty-year collection of motor sporting successes that are the envy of companies ten times its size.

Even before the recent explosion of takeovers and mergers Jaguar was never a big company, and in the 1950s when it was enjoying unbounded success in almost every field, it was still one of the smaller manufacturers in Coventry, let alone the country.

Yet it had a magic which few other motor manufacturers could even aspire to; a magic for producing quite exceptional cars at unbelievable prices, and the man who created the potion was an aloof, totally dedicated, autocratic Lancastrian called Sir William Lyons . . . not everyone's idea of a magician.

He gave the company an aura and a reputation that was quite beyond its size, and in doing so he was buttressed by one of the most talented and devoted teams in the motor industry. This book is about those people, the cars they produced, and the world in which they worked.

It tells of the dark days in the 1970s when Jaguar was on the edge of extinction, and how another Lancastrian, Sir John Egan, who had never run a motor manufacturing plant before, produced yet more magic to save the company.

The Ford Motor Company, the new owners, do not pretend to be magicians, but few know more about making motor cars efficiently. Former Ford man Bill Hayden, the chairman and chief executive of Jaguar Cars, a man of immense talent and experience, has harnessed the company to face the uphill trials of the coming decade, and in so doing has reintroduced many of the disciplines so dear to his predecessor Sir William, as well as quite a few of his own.

He is now a 'Jaguar man', determined to preserve the magic of his product, but at the same time make it the best and most efficiently-built motor car in the world. I think he will succeed.

# 1
# Sir William – The Boss

Throughout his years with Jaguar Cars Sir William Lyons only addressed one employee by his Christian name. Bill Heynes his long-serving chief engineer, and a director, was always 'Heynes'. Equally, Arthur Whittaker, who joined him at the age of seventeen, and became general manager and deputy chairman, was never called anything but 'Whittaker', even in the intimacy of their fire-watching duties at the Coventry factory.

Sir William Lyons, the man who was Jaguar, and a very formidable figure.

The sole exception to the rule was Fred Gardner, who accompanied Sir William from Blackpool, and was in charge of the wood mill. He was the man who made the wooden mock-ups of his boss's body designs. Sir William had the eye, Fred had the hands, and between the hands and the eye there was a unique relationship.

In the pre- and immediate post-war years of the motor industry it was almost a statutory obligation to be a larger than life character, and people such as the awesome Sir Patrick Hennessy of the Ford Motor Company, the tirelessly enthusiastic Lord 'Billy' Rootes of the Rootes Group, and the despotic Sir John Black of Standard Triumph, abounded.

Sir William was larger than life, but it was the intensity of purpose, canalized almost exclusively into Jaguar Cars, that made him so. He was a totally disciplined man who scorned any form of personal flamboyance, and was known to the public because of the success of his motor cars both in the market place and on the motor racing circuits, rather than through his proclamations or public performances.

With his silvery hair and immaculate appearance Sir William must have appeared to the outsider as a benign, uncle-like figure who could be relied upon to give sound advice. Certainly, if asked, he could give a sound opinion with great economy, but even his most fervent admirers, and there were many, would not have described him as benign.

## An Imperious Bearing

As a young reporter on the Coventry Evening Telegraph in the early 1950s I was sent to interview Mr Lyons, as he then was, on the state of the company, because the motor industry was going through turbu-

Sir William and Bill Heynes with the old and the new – an Austin Swallow and a Mk II, similar to the 3.4-litre version which won the Tulip Rally.

lent times. I arrived early having been warned of the disasters that would ensue if I were late, and was summoned to his office at 9.30 in the morning, exactly as arranged.

'Good morning Mennem, sit down'. He was seated erect behind his immaculate desk, dressed in a very dark suit, which contrasted enormously with his spotlessly clean white shirt. He fixed me with his light-coloured eyes, and sat very still. I was reminded of a sergeant major in the Grenadier Guards called Felton, who was so redolent with cleanliness he always appeared to have just been scrubbed with carbolic soap.

Sir William conveyed the same impression of cleanliness with a latent volcanic power as I sat feeling inadequate, and not a little apprehensive, fumbling with my notebook and pencil. I was perceptive enough to realize that this was not going to be easy.

After a moment of preliminary throat clearing I said 'What is your principle problem at the moment Mr Lyons?'

'Labour', he replied, and he continued to look at me steadily, waiting for the next question. I was new to Sir William and I was learning lesson one to great effect; never try to play things off the cuff. It was not one of my most memorable interviews, but I had only myself to blame; I should have learned more about the vagaries of Sir William, and have arrived better prepared.

He made no concessions, and expected a thoroughly professional job from everyone. Blundering about in what appeared an icy, inky void I was getting nowhere, and by mutual consent the interview came to an early end. He must have thought I was a complete fool, but his manner was impassive, and his farewell as curt as his greeting. He had shown not a glimmer of warmth, and had not moved a fraction of an inch to help, but I left the Browns Lane factory cursing, not Sir William, but my own incompetence.

I knew I had been talking to a man of stature; a true leader, and like a boy before his headmaster I wanted to demonstrate that I could do better. He had that effect on far more able people than me.

## A Charismatic Man

Sir William never used two words when one would do, and he firmly believed in that old adage that if you looked after the pennies the pounds would look after themselves.

According to Bob Berry, whose father knew Sir William as a fellow motor cyclist in their Blackpool days, and who worked for Sir William as his public relations manager for many years, he was not a 'cold fish', but equally he showed no personal warmth.

'It is very difficult to explain, yet Sir William, and one would never dream of calling him anything else, was the most charismatic man I have ever worked for'. He was a hard taskmaster who knew exactly what he wanted yet, apart from a brief spell with Crossley in his youth, he had no engineering background, and no training in design.

He was, however, extremely adept at picking the right people, and then motivating them. On the face of it Jaguar was not an ideal company to work for. Pay was not good, and there would certainly have been more money, and more perks – they were virtually non-existent at Jaguar – at say, Standard Triumph.

Most people did more than one job, which was one of the ways he kept costs down, and he would not hesitate to ask his staff to work at weekends, and in the evenings if he thought it was necessary. He took that totally for granted.

## A Fair Man

Walter Hassan, one of the best engine engineers in the country, who had two spells with Jaguar, and

Sir William Lyons stands next to the magnificent D-type and a selection of his cars of the 1950s.

played a major role in the development of the XK120 engine and the V12, says 'I found him an excellent boss', and with a wry smile he points out that in those days it was the boss and the workers, and no one was in any doubt who was the boss.

'It was not strange to us to be called by our surnames. I worked for W.O. Bentley, and he never called anyone by their Christian name, the fashion for Christian names had not arrived' he added.

'He was mean, but we understood why he was mean; he was trying to build something up'. Like most engineers Walter has a logical mind, and thinking back he tries to analyse why Sir William generated so much loyalty. 'He treated us fairly, and we understood what he was trying to do, but he always maintained his aloofness, and when I think about it I cannot explain how it happened, but it did, there is no doubt about that'.

Sir William and Lady Lyons with their Labrador at Wappenbury Hall.

Sir William did not do things on impulse, he carefully considered each move, and calling people by their surnames was part of the school-room strategy of equality. If Sir William had any favourites it was a secret he took with him to the grave, because he never gave an inkling of having any while he lived.

'There were no politics at Jaguar, and everyone was treated equally by Sir William, regardless of their position in the firm', says Berry. He also stresses that Sir William's overwhelming dedication to Jaguar was infectious, and enthused those who worked for him. Few who worked at Browns Lane in Sir William's day would deny that the job satisfaction was enormous.

But there were also those who believed that in the higher echelons there was a good deal of politics, and they would point to the choice of the single camshaft V12 engine as a case in point.

Despite the fact that Lyons was not a qualified engineer he had an extraordinary facility of making the right engineering decisions, and of course his eye for a body line is legendary. On one occasion he asked for a line in a mock-up to be altered by about one quarter of an inch. The following morning he was walking past the mock-up – he did not stop to examine it – and called out to the man in the shop, 'I see you have not altered it yet'. Old Jaguar hands agree that to work for someone who had the magical touch endowed everyone with a feeling of superiority. They knew they were working for a firm that was special.

In achieving success for his company – often synonymous with obtaining what he wanted – he was totally ruthless, and on occasions rules could be bent. When production was of paramount importance his dealings with the trade unions were not beyond reproach. An example was the occasion when a foreman in the paint shop was struck by one of the workers, which would normally have been a matter of instant dismissal. Since a strike would have been most unwelcome at the time, a compromise solution was arranged.

Sir William was also described by one of his senior staff as the most highly paid progress-chaser in the motor industry. Certainly he was always demanding the impossible, but achieving it by pushing his staff, in particular, but other company's staff as well, beyond their normal levels of achievement.

Late one year he said that he wanted new body panels for the front end of the Jaguar 420 by July the following year. He would announce this in a matter of fact way, as if he were asking for another cup of tea. His own staff said it was not possible; Pressed Steel, the body builders thought it was hilarious. It was produced in July.

## Natural Authority

Jaguar had their fair share of trouble on the shop floor, but in Coventry, if you worked 'at the Jaguar' you considered yourself something above the common rung of car worker. This was particularly so before the British Leyland débâcle. The company's successes at Le Mans, the triumphal entry of the team into Coventry after their victory in 1953, with laurel wreaths on the front of the C-types, and the mechanics draped over the rear of the cars, as crowds packed the streets of the city in a manner rarely seen before, played a large part in maintaining the mystique.

Only one motor race rated in Sir William's view, and that was Le Mans. This is the principle reason why Jaguar had to wait until the 1980s to win the World Sports Car Championship. Although they were eminently successful at Le Mans, and in other national races around the world, they never tackled the Sports Car Championship. When Jaguar were racing at Le Mans Sir William was a constant visitor, and rarely left the pit counter throughout the twenty-four hours. F.R.W. (Lofty) England, the service manager, was also racing manager – as I pointed out earlier, most people at Jaguar had two jobs – and he was in charge of the racing activities, but Sir William kept a very close eye on everything.

He was desperate for victory; for a small firm it was a costly business, and by nature Sir William was a winner, and true to form, as he listened to shouted information from Lofty England, he remained, outwardly, completely impassive.

When victory came he allowed himself the indulgence of a big smile, a few handshakes, and 'well done' to mechanics such as Frank Rainbow, and one or two others, but nothing excessive. Champagne was not squirted about the place because that would have been considered wanton and wasteful. It was all terribly British.

Sir William did not subscribe to the philosophy of the good loser. The object was to win, and in 1949 when Jaguar entered the one-hour production race at Silverstone, every possible step was taken to ensure that they would win.

## Sir William – The Driver

They hired the circuit, drove for over an hour, ensured their lap times were fast enough, and checked every possible detail, and they won.

Sir William was a very enthusiastic driver, and I can recall being overtaken by him – he was driving a Mk VII, and I was at the wheel of a side-valve Hillman Minx – on the way to Silverstone. For a while I attempted to keep up with him, but soon gave up the unequal struggle, and when I arrived at Silverstone I commented on the Mk VII's lively performance.

'I always try and maintain an average speed of over 50mph', he said. This, of course, was in the days before the 70mph speed limit in Britain, but even so it required some enterprising motoring, and I doubt if there were many chairmen of motor companies at the time, who drove themselves, and if they did, drove with such enthusiasm. Some, who were good drivers, and were close to him, questioned whether he was a 'good' driver, but he certainly enjoyed his driving, and an amusing incident happened at Silverstone when they were preparing for the race, which is worth repeating, for amusing incidents and Sir William were not commonplace.

According to Walter Hassan, who had been driving the XK120s around the club circuit, and exceeding the lap record, Sir William expressed a wish to drive round, and took Bill Rankin, who was then the boss of advertising and publicity, with him.

The story goes that Bill was most concerned at the speed at which they were approaching the corners, and his unease was conveyed to Sir William, who calmly announced that he had left his spectacles behind, and Bill would have to tell him where to brake. Bill Rankin arrived back looking very sickly.

It took a long time before the Jaguar was accepted

as a gentleman's carriage; the ridiculously low price did not help in that respect, nor did the slightly exaggerated lines of some of the earlier SS models, and its predecessors collected the sobriquets of the Sexy Six, the poor man's Bentley, or the Bentley of Wardour Street.

But by the standards of their day the SS and early Jaguars, were comparatively quiet, comfortable cars, and with the arrival of Mk VII saloon they could stand comparison with any luxury car for quietness and comfort. Sir William was meticulous to an infinite degree; he would, for instance, write an important letter a dozen times before he was satisfied that it said exactly what he wanted it to say.

## A Sensitive Man

Sir William saw his motor cars with blinding clarity through the eyes of his customers, an attitude which might have been considered a gross presumption, but he had a very shrewd idea of his customers and what they wanted, and his decision was that they wanted a car that was stylistic, but not fashionable, and one that was, above all, comfortable and quiet to drive.

He marshalled all his capacity for detail to bring this about. People involved with him on the development of prototypes say that his sensitivity to noise was quiet remarkable. One of the first comments he made when he heard the XK120 engine running for the first time was 'What's that whine?' He also had an acute feeling for vibration, and as a result he distilled what was to become the very essence of Jaguar; a car that was quiet and comfortable to drive, with a distinguished shape.

By the time he had moved to Browns Lane in 1952 the people around him were sympathetic to his way of working, and after taking a car out on a test drive he would tell the assembled group what he thought of it, and they would listen very intently. They knew what the standard should be, the only argument would be on how to attain it, but they managed.

Sir William was a man you never took lightly, because he never took anything lightly. He had no small talk whatsoever, and he never said anything unless he meant it, and it was necessary. But neither did he rule by conscious intimidation, or indulge in the barrack room behaviour or language that was common in the higher echelons of some motor manufacturers.

He would not tolerate waffle from his staff, but if they had something to say he would listen, and if he approved of an idea he would let them run with it. For instance Bob Berry, then a lowly member of the organization, suggested the names XJ6 and E-type. He also persuaded him that the name F-type would be totally unsuitable. It was, however, a monumental error to tell Sir William what he should do, and as far as I know no one made that mistake twice.

## An Understanding Man

He had a no-nonsense, simplistic approach to business which worked extremely well. His tightness with money, born of starting a company from virtually nothing, did have its downside, and the company was short of equipment when he left, but he was generous to people who had a genuine problem.

One of his staff, for instance, had been very ill and Sir William decided that he and his wife needed a holiday. They were flown to the continent and booked into a splendid hotel, but Sir William took infinite pains to ensure that he was never personally involved. His aloofness never broke down.

It did not break down when his only son John was killed on the way to the Le Mans race. Those close to him knew that he was terribly upset, but he never allowed it to show; the iron discipline never broke down in public. He also had two daughters, both of whom survived him. Lady Lyons and Sir William enjoyed Wappenbury Hall south of Coventry, which he bought very economically in 1937, and kept it as a very private place. Few people at Jaguar were invited to the Hall. He also enjoyed the company of his labrador dog, but as a member of his entourage he expected it to be impeccably behaved, and one of his staff, with a reputation for training dogs, was summoned to help. Needless to say the whole business was transacted with considerable formality, but on one occasion Alan Hodge, the instructor, became rather exasperated when Sir William consistently stood on the wrong side of the dog.

'It is a long time since I was at school Hodge', said

Sir William, retired, but looking as immaculate as ever.

Sir William, 'let's have a break for a drink'. Asked what he would like, Alan suggested that a gin and tonic would be admirable. He went in search of the drink trolley on which there was no lemon and no ice. Alan dismissed their absence as of no importance, but Sir William insisted 'do you like ice and lemon?' When Alan replied that he did Sir William went off in search of them commenting 'If a job is worth doing it is worth doing well'.

When Lady Lyons joined them she asked Alan if he would like another drink. 'Alan would like another drink', she told her husband. 'He has had one', replied Sir William.

The training of the labrador extended over several months of evening and weekend lessons, and eventually the subject of a fee was raised by Sir William. Knowing that value for money loomed large in his mind, Alan suggested a figure for each lesson which was considerably below the one he normally charged.

'Would £5 be all right?' he asked a little nervously. Sir William replied that that sounded very reasonable, and gave him £5.

There was never any doubt that the overwhelming focal point of his life was Jaguar Cars, and he only took a perfunctory interest in matters that were unrelated. He had no ambition to own yachts or aeroplanes, and although Lady Lyons constantly attempted to persuade him to take the boat when he visited South Africa, he cancelled it many times. Sir William making polite conversation at the captain's table does not spring readily to mind. Apart from which he was not always convinced of the value for money provided by majestic liners. People of Sir William's background and generation were much keener on value for money than people appear to be today.

On one occasion he was seeking a jewellery case as a present for Lady Lyons, and a very well known and respected jeweller was summoned to present some examples. They appeared eminently presentable to a colleague who was with him, but after a careful scrutiny, but without looking at the prices, Sir William announced 'Fred (Gardner) could do a better job than this'. And it is reported that he did.

## An Unusual Luxury

As a man who hardly ever used a chauffeur, he could see no reason why any other able-bodied man should use one, and he was never known to darken the doors of the flesh-pots of the world, Sir William afforded himself one extravagance apart from his modest golf: in the last week of the London Motor Show he hosted a reception at the Grosvenor Hotel in Park Lane. Although it was concerned with the Motor Show, and the guests were journalists and others connected with the motor industry, by Sir William's standards it was an extravagance.

It was the one he really enjoyed. I was fortunate enough to attend all of them, and it was here that you saw him at his most relaxed. People like Bill Heynes and Arthur Whittaker who had known him for years, maintained that he had a good sense of humour, but I found that he kept it under firm control.

It was at one of these receptions that he regaled me with a story of his pre-war visit to a body plant in Coventry. After touring the plant he approached one of the press operators and asked how many of his particular body parts he produced in a day.

In a rich Coventry accent the operator said 'I don't know, but I'll tell you what, every time it goes bang it's sixpence for me'. At the recollection Sir William had a quiet chuckle.

In the Earls Court era of the Motor Show an invitation to the Jaguar 'do' was most sought after, and some surprising people were not above pleading for an invitation. Bob Berry maintains that juggling with the invitation list was one of his most difficult jobs of the year, because Sir William treated it very much as his personal party.

As a perfectionist in every thing he did, it must have given him a good deal of satisfaction to know that his sole Jaguar extravagance was considered to be the best of its kind.

# 2
# Early Days

In the beginning was a man called William Walmsley, the son of a wealthy Cheshire coal merchant, and a motor cycle fanatic. When Walmsley senior retired in 1920 they moved to Blackpool and became neighbours of the Lyons family. An Irish musician who had settled in Blackpool, Mr W. Lyons had graduated to the piano business, and he had a son called William, who was also an enthusiastic motor cyclist.

If the young William Lyons had not met the young William Walmsley he would, no doubt, have eventually found his way into the creative side of the motor industry, but it must be said that it was fortuitous that the Walmsley family moved to Blackpool, and equally fortuitous that both possessed such accommodating parents.

Neither young man showed the slightest interest in his father's business, an attitude which in those days was generally interpreted as an act of outrageous ingratitude. The First World War and its traumatic impact was still very fresh in the mind, but the tradition that a young man should get down to doing something sensible as quickly as possible was still strong in the northern middle-class mind.

The young Lyons was not covering himself in glory in that respect. Having left Arnold House school in Blackpool, aged seventeen, where again, not covering himself in academic glory, but where with the exception of cricket, he had been successful at sport, he spent a short spell with Crossley Motors at Manchester.

At the time they were a well respected firm having made a solid range of motor cars before the war, and a considerable number of military vehicles during the war, earning them a reputation for reliability and durability. They went on to make a rear-engined car, which was way ahead of its time and unsuccessful, and in 1938 they stopped making motor cars. However, William Lyons had no intention of waiting to discover the fate of the company, and was soon back in Blackpool. Battling through a relatively large engineering firm did not commend itself to the young Lyons as a route to running a successful business of his own, an idea that was already at the forefront of his mind.

Sir William was a motor cycle enthusiast before turning to four wheels.

Since a touch of nepotism had been used by Lyons senior to get his son into Crossley Motors he was not best pleased to see him back so soon. A short spell in the piano business followed, with the young Lyons dreamily considering the possibilities of the burgeoning gramophone business, but before long he had joined local motor retailers Jackson Brothers, and subsequently Brown and Mallalieu as a junior salesman. He was still able to indulge himself in his hobby of motor cycling, and owned both Harley Davidson and Indian machines which he rode in spirited fashion in both hillclimbs and speed events on Southport sands.

The other William, who was about ten years older than Lyons, had returned from war service in the army, and having spurned the coal business, was busy uncrating and refurbishing ex-WD Triumph motor cycles in the family garage at Stockport. To boost sales, which were not flourishing, he decided to offer them with a sidecar, and his idea of a sidecar was very different from the common concept at the time.

## The Swallow

Soon after the motor cycle had been invented efforts were made to provide accommodation for a second person. What most people had in mind was something suitable for a lady, and appendages were created which either trailed at the rear, or were pushed at the front, but for a variety of reasons neither solution proved successful. By 1906 several sidecars were in production, and they were widely used during the First World War.

They were cumbersome pieces of equipment, reminiscent of a bathtub with a wheel attached, and I can well remember an uncle of mine visiting us in the early 1930s with a Matchless machine and yellow sidecar that strongly resembled a giant banana.

Using aluminium on an ash frame the young Walmsley produced a sidecar not dissimilar to a large cigar tube. When his family moved to Blackpool production continued at the same frenetic rate of about one a week. Considering that Walmsley did almost everything himself (his only assistance was from his sisters who coped with the upholstery) his productivity was reasonable. As neighbours and motor cycling enthusiasts the two Williams soon met, and William Lyons was extremely impressed by the Swallow sidecar which by then sported such luxuries as a polished aluminium disc wheel – the aerodynamic virtues of which were probably unknown – aero screen, and close fitting hood. They were sold for thirty-two guineas, complete with hood and a few accessories, which was a small fortune in those days, but the young Lyons bought one. It is not recorded whether he obtained a discount, but judging by his shrewdness in

Proper premises at last. The names over the Blackpool works in Cocker Street, read W. Walmsley and W. Lyons.

In 1927 the first car was produced, an Austin Swallow two-seater. Production at Blackpool was two cars a day.

A Swallow Sports sidecar complete with disc wheels, built by William Walmsley and Bill Lyons in the early 1920s, from which everything began.

subsequent years it is unlikely that he paid the asking price.

He was very impressed with the sidecar, and quickly realized that if these stylish vehicles were produced in sufficient quantity the price could be reduced, and there would be a good market for them. Encouraged by Walmsley's father, in particular, he suggested that the two of them should go into business together, and Walmsley, after a good deal of persuasion, agreed.

As Sir William pointed out later in life there were some misgivings on both sides, because although Walmsley was a talented man, he did not possess the burning commitment to success that was the very backbone of his younger partner, but the partnership lasted until 1934 when Walmsley became more interested in model railways than motor cars. More important at the time perhaps, their respective parents agreed, for they were persuaded, apparently with ease, to provide bank guarantees of £500 each to float the Swallow Sidecar Company. There was a slight delay to proceedings because William Lyons would not be of age until 4 September 1922, but at the age of twenty-one he was working for himself, in a business of his choice; a pattern that was to continue for fifty years.

At this very early age William Lyons already had an intuitive instinct for his customers, and what they wanted, and very soon production had moved into their first factory at Bloomfield Road, where they employed twelve people, and were producing even more sophisticated sidecars on chassis built by Montgomerys of Coventry. That rapier-like eye for line, and the ability to make a modest change that would alter the character of the vehicle totally, was already hard at work, and paying dividends. In four years they had moved to a bigger plant at Cocker Street which they rented from Walmsley senior, and the workforce had increased to thirty-two, including a young typist called Alice Fenton, who moved down to Coventry with him and was home sales director of Jaguar Cars when she died in 1960. It is interesting to note that the move was accomplished in forty-eight hours, with no outside aid apart from a pantechnicon and a driver.

## Enterprise and Vision

His restless enterprise, vision, and canny facility with financial matters were also very much to the fore at this period. While other manufacturers of sidecars, and there were many, attempted to promote their

AGENT'S
SEASON TICKET
(Not Transferable).
Price 15/-
Tax included

THE SOCIETY OF MOTOR MANUFACTURERS AND TRADERS, LTD.
Thirteenth International
MOTOR EXHIBITION
OLYMPIA
November 7—15, 1919

No. 1918

Signature of Holder
W. Lyons

Name of Member of Agents Section, Ltd.
Metropole Garage

Sir William's pass for the Olympia Motor Exhibition in 1919.

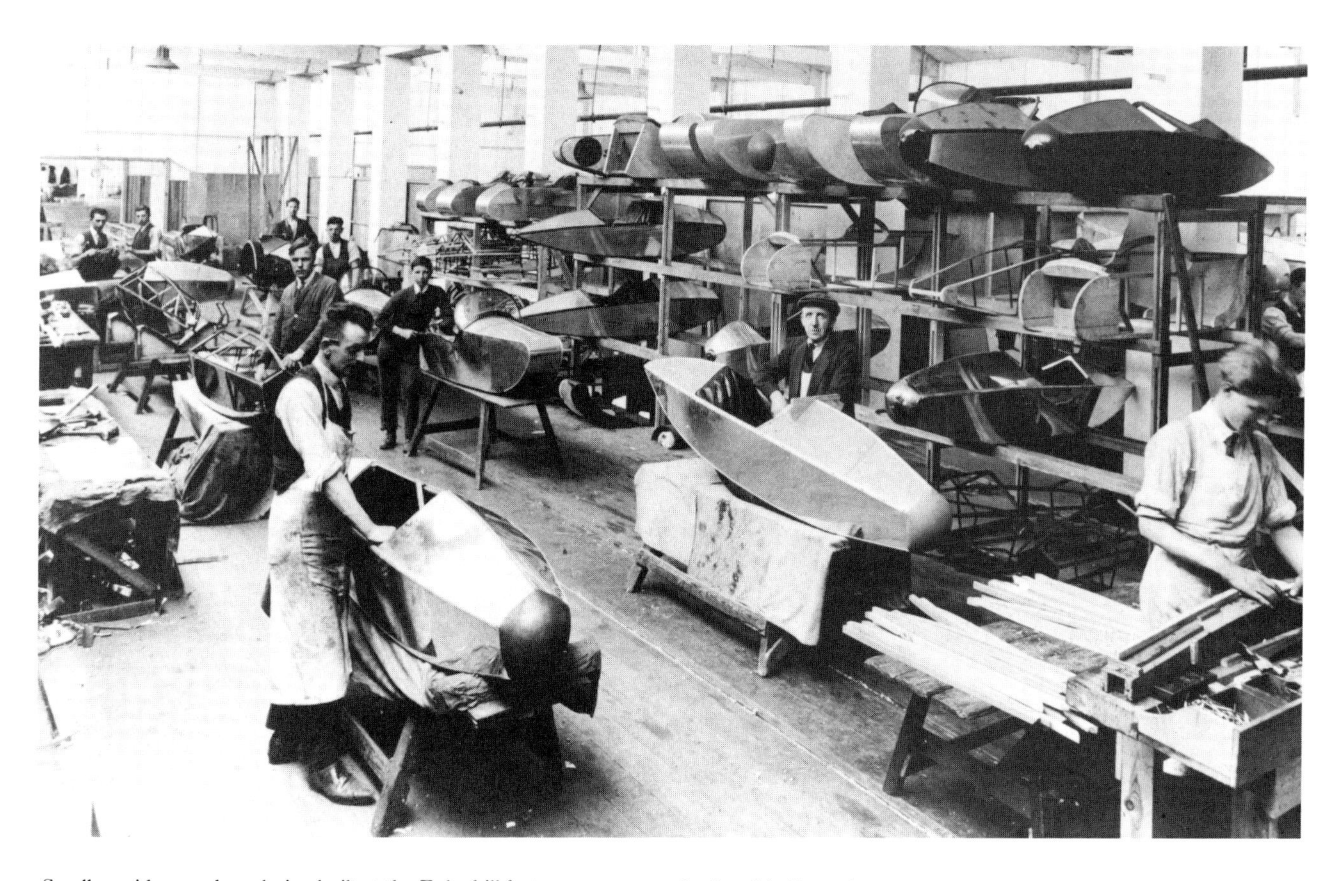

Swallow sidecars, here being built at the Foleshill factory, were genuine hand-built products, created by craftsmen.

wares through sporting events Lyons appreciated that it could be an expense of spirit in a waste of shame, and while he and Walmsley still took part in local sporting events, they restricted their wider sporting activity to the Sidecar TTs of 1924 and 1925. In the former they finished second and third.

As opposed to most other sidecars, they were making a thing of beauty, but they never lost sight of the fact that attractive or not it had to be produced at the right price. They were constantly seeking means of reducing production costs, by using different types of materials, or buying more cheaply from their suppliers, and obtaining the maximum effort from their employees – characteristics which never deserted the Lyons side of the partnership. The Swallow Sidecar Company in Blackpool was a microcosm of Jaguar Cars, Coventry.

It was at this time that he made his first business deal with the police selling Swallow sidecars to the Nottinghamshire police to fit alongside their Brough Superior motor cycles. At a time when the motor industry, both two- and four-wheeled, showed a singular lack of interest in Europe, William Lyons in co-operation with chassis manufacturer Charles Hayward (who produced a Universal chassis which could be fitted on either side of a machine) stepped up sales to the continent through Emil Frey of Zurich, whose son is now selling Jaguars in Switzerland and Germany.

In the spring of 1927 the first Austin Seven Swallow two-seater was produced at Blackpool, and changes came fast and furiously. Motor cars were now William Lyons' true love, and although he went on producing sidecars at the rate of 4,000 a year right up to the beginning of the Second World War, most of his energy and inspiration went into the four-wheelers.

Because suppliers were at hand, and the skilled labour was available, the factory was moved to

Foleshill, Coventry, in 1928. A year earlier, as an indication of the route the company was taking, the name was changed to the Swallow Sidecar and Coachbuilding Company. To have a solid sidecar business bringing in the cash must have been some comfort to Lyons and Walmsley when they launched themselves into the unknown waters of specialized coachbuilding on extremely modest family saloons, something which had hardly been attempted before.

Specialist coachbuilders were rather grand people who created bodies for cars with such illustrious names as Rolls Royce and Hispano Suiza, not for motorized prams like the Austin Seven. So they were taking a chance, and it was comforting, and profitable, to have the sidecar business ticking over in the same Coventry plant.

They continued to build eight different basic sidecars ranging from a semi-sport to a luxury saloon, and strange to contemplate in this day and age, prices were coming down, the streamlined Ranelagh saloon, which was the last word in luxury costing £31 10s.

During the Second World War Swallow Coachbuilding produced hundreds of sidecars for the three services and the National Fire Service, but in 1945 Jaguar Cars had been formed, and there was no room for sidecar manufacture. At the end of the year the assets of Swallow Coachbuilding were sold to the Helliwell Group. Three years later they sold it to Tube Investments Ltd., who continued to produce Swallow sidecars, and then the Swallow Gadabout scooter, which was several years ahead of its time, and the Swallow Doretti sports car, based on the Triumph TR2.

It was in a Swallow Doretti, being driven by his test driver Ken Richardson, that Sir John Black, chairman of Standard Triumph, had a serious accident outside his Banner Lane factory in Coventry. He retired soon afterwards. The Swallow Doretti was about £150 more than the Triumph TR2, but it was more luxuriously appointed, and was selling reasonably well when production stopped. Against formidable opposition in the 2-litre category the manufacturers clearly thought it had no long term future. But Swallow Sidecars soldiered on, and in 1956 the company was bought by Watsonian, and operations moved to Birmingham, where the name conceived by William Walmsley over seventy years ago, still continues.

## SS Cars

Walmsley's technique of using an ash frame and aluminium panels had worked extremely well, and linked with William Lyon's eye for the right line they had earned themselves a considerable reputation for producing stylish sidecars. William Lyons had clearly been thinking for some time that the same technique, or one very similar, could be applied to motor car bodies, and with his eye for styling, he believed they could start a minor revolution in the motor industry.

Today, coachbuilders are few and far between, but at that time they were prolific not only in London, but in the provinces where firms like Rippon in Yorkshire and Mann Egerton in Norfolk practised their art. From such couture establishments one was able to buy, at a price, a one-off body, but they were rarely prepared to embark on anything below a medium-sized car.

William Lyons was not planning one-off models, he envisaged series production, and he also had in mind something very much smaller than a medium-sized car. He had bought a second-hand Austin Seven; not much bigger than one of his sidecars, and decided that it would be ideal for one of his conversions. It is not recorded whether he anticipated the depression; with his acute feeling for the economy it would not have been surprising if he had, but the choice of an Austin Seven proved to be fortuitous, for when the full horrors of the depression descended on the country, there were still sufficient people left who could afford the £174 for a motor car that was definitely different, and the company survived the depression virtually unscathed.

It was also fortunate for the company that the British motor industry was being led by engineers whose eye for style was zero, and with very few exceptions the cars being produced were indescribably ugly. Against this background William Lyons' star shone all the brighter.

Austin had produced a Seven before, but it was a big motor car, and the one they produced in 1922 was much more in keeping with the times, and a great advance in every respect on comparable cycle cars being produced at the time. The body was ugly, as Lyons duly noted, but it was a four-seater, it had four-

Somewhat bigger than previous models is the 1927 Morris Cowley Swallow in two tones, which was quite unusual at the time.

wheel brakes and it was easy to drive; not an unimportant point if you intended to appeal to women motorists.

It was powered by a four-cylinder side-valve engine of 747cc, which produced 10.5 brake horse power. Its top speed was 52mph (83.5kph) and fuel consumption was claimed to be 43mpg (69kpg). As with other motor cars they re-styled, Swallow did nothing to the mechanical parts of the car, and although the Austin Swallow looked a racy version of the original Seven it was, in fact, a similar performer. This did not inhibit sales.

By this time seventeen-year-old Arthur Whittaker, a former apprentice at the Imperial Garage, Blackpool, had joined Swallow in the capacity of a part-time salesman, a job he did not particularly enjoy. He preferred using his hands, and soon inveigled himself into the works where he helped to put the first Swallow body on a motor car. It was a burnt-out Austro-Daimler belonging to William Walmsley. He rose to be deputy chairman and when he retired in 1968 was one of the longest serving members of the company.

The other happening of the period was of a much more personal nature. In 1922 William Lyons became engaged to Greta Brown whose father Albert Jenner Brown was a schoolmaster from the village of Cuddington, near Thame, Oxfordshire. But her grandfather had been a headmaster in Blackpool, and when her father returned there she met, and started courting a slim and rather serious young man called Billy Lyons. They were married at St Stephen on the Cliffs, North Shore, Blackpool, on 15 September 1924.

## The Austin Swallow

The first Austin Swallow appeared late in 1926, and was announced to the public in May 1927. It was an immediate success. Unrecognizable as an Austin apart from the badge on the radiator, and possibly the transverse leaf springs, it was a two-seater with a rounded body, separate headlamps and side-lamps mounted on cycle-type front mudguards, and all the interior refinements missing from the original Austin.

By the following year production was storming ahead and a four-seater saloon body was added to the range, the cycle-type mudguards were replaced with full-sized wings, and Vee-type windscreens with an opening panel on the driver's side were fitted. For £190 the car was available with either hard or soft top,

The Austin Swallow saloon, all curves and V-windscreen, sold for £187 10s in 1929.

and the saloon cost £187. Chassis were delivered direct from Birmingham, fifty at a time, and because of the limited space at Cocker Street, the co-operation of Blackpool North railway station was stretched to the limit.

It was imperative that they move to Holbrook Lane, in Foleshill, Coventry, and although this was not achieved with the same alacrity as the move to Cocker Street, it was still done with commendable speed, and with considerable juggling production was maintained. Blackpool was nothing more than a memory.

## Variations on a Theme

Apart from the conversions to the Austin Seven, Swallow had also produced a two-seater Morris Cowley Swallow for £210, but it seemed that they thought this was running a little too close to the recently formed MG, and only a handful were made, despite the fact that the MG was considerably more expensive. At the 1929 Olympia Motor Show, Swallow showed, in addition to the Austin Swallows, a Type 509A Fiat, a Standard Big Nine, and a Swift Ten, all with wood and aluminium bodywork, but longer and sleeker than the Austin. William Lyons was now getting to grips with his vision of what a motor car should look like and how it should feel to drive; it was still some way off, but he was getting there fast.

Henlys, a very wealthy and powerful distributor of cars, were handling Swallow products in the south of England, and this was the beginning of a long and successful association between Lyons and Henlys.

By 1931 an attractive Wolseley Hornet Swallow was added to the range, and most important a Swallow-bodied Standard Sixteen followed shortly afterwards. It did not sell very well, but it heralded the association between Swallow and the Standard Motor Company who were to produce engines and modified chassis for the new range of SS cars.

In the Autumn of 1931 the Swallow Coachbuilding Company (the Sidecar had been dropped) announced that '. . . the SS is coming . . .' and on 9 October it arrived, and was one of the sensations of the London Motor Show held later that month. It was a sensation for several reasons, but one of the principle reasons was that it cost £310, a figure which literally left the opposition gasping. How did they do it?

By 1931 this Austin Swallow had come down in price by ten shillings since its introduction four years earlier and cost £178 10s.

This Austin Seven Swallow Saloon produces a few giggles among the motoring intelligentsia today, but for the customer who wanted something different for under £200 in 1932, there was a lot to be said for it.

*The Autocar* magazine in a road test report a little later, had this to say about the SS1: 'The most modern lines, long, low and rakishly sporting, the general effect being that of a powerful sports coupe costing £1,000, although the actual price is a third of that figure . . . performance in keeping with its looks . . . very steady on bends . . . steering which is light and positive . . .' Even Lyons would have found it hard to improve on that report.

Harold Pemberton, a respected motoring correspondent of the *Daily Express*, also produced a eulogistic report. His line was that the senior salesmen from Henlys had been summoned to a conference and asked to state the sort of motor car they could most easily sell. They were unanimous on one point: 'Give us a car with a £1,000 look, but which costs £300, and life will be easy'.

The result, he said, was the SS1. William Lyons would listen if he thought people were talking sense, and when one remembers the close and special relationship between Lyons and Henlys, I have no doubt that their observations corroborated, at the very least, his own views.

## A Marque of their Own

It is interesting that Lyons should choose to leak the story of the SS1 some time before its official announcement, because he used a similar tactic many years later with the E-type. When he wanted to exert an extra twist of pressure on his staff he presented them with a target, and then pointed out in a matter of fact manner that he would like to see this or that ready by next Friday. Because none of his staff wanted to let him down prodigious efforts were made to ensure his 'requests' became realities. It worked with the SS1 and the E-type.

The SS1 built in 1931 was the first car to be introduced by the Swallow Coachbuilding Company as a marque in its own right, and William Lyons had now moved to assembling his own cars, and the goal of actually building them was in sight. It must not be forgotten that the other William was still in the company, and making a contribution, but the powerhouse was Lyons.

Captain John Black, as he was then, was in the Royal Tank Corps at the end of the First World War, and although he had studied to be a solicitor before joining the army, like many ex-servicemen he tried his hand at chicken farming on demobilization, and was as unsuccessful as the vast majority. He then had the good fortune to marry one of the Hillman daughters, and subsequently joined the struggling Coventry company. He later moved to the Standard Motor Company, and did a very good job introducing the successful Flying Standard range of cars.

A little older than William Lyons, he was also a thrusting personality, and they got on well, which was fortunate because there was a lot of internecine warfare in the British motor industry, which lasted well into the post-war years. Lyons did not, for instance, hit it off with Sir Herbert Austin. It was agreed that Standard would produce a modified Sixteen chassis for the SS1 and another modified chassis derived from the Standard Little Nine for the SS11, which was also introduced at this time.

The engine for the SS1 was the long stroke 2,054cc side-valve unit, presented in untuned form, but with a stiff seven bearing crankshaft capable of some development, and this was coupled to the Standard's reasonably close ratio gearbox, standard axles and steering mechanism.

The chassis was modified to give a much lower overall line, and it was lengthened by 3in (7.5cm), and the front semi-elliptic springs were mounted outside the chassis frame, and the engine set back 7in (17.5cm) to give that much sought-after sports car look. To allow three people to sit abreast the centrally-mounted handbrake took on an unusual shape, but there was a centrally-mounted four-speed gear lever, and an extensive display of oval-shaped instruments. The brakes were cable operated, and remained so for eighteen years, but according to contemporary road tests they were considered perfectly acceptable. At about this time the motor industry in the United States was introducing hydraulic brakes to mass produced cars.

However, if they did the job Lyons could see no point in changing them, because they had the virtue of being competitively priced, and these were the sort of considerations that helped him keep the price down to

A Wolseley Hornet Swallow outside Gretna Green. In its day a dashing car for an elopement.

a 'magical' level. He did, however, indulge in wire wheels, of which he was a great admirer, and there is little doubt that they did, in the eyes of most people, enhance the appearance of his cars.

Onto these well-tried mechanical parts William Lyons built a rakish, somewhat claustrophobic two-seater. In retrospect it was not his finest effort, but it was his first real attempt at producing a car to which the description 'Space, Pace and Grace' would rightfully apply. His technique of setting deadlines could be nerve racking – no one in the trim shop could get the fabric on the roof of the prototype right, and the cry went out from the Holbrook works for a real expert trimmer.

Coventry, of course, had experts on anything to do with the motor industry, and someone always knew where they could be found. Percy Leeson, who had been sacked twice for fighting, was the man they wanted, and he duly presented himself at Holbrook Lane. 'If I can't do it nobody can', he pronounced with a certain amount of immodesty. He had a good deal to be immodest about, because after working long into the night, watched anxiously by Lyons and Walmsley, he finished the job, and stayed another forty years with Jaguar.

Compared with the equivalent Standard Sixteen's height of 5ft 8in (1.7m), the SS stood at only 4ft 7in (1.4m). It was priced at £310, and the SS11 which was powered by 1,052cc Standard engine cost £210, and both were offered in half a dozen different colours. The SS1 would reach 71mph (114kph), and 60mph (96.5kph) in third gear; a very acceptable performance for a 2-litre car in the 1930s. It was an outstanding success at the London Motor Show, and Henlys loftily offered to buy half of the first year's production, and one of the very first Dinky toys was of an SS1.

## Sexy Six

It carried the Swallow badge on the vertically stripped radiator, although the SS hexagon motif was in use in catalogues, and advertisements, and the public were already asking what the initials stood for. Some of the coarser speculators thought it was 'Sexy Six', but the majority opted for 'Standard Swallow', or 'Standard Special', but the truth is that we are still speculating, because John Black and William Lyons never revealed what they stood for; a rather unnecessary conspiracy, I would have thought.

The Swift Swallow followed a well-set pattern with lots of curves, a V-windscreen, two-tone paintwork, and marine-like air intakes.

In post-war years I asked Sir John Black, as he had then become, what SS did stand for. Like William Lyons he was always immaculately turned out, indeed he never moved without a valet, and during business hours he did not smile a lot.

'What would you imagine Mennem', he said, and walked off. I imagined it was Standard Swallow, and still do.

Swallow had paid £500 to the Standard Motor Company towards the cost of dies and tools, and in turn paid Standard £130 for the SS1 chassis and £82 for the SS11, in what transpired to be a satisfactory arrangement for both companies.

In addition to improved versions of the coupe models – the 1934 model with four windows was more gracious and less claustrophobic – versions appeared with four-seater open and saloon bodies, and four different engines were available; a 20hp and 16hp for the SS1, and a 12hp and 10hp for the SS11. Remarkably, the sports four-seater sold for the same price as the coupe and, in 1933 the first customer was, appropriately, John Black of the Standard Motor Company.

In late 1934 the SS1 Airline saloon was announced. There was a fashion for streamlined cars – the Chrysler Airflow was one example – at the time, and William Lyons admitted years later that he had allowed himself to be influenced by the trend, but did not like the Airline saloon, and in fact he disliked it more than any other car he had been involved with. They were also to produce the SS1 Drophead, which was a very attractive motor car, and in early 1935, the first two-seater sports car called the SS90 and, after much effort on Lyons' part, obtained a stand of their own for the first time at the 1934 London Motor Show.

Other momentous things were also happening. Towards the end of 1934 SS Cars Ltd, was floated as a public company, William Walmsley left, and extra land at Foleshill had been acquired for a mere £12,000.

## Departure

It was revealed in the prospectus that sales in the previous three years had increased by 100 per cent, and that profits had risen from £12,447 to £37,645 in the same period; a formidable achievement for a company whose top selling car cost around £300.

A public company had no appeal to William Walmsley, and the twelve-year partnership was dissolved. It probably would not have lasted much longer in any event, because the two were growing apart. Walmsley was creative, but a dilettante; a warm-hearted man who would create a new sports car and then adorn it with a fire bell . . . not the sort of antics that appealed to his partner. Most people would have found him a more amiable companion than William Lyons, and when he left the company he was very supportive of Clifford Dawtrey, who had been sacked by Lyons. Like many at Swallow, and subsequently Jaguar, Dawtrey did two jobs; he was an inspector and also prepared the first SS handbooks, but when he became interested in building streamlined caravans in his spare time, he was given the sack.

You worked for William Lyons 100 per cent or not at all. Despite the assistance of Walmsley, and several attempts to restart in the caravan business, he had no success, and died tragically. Lyndon Smith another ex-Swallow man was also helped by Walmsley, but this time there was a much more successful outcome in that Lyndon Smith started the Blue Boar group, which became enormously successful.

Walmsley suffered from pernicious anaemia throughout his life, and the death of his only son Bobby, flying a Typhoon over war-time France, was a severe blow to him. His health gradually deteriorated, and he died back on the Lancashire coast in June 1961, aged sixty-eight.

## Improvements

The press had been flattering about SS Cars; in its efforts to boost a new British product, perhaps it had been too flattering, as it was, in my view, in post-war years . . . and I was part of it at that time. But William Lyons knew some changes had to be made. In the sporting field the SS had done tolerably well at local level, but in its excursions into international competition had done less well. In concours d'elegance at home and abroad it had been consistently successful,

It is not surprising that the SS100 Saloon earned the sobriquet Sexy Six, or Poor Man's Bentley among motoring's upper echelons, but it was dramatically different.

so clearly the styling was right, but the performance could be improved. At first he looked at a Studebaker straight-eight. This was whisked before him in Coventry for his assessment because Henlys had the sole rights for distribution of this American car in the UK. The idea was turned down. Another suggested solution was supercharging, and this also was turned down.

For 1935 the cars were considerably improved, using a high compression head evolved with the co-operation of Harry Weslake, a higher lift camshaft, twin RAG carburettors, modified cooling and a bigger sump. At this time the high ratio back axle was standardized on all SS1s. But it was at this time that William Lyons realized that if he was to keep his cars ahead of the rest he would have to set up his own engineering department.

It heralded the appointment of one of the key men in the company's history, a man who many believe has been enormously underrated – William Munger Heynes. He was well recommended by Edward (Ted) Grinham, Standard's chief engineer, but once again it illustrated Lyons' ability to pick the right people. More than anyone it was Bill Heynes who conceived and fought for production of the E-type.

He was a short, dark-haired man with a light voice and twinkling eyes, an engineer of the old school, who began his engineering apprenticeship at Humber, in

**Bill Heynes**

I have not met an engineer who worked with, or knew Bill Heynes, who did not have the highest regard for him both as a man and as an engineer. Many say that he was one of the most underrated engineers of his era; that his achievements have never been fully appreciated.

An engineer with oily hands, in the tradition of his time, he was one of the trio – Sir William and Arthur Whittaker were the other two – who put SS Cars and then Jaguar on their feet, and he was the leading light in the design of the XK engine, one of the most famous of all time. Dapper and diligent his hands floated across an engine as though it were a musical instrument, and he was a great advocate of that engineering adage that 'if it looks wrong, it cannot be right'.

In his younger days I recall him as a man with a ready smile, and eyes that twinkled at some inner thought, as he explained his engineering schemes. He had great ability as a leader, was an excellent picker of men, and from nothing produced an engineering team that worked wonders at Jaguar. He loved motor racing; I think the glamour and the excitement appealed to him, but he also appreciated that it helped enormously in attracting, and keeping, a talented engineering team.

Although the racing programme of the 1950s put considerable stress on his engineering department, he was sad when Jaguar pulled out of motor racing.

William Mungo Heynes CBE, was one of six boys, and born to a Leamington Spa cabinet maker and his wife on the last day of 1903. Like many Edwardian families it was governed by strict principles, but Bill Heynes had a happy boyhood coping, among other things, with five individualistic brothers. His ambition was to be a doctor, but the fees involved proved too much for the Heynes family, so Bill decided he would be a vet instead, and took some of the examinations. But this was frowned upon as a suitable occupation – vets were considered a rather rough lot – and after an unsuccessful period working with his father, an obliging aunt with the right connections, pointed him in the direction of the growing motor industry, and Bill Heynes was apprenticed to Humber at the age of twenty in 1923.

Encouraged by his seniors, who were constantly eager to pass on their knowledge to a receptive trainee, he quickly demonstrated a flair for design, and forward thinking, and his first design exercise for an Institute of Automobile Engineers' paper was for a four-cylinder motor cycle engine with twin overhead camshafts and hemispherical combustion chambers. Subsequently he designed a four-speed synchromesh gearbox for the Hillman Minx, and several independent front suspensions for the same model.

He married Evelyn Blunt in 1932, and three years later he moved to Swallow Road, as chief engineer of SS Cars Ltd, with one assistant, a draughtsman, and an urgent request to have two cars ready for the Olympia Show which was six months away. He built up a small team of engineers – it never became very big – and with them produced miracles, always managing to produce that extra horse power from the XK engine while still retaining its reliability.

He became vice chairman (engineering) in 1961, and was responsible for the first XJ6 which appeared in 1968. In the following year he retired, perhaps a little disappointed that his twin overhead camshaft V12 engine had never gone into production. He spent his remaining years on his farm in Warwickshire, but the death of his wife in 1988 caused him great sadness, and he died in the following year.

Sir John Egan said: 'Everyone at Jaguar today owes a massive debt to Bill. He will be sadly missed by all of us.'

Coventry, in 1923. He rose to be head of the technical department of the design office, which he held from 1930–4, when Humber produced the Snipe and the Pullman. He was a versatile engineer with a flair for design, having designed a four-speed synchromesh gearbox for the Hillman Minx, and he had also been involved in various designs of independent front suspension systems for the Minx. He joined SS Cars as chief engineer, and with the minimum staff got down to producing two new cars for the Olympia Motor Show six months away. A daunting task, and when I asked him many years later how he did it he shook his head, smiled, and said 'You just got on with it, it was as simple as that'.

Another very important appointment was made a year earlier when Ernest William Rankin, a slim, intense Londoner, joined SS Cars as advertising and publicity manager. He was a very talented man, and a very loyal one, because in later years he could have earned much more than he did at Jaguar Cars, but he stayed with them.

He was thirty-five when he joined the company, a veteran of the First World War in which he had served as a Lieutenant in the Middlesex Regiment, and for six years he had been advertising General Motors' products when they operated from Hendon. In a competition held to brighten the image of Watney's brewery, he not only won, but created the 'Red Barrel' which is now so well known.

Previously the work had been done by Henlys, under the wary eye of Lyons. Now Bill Rankin, as he was always known, got down to the job in a very professional way, and after a débâcle over the bill at a Blackpool gathering of the SS Car Club, which William Lyons had to pay, Bill Rankin was told in forthright manner that either he became secretary of the club or it closed down. This suited Bill because he was a great believer in fostering a relationship between the marque and its customers.

He worked tirelessly to promote the company at motor sport events, motor shows, and any promotional activity he could think of, and as a young man I wondered on occasions whether he ever left the factory. In the Second World War he served at Dunkirk, and in the Western Desert and Italy, leaving with the rank of major.

## Value for Money

The company had had to overcome some problems with the early SS1s such as leaks in the windscreens and sliding roof, as well as the engine fumes and sticking carburettors, while the SS11 was seriously under-powered and although it looked neat and attractive its performance was bordering on the pathetic, and it had plenty of direct competition.

Although the performance of the SS11 remained poor, the SS1 improved considerably and by 1934–5 the motoring magazines were reporting cruising happily at 70mph (113kph), and maximum speeds of 84.5mph (136kph), and the value for money was breathtaking.

Most expensive of the cars in the range were the 20hp drophead coupe at £385, and the two-seater SS90, of which not very many were made, at £390. For £335 you could buy the 16hp tourer. The racy lines of the SS cars attracted customers from show business, including such superstars of their day as George Formby, as well as a brash clientele that did little to enhance its reputation. It was also driven by many of the major motoring names of the day, and John Cobb, who was used to driving some of the finest machinery available, was fulsome in his praise of the SS1.

The police were also showing some interest in the SS marque, and sales were good. Henlys, under the enterprising Frank Hough staged some truly magnificent sales campaigns, and with their domination of the south of England their role was crucial. Without doubt the SS car had made a big impact, and thanks to the efforts of Rankin, the unstinting efforts of the service department at Foleshill (who tended to treat customers like personal friends, taking them home to tea while work was done on their cars) and, of course the whole team, progress had been made in three years that drew the respect even of its competitors.

It still had a long way to go, and no one realized this more than William Lyons. The car population of Great Britain in 1935 excluding the Channel Islands and the Isle of Man, was 1,505,019, and ownership started with the lower middle classes who tended to buy used cars. If the working classes had any personal transport, it was either a motor cycle or a bicycle.

He was appealing to a very conservative audience, many of whom were extremely wary of this rather 'flashy' motor car, and even the low price was a handicap to its image in that many were convinced there was 'a catch in it somewhere'. Rankin realized this and wrote to dealers suggesting how they should tackle the problem. It would be some time before company chairmen rode in Jaguars as a matter of course. As value for money, however, the cars went from strength to strength and it is interesting to note that standard equipment on the 1934 SS1 coupe costing £335, was a speedometer, ammeter, oil pressure gauge, fuel gauge and water temperature gauge as well as an electric clock. There was also an opening rear window and remotely controlled blind. There were fifteen different basic colours and nineteen combinations of exterior and interior finish.

The hexagonal SS badge appeared on the motor cars, trafficators became standard equipment, and so did reversing lights. A wireless was available for sixteen guineas – expensive – plus £3 for fitting, but the aerial was fixed, and such luxuries as heating, demisting and windscreen washers were still to come.

## Overseas Markets

In the 1930s the British Empire was not at its zenith, but it was still going strong, and in general the motor industry believed that if it had to export, then the proper place was to the Empire where they knew more or less who they were dealing with. There was not a great enthusiasm for exporting in those days; people complained about dust and water getting into their vehicles, which was all very tiresome, and on the whole it was much simpler to provide for a growing home market.

William Lyons foresaw the potential of overseas markets with his sidecars, and he realized that when selling specialized cars such as the SS, the bigger the market-place the better. At first the sales department of SS Cars consisted of William Lyons assisted by Alice Fenton, though it must be remembered that Henlys did a lot of the work that would normally have been done by a sales department.

Nevertheless it was a shoestring operation, and when it is remembered that he took a personal interest in every other department it is not surprising that he was often at his desk by 7am. Lyons was determined to tackle the Continental markets as well as more distant places such as India, South Africa and the United States.

With the help of the Standard Motor Company he appointed agents in the Netherlands, Denmark, Portugal, Austria, and his old friend Emil Frey stayed with him in Switzerland. The French Motor Car Company looked after India, and John Clarke of Johannesburg took care of South Africa. In India and South Africa they used right-hand drive, but the cars he sold to the Continent were never modified to left-hand drive in this country. Some might have been converted on the Continent, but the problem of right-hand drive was not as great in those days when a lot of cars, particularly in Italy, were built with right-hand drive.

In mountainous country the theory was that with right-hand drive the driver had a better view of the edge of the road, and was less likely to fall over the edge. It must also be remembered that traffic density on Continental roads was derisory compared to today and, therefore the position of the steering wheel was not so critical. In any event left-hand drive cars were not produced until after the war.

By 1933, without the aid of a conveyor belt system they were producing 1,394 cars a year, of which 131 were exported, and in the following year the figure had gone up to 1,574, with 219 exports. The export figure never rose beyond 252 in pre-war years.

## The American Market

Although William Lyons distrusted the fickleness of the North American market, its potential fascinated him. I can recall him saying, when exports to the United States were booming in the post-war years, that he did not believe in putting all his eggs in one basket, and despite their success in North America, exports to that market rarely amounted to more than half the total.

Before the war SS Cars sold under fifty cars in the United States and another ten to Canada, but according to the ballyhoo in some American newspapers at

The final production line for Standard Swallows, at the Foleshill factory, when things moved at a more leisurely pace.

the time, you would be forgiven for believing they had sold many more. Sales arrangements were untidy to say the least, a state of affairs that Lyons must have found extremely irksome.

With the biggest motor industry in the world of its own the United States had only been a happy hunting ground for specialist car manufacturers such as Rolls Royce, Mercedes-Benz, Bugatti and others of that ilk. But the Wall Street crash of 1926, and the depression that followed put paid to most imports, and it was very adventurous to exhibit at the New York Show in 1935.

But one of the men principally involved appeared to be an adventurer, to put it at its mildest. Although British Motors took on the agency for SS Cars in 1934, one Richard G. Taylor appeared to corner the market by registering the name SS in the United States. He was certainly photographed with a fleet of SS Cars in Coventry that were said to be going to America, and with him was Captain Strickland, the Coventry MP, and the ubiquitous Bill Rankin. Interviews he gave in America said that he had been selling cars like wildfire, and despite the fact that he had been so badly shot up in the war (he could hardly stand up) he claimed he had covered well over a thousand miles in a day in an SS Car: they were so quiet and comfortable.

It seemed at one time that SS Cars would be the only imported car at the New York show, but at the last minute a PA MG was produced as well as a Type 57 Bugatti. SS Cars exhibited the Airline, and a few were sold, and the intrepid racing driver and war hero Richard G. Taylor, complete with wide brimmed fedora hat, disappeared from the scene.

The next thing that is heard of sales in America is that in 1936 Hilton Motors announce they are selling thirty-five SS Cars, and that substantial savings can be made, which was not altogether surprising because the SS Jaguar with an overhead valve engine was now available, and these were powered by the old 20hp side-valve engines.

They had dipped their toe into the ocean of the American market – which is more than many other manufacturers had attempted – and learned a lot that would be of great help when they made their real thrust into North America ten years later.

# 3
# The Trial of Trials

William Lyons, Bill Heynes, Arthur Whittaker, and Bill Rankin had all taken part, with some degree of success, in local and national rallies, and it would have been difficult to find another company where the hierarchy drove their own products with such zest – even harder today.

As an intensely competitive person Lyons was attracted to competitive motoring events, but as has been pointed out, his approach to almost everything was direct and uncomplicated, and he could see no virtue in competing unless there was a very good chance of success. Indeed he was extremely conscious of the damage that could be caused by the adverse publicity of failure. He even did his best to persuade several private entrants not to compete in events in which he thought they had no chance of success.

The general picture in the early days of SS competition was that they did well in the Concours de Confort and Elegance, both at home and abroad. These events had considerable standing in pre-war days, and when it is remembered that they were competing against motor cars that cost at least twice as much, it was a considerable achievement.

However, the cost factor did come into it on the question of performance, and the side-valve Standard engine, even with aluminium head was never truly competitive, and it was not until they had the 100hp-plus overhead valve 2½-litre unit that they began to win international events.

Jaguar started to export to the United States before World War II, and this 1936 2½-litre SS Jaguar Tourer is one of them. No nonsense about left-hand drive in those days.

This competition version of the SS100 had quite a history. It started life as a 2½-litre, and made best performance in the Alpine Trial of 1936, driven by T.H. (Tommy) Wisdom, and his wife Elsie. It was also driven successfully in hillclimbs by Sammy Newsome, and with a 3½-litre engine Tommy Wisdom lapped Brooklands at over 118mph (190kph).

In the centre is E.W. (Bill) Rankin, who was the very successful advertising and publicity manager for SS and Jaguar Cars, and I am not sure of the others. They won the team prize in the 1937 Welsh Rally, I do know that.

Competitors were somewhat casual in their attire as this photograph of a 3½-litre SS100 illustrates.

This 2½-litre SS100 (it was actually 2,663cc) cost £395 in 1937.

The parts for this 3½-litre SS100 were kept at Sir William's home at Wappenbury Hall during the war, and put together soon afterwards for Ian Appleyard who competed in the car quite successfully.

The SS11 Tourer was very smart and cost £265 in 1935.

The SS1 Tourer was a much more attractive model than the saloon or coupe.

Arthur Whittaker, deputy chairman of Jaguar Cars, who joined Sir William in Blackpool and was one of the stalwarts of the company. He had the magic of buying everything from suppliers at the right price.

Ernest Rankin, usually known as Bill, did a tireless and magnificent job for Jaguar as their public relations and advertising manager.

## The Monte Carlo Rally

Pre-war and immediate post-war Monte Carlo rallies were very different events to what they are today, and they certainly appeared to be held in much colder weather. At that time the object of the Monte Carlo Rally was to get from one of the many starting points to Monte Carlo, a distance of up to 2,000 miles (3,219 kilometres), with the least loss of marks. There were driving tests and a hillclimb to La Turbie in the case of a tie. Support vehicles were unknown, and the competing cars had to carry all their own spares. A comment among British competitors at the time was that the most important item to carry was a dinner jacket, because it was impossible to get anywhere in Monte Carlo without one.

In 1933 an SS1 driven by V.A. Prideaux Budge and his crew took part in the Monte Carlo Rally, the first international event for the marque. The British starting point for the Monte was John o' Groat's. The winner started in Tallinn, the capital of Estonia. There were, of course, no car heaters at the time. The 20hp SS had only progressed a little into France when it encountered a parked vehicle on the blind side of an icy bend. It took some time to straighten the axle of the SS, and it was time they were never able to recover and they finished 58th. The best British car home was a Bentley powered by a Gardner diesel engine which came fifth.

The company would have to wait until 1956 when a most unlikely car, the big Mk VII saloon, driven by Ulsterman Ronnie Adams, and crewed by Biggar and

Soon after the war Sir William started shipping Jaguar Mk Vs to the United States, and they crossed the Atlantic in style.

Even the most devout enthusiast would have to admit that the SS1 Coupe was slightly over the top, but it was not a motorcar that could be overlooked.

The Hon. Brian Lewis, a competition driver and a motoring journalist in the SS90. In his capacity as a motor journalist he was critical of some aspects of the SS90, which was not outstandingly successful.

Sir William was always an enthusiastic motorist, and he drove an SS100 several times competitively.

Johnstone, won the event in fine style, but by then they were getting a little blasé. That was far from the case in the thirties.

## The Alpine Trial

The Alpine Trial, which in post-war years was called the Alpine Rally, was a high speed race over mountain roads, and until it was abandoned following the disaster in the Mille Miglia, was considered to be the most demanding of all rallies staged at the time. It was very brave of SS Cars to enter a team for the event in 1933, and three tourers were loaned to Humphrey Symonds, Charles Needham and Margaret Allan, all of whom had won a Glacier Cup for a penalty-free run in the Alpine, so they were experienced competitors. One car was painted red, the other white, and the third blue.

Georg Koch, the Austrian distributor also drove a SS1 tourer which had been prepared in Coventry, and another Austrian Graf Orssich drove an SS1 coupe. Out of the five starters three finished, and the highest placed was Koch who was fourteenth overall and sixth in his class. Needham, suffering as the two other team cars did with overheating, was also troubled by steering that needed frequent greasing, but still managed to finish eighth in his class. The two other team cars failed to finish.

They had another go in 1934, with two SS1s and an SS11, and F.W. Morgan in the big SS won a prize for finishing equal fourth in its class, while the other big car had the honour of finishing. The SS11 ran out of time when the drivers overslept on the fifth day, and they were excluded without turning a wheel.

In 1935 the SS90 had been introduced, a good-looking two-seater that changed little outwardly when it became the SS100. It was powered by the 2.7-litre (20hp) side-valve engine in twin carburettor form, and was fitted with a close ratio four-speed gearbox and a choice of back axle ratios. In production form it had an 18-gallon slab tank mounted at the rear with the spare wheel. It sold for £395, but only about fifty were made, so it now has a rarity value which is reflected in the price; a good model will fetch more than an SS100.

Its top speed on a special 8ft (2.4m) × 8in (20cm) chassis was about 90mph, and in competitive events it lacked horse power. The Hon. Brian Lewis came third at Shelsley Walsh, and other SS models put up a reasonable show in national sporting events, but it was the advent of the 2½- then the 3½-litre overhead valve engine, which arrived with the name JAGUAR that rejuvenated the company's sporting life.

# 4
# Coventry

It is extremely difficult to be precise about the number of different makes of motor car built in Coventry since 1901, but ninety-six would be near the mark. Most were assembled from parts produced in the city, and while some had a lifespan of fifty years, others died at birth, whisked from this world by a shortage of cash.

Some were built in factories of grand if unsuitable proportions – the Triumph works was, for instance, on several floors, in buildings on different sides of the road – but many were constructed with great skill, diligence and enthusiasm in extended garages or sheds.

Men who had escaped the devastation of the First World War, and seen the internal combustion engine achieving the unimaginable in the sodden Somme or deserts of Arabia, had a touching faith in its peacetime potential. Flimsily buttressed by their gratuities they came to Coventry, already the home of the motor industry such as it was, and started in the motor-car manufacturing business.

Their enthusiasm was irreproachable, but their credentials in other matters, such as engineering skills, business acumen and so forth, were often questionable. Most failed, but a few succeeded. One was Sir John Black, managing director of the Standard Motor Company, who went to Tiffins grammar school at Kingston upon Thames, and was articled to a local solicitor when the First World War started.

He returned as Captain Black of the Royal Tank Regiment, and like many others first tried his hand at chicken farming, but when this lost its rural attractions and financial fulfilment, he joined the Hillman Motor Company, and subsequently married one of Hillman's six daughters.

A little later he took over the Standard Motor Company from Reginald Maudsley, and built it into a very successful company. Sir John had learned something of internal combustion engines during the war, but he was no engineer. He was however, a great doer and a man of immense character and personality. He, it could be said, succeeded, but I doubt very much if he thought so, for beneath his posturing and immaculate appearance lay a sensitive and tortured man.

Clearly, most did not do as well as Sir John, and today, of the ninety-six names that once adorned Coventry-built cars only two remain in the city: Jaguar and Daimler.

The city to which William Lyons moved in 1928, had recovered from a recession in 1921, and a serious strike in 1922. Unemployment in the West Midlands had reached 33.1 per cent in June 1921, but after the strike a year later it began to decline, and by December 1925 it had fallen to 7.2 per cent. The depression which hit other parts of industrial Britain with such severity had, by comparison, a miniscule effect on Coventry.

Indeed when re-armament started in 1936 Coventry was a magnet for the unemployed who arrived in their thousands. The city missed the industrial revolution, but started its own revolution around the end of the nineteenth century, and it was one that lasted until well into the 1970s. From being a quiet Warwickshire town which had not changed in size since medieval times the population increased fivefold in the twentieth century.

## An Individual City

The three spires which towered over Coventry in the nineteenth century presided over a city of delightful cobbled streets, half-timbered buildings, and more recent buildings remarkable for their solid workmanship rather than their inspired design. Unspoilt commons nudged the edges of the city, and maintained a communion between town and country which was not to survive the next century. The extensive commons were a delightful feature of the city, and the Commoners Rights were not abolished until 1927.

George Eliot in Middlemarch gave a sound portrayal of Coventry; a place renowned for its individualism, industry, and the upright, conventional thinking and attitudes of a society dominated by the self-employed. Coventry thought of itself very much as a working town, and its prim and somewhat pedestrian attitude to life never attracted the gentry or the nobility. If they were missed there appears to be no mention of it.

Even in scholastic life the trades people of Coventry put great emphasis on being taught practical things which they hoped would help them in life, and the many charity schools supported this view, while the grammar school was criticized for sticking to classics. This rugged individualism and shrewdness, endemic in the true Coventrian, and many other Midlanders, was born of a way of life.

Principle occupations of Coventrians in the nineteenth century were ribbon-making, dyeing and then watch-making, and while there were some factories for ribbon-making, and allied occupations such as Cash's nametapes, a great deal of the work was done in the home. Ribbon-making petered out towards the end of the century – although with considerable ingenuity some firms contrived to continue until the 1920s – and was replaced to a large degree by watch-making, and again much of this work was done in workshops attached to an individual's house.

The Coventry watch trade never aimed, or appealed to the mass market, and in 1909 J. W. Player produced perhaps the most complicated clock ever made in Britain, which had a perpetual calendar, and also produced a host of astronomical information. It cost £1,000 to make in 1909, and not altogether surprisingly the firm went out of business in the following year. Indeed, by the end of the century the watch-making industry was declining, but again some firms kept going until the 1920s. It was not, however, an industrial force in the city.

However, these two industries made piecework a way of life in Coventry and this was to cause considerable problems after the Second World War. Because the men and women involved in ribbon-making, and later in the watch trade, could not be paid for the time they spent working, since only they knew how much time they had spent on the job, they were paid instead for what they produced, and the practice in such a relatively small and uncomplicated system worked well. In the complications of a modern motor plant it had many crippling disadvantages, but since old customs die hard it took some time before it

Jaguar were still operating from the Foleshill factory when this photograph was taken of their immediate post-war push-rod engined models.

was replaced by measured day work and there were inevitably some casualties.

As ribbon-making and watch-making died, the bicycle appeared. It was fortuitous for Coventry that James Starley invented the Rover Safety bicycle in 1884, and a number of other enterprising businessmen realized that here was an outlet for their talents. The Dunlop pneumatic tyre was launched in 1889, and then Coventrian Charles Kington Welch invented the detachable pneumatic tyre which he sold to Dunlop. Later Henry Sturmey produced the Sturmey Archer 3-speed gear. Very soon the bicycle industry was enjoying a boom.

An old-established Coventry family, the Rileys, who had been involved in ribbon-making and also in manufacturing textile machinery, turned to bicycle-making and then to cars, and were one of the very few car-making families to emanate from Coventry.

## Coventry becomes Motorized

The bicycle industry brought a dynamism to the city which has never entirely deserted it, and it also brought the first big influx of labour, mostly farm labourers from the surrounding country; they were lonely, illiterate men who inhabited what had become the slums of the Rope Walk and the Chauntries, and they presented new social problems for the city.

They were not the only imports into the city; names which became famous throughout the world as the trade names of bicycles were newcomers towards the end of the last century. James Starley and George Singer came from Sussex, while William Hillman came from Greenwich. Thomas Humber was a Nottinghamshire man, and Daniel Rudge had been a Wolverhampton publican. Others came from further afield, like Siegfried Bettmann who was born in Nuremberg, and came to Coventry via Paris and London intent on exporting bicycles, which he did most successfully. He sold them under the name Triumph because it was a word generally understood throughout Europe, and he later developed the Triumph motor cycle and car business.

The bicycle industry brought the first taste of volume production to the city, and in 1907 the Rudge-Whitworth Cycle Factory, the largest industrial unit in the city, was employing 1,800 people, more than three times the size of any previous factory.

Although the real founder of the motor vehicle industry was Gottlieb Daimler, a German who carried out his experiments on a motor bicycle before turning to a four-wheeler, it seems that an Englishman named Edward Butler was the first man to have produced a motor cycle. As far as can be gathered it ran in 1884. Until the first safety bicycle was produced, also in 1884, the standard machine was the high bicycle, or 'penny farthing', but these required not only a considerable amount of skill to mount and propel, but also a

**Motoring Magazines**

The modern motoring magazine was founded in Coventry by a member of an old Coventry family, William Isaac Iliffe. His father William Iliffe had owned a corner shop at Smithford Street, a part of medieval Coventry that has now disappeared.

He sold books, stationery and wallpaper, but more importantly he had a growing jobbing printing business. Originally William Isaac was apprenticed to the ribbon-making trade, but when the trade suffered its first major setback in 1860 he returned to his father's printing business.

The bicycle business began in Coventry, but he noticed – long before the advent of the Safety Bicycle – that while the city was producing the machines, the magazines catering for their riders were being produced in London. So in 1878 he started *The Cyclist* in collaboration with Henry Sturmey, of three-speed gear fame, and then in 1895 he started *The Autocar*, which is now published under the name of *Autocar and Motor*.

*The Cyclist* was such an outstanding success that it soon absorbed two of its rivals and the editorial side moved to London, where it was produced under the title *The Bicycling News*. Work continued in Coventry, and when Iliffe wanted an assistant editor he recruited a young man called Alfred Harmsworth. Later he became Lord Northcliffe, not only the creator of popular journalism in this country, but of his own newspaper empire. He was not a journalist in the sense that Lord Northcliffe was, but he was needle-sharp, and as far back as 1879, realizing that the two weekly newspapers in Coventry were very dull, he brought out *The Coventry Times*, and twelve years later an evening newspaper, *The Midland Daily Telegraph*, which was to become *The Coventry Evening Telegraph*, still published today. The Iliffe family, however, sold out their interests in the Coventry and Birmingham newspapers some years ago.

A trilby hat and aero screens do not seem to be an ideal combination, but this competitor in the MCC Torquay Rally appears to be coping with equanimity.

good deal of nerve. As a result a less adventurous type of three-wheeler was produced, usually driven through the single rear wheel, with the rider seated between the two front wheels, and it was on this type of machine that Mr Butler fixed his twin horizontal cylinders, which were water-cooled through a water tank mounted in the rear mudguard, and drove the rear wheel through an epicyclic gear.

Nothing much more was heard of the Butler Tricycle, but it was not until 1896 when the first Motor Car Act was passed, and the law allowed a speed in excess of 4mph, with the requirement that the vehicle should be proceeded by a man with a red flag, was dispensed with. Mr Butler must have been a very frustrated man, since Continental manufacturers had no such inhibitions.

The motor cycle industry did not take off with the same vigour as the bicycle industry, and in the very early years of the twentieth century there was a slump in the motor cycle industry. As manufacturers overcame the technical problems, many of which were caused by suppliers, business picked up and by 1905 there were twenty-two motor cycle manufacturers in Coventry. In 1909 Triumph sold 3,000 machines. The motor cycle industry was growing in parallel with the motor car, and contemporary accounts say that it was impossible to exaggerate the immense self-confidence with which young men working in Coventry approached the making of motor cars before 1914.

At the Daimler factory (and it was one of the few real factories), they could not conceive that proper motor cars were made anywhere else, and unlike Henry Ford, the majority believed that the motor car should be confined to those sufficiently informed to understand and appreciate its intricacies. This attitude was to change after the First World War.

A Mk V saloon fits comfortably into the surroundings of Wappenbury Hall, Sir William's home.

## Expansion

With its knowledge of volume production Coventry was invaluable during the war, and a centre of munitions production, high wages and lurid tales of extravagance. But the war did bring some benefits in that a number of new factories were built which served the city well in post-war years. Coventry did suffer a recession immediately after the war, but in addition to the expanding motor industry – fifty-nine new motor manufacturing firms came into being in England in 1920 – there was enormous growth in the machine tool industry, in electrical equipment, telephones and artificial fibres.

It was a prosperous city, and every manufacturer had to pay what were considered good wages at the time, otherwise it was difficult to get the right people. The motor industry paid good wages, but continuous employment was something that was still to come. Everything hinged around the Olympia, and then the Earls Court Motor Shows. Stocks were built up for the show and then it depended on how the car was received whether you worked for nine months or less, but for the normal factory worker it was almost unheard of to find employment for twelve months of the year. In places where there was grievous poverty permanent employment would have been looked upon as heaven, and in Coventry temporary work was generally accepted.

In the 1930s the motor manufacturers were represented by the Coventry Engineering Association, while the trade unions, with a large number in engineering, were combined for negotiating purposes in the Confederation of Shipbuilding and Engineering Workers. The Coventry District Committee included a number of skilled craft unions such as the Metal Mechanics, the Birmingham and Midland Sheet Metal Workers, and the Vehicle Builders, while the Transport and General Workers had taken over the Workers' Union in 1929, to look after the mass of unskilled workers. The core of the trade union movement in Coventry, however, had been centred round the skilled unions which amalgamated in 1921 to form the Amalgamated Engineering Union (AEU).

It included the Toolmakers, long considered the aristocrats of the engineering trades, the Steam Engine Makers who claimed to have been founded in 1826, and the Amalgamated Society of Engineers who harked back to 1851. This group had given the local Labour movement much of its leadership, and before the dispute in 1922 its membership was 11,000.

This particular vitriolic dispute was over the employers' right to decide when overtime should be worked, and its outcome was a disaster for the trade unions. As a result membership faded so that by 1931 the District Committee exercised authority over only about 2,400 members. It was not until re-armament started at the end of the decade that recruitment increased, and the organization improved.

So the trade unions were not a problem to William Lyons and his new company when he arrived at the former munitions factory in Foleshill in 1928. Just before the war a new District Committee of the Confederation of Shipbuilding and Engineering Workers was formed, and the secretary for this powerful Committee was a man called J.L. (Jack) Jones, who rose to be General Secretary of the Transport and General Workers Union.

A powerful Liverpudlian, very much to the left of the Labour party, he had fought for the Republicans in the Spanish Civil War, and had battled his way to the top of his union. During the war there was another big influx of people into Coventry, and a mass of negotiations to be carried out over production problems, pay rates and other matters. He was very much involved.

The idea purveyed by wartime propaganda films, that it was all shoulders to the wheel and no effort spared, is a little short of the truth. During the 'phoney war' it was difficult to recruit people into the shadow factories engaged in war work, but this changed after Dunkirk, and when the USSR came into the war, and the British Communist Leader Harry Pollitt visited Coventry in June 1942 urging an all-out war effort, and a second front, membership of the Coventry Communist Party is said to have increased from 70 to 1500.

For many men and women who had suffered from the Depression of the inter-war years, working on 'war work' was the first opportunity they had had to earn good wages, and there were plenty of trade union officials determined to ensure that in this bountiful era they were not denied their rights.

Many of the shop stewards in the shadow factories were communists, and the workers, living in hostels and strangers to Coventry, looked to them rather than the remote trade union officials, or the traditional Labour party for leadership. During this wartime period the shop stewards were also active politically, and as members of the trade union movement. They became very powerful, and many of them were still ensconsed when the war was over, and I can well remember meeting the charismatic Jack Jones, and some of the stony-faced Communist shop stewards who still operated in the Coventry motor industry, and were still trotting out their Marxist liturgy with utter conviction, and devastating effect.

Like many others before him William Lyons came to Coventry because of the special facilities it offered anyone aspiring to be a motor manufacturer. It developed into a personal relationship which lasted for forty-four years, and during war and peace it overcame many trials and tribulations. Like any close relationship it had its peaks and troughs, but without doubt the cars and the company he created enhanced the city of Coventry, and equally the city, which had changed so much during his working life with it, made a decisive contribution to the success of Jaguar Cars Ltd. It is good that the two still remain synonymous.

businessman'. As Walter Hassan, who is soon to enter this story, would say, 'Sir William was a coachbuilder'. But as a coachbuilder he was a very good judge of engineering, and it was this ability to listen to what other people had to say, and then decide on something which would still be in favour several years ahead, which saved the company a great deal of money.

## Leaps Ahead

Today some manufacturers make as many cars in a week as SS Cars were making in a year, but as a specialist car manufacturer their production was good, higher than MG who were supported by Nuffield, a giant of the time. Yet SS Cars made few changes to their models, and those that they did make were usually minor ones. Even in 1935 when there were major changes to their 1936 model range, the SS1 and SS11 were retained for a short while still powered by the old side-valve engines.

As a sales incentive prices were dropped to £235 for the 10hp saloon, and £330 for the 20hp Airline saloon; a very attractive buy.

When the Standard engine was to be converted to overhead-valves, the minute management team of SS Cars had in mind a figure of around 90bhp, which they believed would be sufficient to propel their new saloon at over 80mph (129kph), and the new SS100 sports car at over 90mph (145kph). In fact in standard form it gave 104bhp at 4,500rpm. It retained the same bore and stroke of 73x106mm, and the seven bearing crankshaft, but the new version had light alloy connecting rods, which it is claimed contributed to the low oil pressure. It had aluminium pistons which operated in a chromium iron block, and two SU carburettors were supplied by an electric pump.

The four-speed synchromesh gearbox – much admired by the contemporary press – was designed and built by the Standard Motor Company, using a single dry-plate clutch. Standard agreed to produce these engines exclusively for SS Cars, but this time they

The SS100 was a very elegant sports car, but was rather short of weight at the stern.

Ted Robins performing at the Prescott Hill Climb in a 1938 SS100.

It could take three men to fill up a 2½-litre SS100 in Inverary in pre-war days.

in fact it was the tourer which did most of the testing. But at the time both of these cars were overshadowed by the saloon.

## The Jaguar

The public were still using the name Standard when referring to SS motor cars, and it was decided that it was high time their products had a new, distinctive name; one to go with the new model. Bill Rankin was very much to the fore in this exercise; William Lyons being much too busy with other matters to devote any time to ploughing through lists of names.

In the motor and aircraft industries at the time animal names were popular, particularly those of predatory animals, and in discussions with the Nelson advertising agency, the name Jaguar kept re-appearing. It was put to Lyons, and he liked it, but there was one snag; Armstrong-Siddeley, who were in Parkside on the other side of Coventry, had built a Jaguar aircraft engine. Approaches were made to the company and they were told that the engine was now obsolete, and it was with pleasure that they offered the name. So, SS Jaguar it became.

For many years after the war there were a number of journalists who could recall the launch of the SS Jaguar, and the enormous impact it had made on the motoring world at the time. Thanks to Bill Rankin it had all been carefully contrived, and his contribution to the success of Jaguar should not be underestimated. It was his idea that a lunch should be staged at the Mayfair Hotel, in London, where the new SS Jaguar would be launched, and where guests would be invited to guess the price of the new model; a sure-fire way of getting some acreage in the newspapers.

Apparently guests at this trade lunch were most impressed with the new SS Jaguar – news of which had been well and truly leaked, so it was not a shattering surprise – and then they set about guessing the price. The price of the original SS1 had surprised everyone, and they were not to be taken in so easily with this one, and the average price worked out at £632; still a remarkably low estimate. The 2½-litre was priced at £385 and the 1½- at £285. William Lyons was keen that he should not lose contact with the lower end of the market.

With their own stand the new SS Jaguars were stars at the Olympia motor show in 1935, and by the end of the year deliveries had started.

## A Sporting Success

The launch of the Jaguar SS100 – at £395 their dearest model – was a relatively modest affair, the feeling being that with this car actions would speak louder than words, and in the Alpine Trial of 1936 they got their action when a car driven by Tommy Wisdom, and his wife Elsie (who was always known as Bill) made a penalty-free run, and if there had been a general classification, would have won it. They had been

An impressive line-up of Mk V police cars. Jaguar's connection with the constabulary started before the war.

In pre-war days a sports car was supposed to be capable of coping with some off-road activity as this 2½-litre SS100 demonstrates on the Lawrence Cup Trial.

competing against cars of the calibre of 328 BMWs, so the *cognoscenti* began to take notice. Because the French found themselves outclassed in Grand Prix racing they conveniently transformed those events staged in France, into sports car races, and that year Australian F.J. McEvoy won his class driving an SS100 in the Marne Grand Prix. Later Casimiro de Oliveiras won the race at Vila Real outright in an SS100 after a very hard battle against BMWs, Adlers and Aston Martins. It was the company's first outright win in a continental race. In the Monte Carlo Rally the Hon Brian Lewis had taken second place in his class in the coachwork competition and another second in the Engine Appearance Competition, which said something for the cleanliness of the new engine.

In the SS100 the 2½-litre was giving about 115bhp, not quite enough to give it a top speed of 100mph (161kph). In fact *The Autocar* gave it a top speed of 91.84mph (148kph), after a two-way run, and a 0–60mph (0–96.5kph) figure of 13½ seconds. It was a bit twitchy to drive (Walter Hassan thought the 3½ was 'a pig' to drive), the suspension was very hard, the tyre wear – heavy, and it had a poor lock. But the engine was not temperamental, it was light, weighing only 23½cwt, but very strong, and performance-wise it would cope with almost all of the competition.

A lack of independent front suspension and weight over the back wheels, were its main drawbacks. While the drawbacks were to continue it was soon to get even more power.

The work-force in Coventry was growing rapidly and numbered about 1,500, and the skills required

Motorcycle production went on throughout the war, and here in military guise, are a line up of Swallow sidecars.

The SS100 Coupe which was built just before the war, but never went into production.

were changing equally rapidly as the change over from the old Swallow construction methods of metal on ash frames, were changed for all-metal bodies.

## All Steel Bodies

SS Cars began importing labour to Coventry; people with specialized knowledge of the new body building art, and these were to be found at Briggs in Essex, the plant that produced bodies for the massive Ford Motor Company. Lead loading was used to smooth out tricky curves, and the SS Jaguars, and subsequent Jaguars had plenty of those. Dramatically different working methods, along with a whole series of new suppliers were brought into operation, and it inevitably caused problems.

Along with the all-steel bodies came two new overhead-valve engines: a 3½-litre and a 1.8-, both derived from Harry Weslake's design. The 1½-litre was based on the Standard Fourteen, and had a bore and stroke of 82x106mm (1,776cc), which gave 65bhp at 4,500 rpm. It was equipped with a single downdraught SU carburettor, a mechanical pump, and a manual choke. The 3½-litre was not sinply a bored out 2½, the bore and stroke were 82x110mm (3,485cc), producing 125bhp at 4,250rpm. It had twin SU carburettors and twin electric pumps, an automatic choke and a 14-gallon petrol tank, not much for a car that was doing just a little over 21mpg (33.8kpg).

The cars were launched at the 1937 Motor Show (they were annual events in those days) and, as they would say in show business, were greeted with rapturous applause. For reasons of economy the range was restricted to a saloon and a drophead coupe, both of which could be fitted with any of the three engines. The SS100 was equipped with the new 3½-litre, or the 2½-litre engine. The new bodies were not dissimilar to the previous models, but they were wider, had bigger doors and considerably more interior space. Despite the improved performance of the 1½-litre, they found the big, heavy body hard work.

They were, of course, incredible value for money, the 1½-litre drophead coupe selling for a modest £298, while the 3½-litre version cost £465. At this time the famous Lucas P100 headlights were standard on SS Jaguars, but William Lyons managed to buy them at half price. No one is quite certain how he managed to pull off individual deals, but there is little doubt that he did convince his suppliers that it would enhance their products to have them adorning his cars.

He had had two good years, and in 1936 orders had more than doubled on the previous year. His cars totally dominated the 20hp class, and he was now getting repeat orders – one in three of his customers owned an SS motor car. By 1937 net profit had gone up by £10,000 on 1935 to reach £34,292. However, the winter of 1937 brought trouble.

When a manufacturer is depending on a number of suppliers for the body alone, they all have to produce on time, or clearly the whole system breaks down. The suppliers were not producing on time and for several months, despite the efforts of Lyons and his staff, the works were at a virtual standstill, and the increased workforce was doing very little. This did not suit William Lyons in the least, and it is not difficult to imagine that there were some very abrasive meetings between him and his suppliers.

All was not always sunshine and light with his staff; they were not always a happy band of brothers. Harry Gill, one of the managers, had been with Lyons since the beginning. He was a forthright Yorkshireman – and you can read into that what you like – who had joined Swallow Sidecars from school, and was now an integral part of the organization. At this time W.C.E. Orr, or Ted as he was usually known, joined the company as works manager from the Standard Motor Company, and some forcible views were expressed by both of them on how things could best be achieved.

By the spring of 1938, after an exhausting winter, everything was slotting into place. Production was running at the rate of up to 100 cars a week, and by July the figure had increased to 150 a week, by far the highest ever achieved by the company, and although it had been feared that the company would make a loss because of the bad winter, this was not the case. In the autumn Lyons told shareholders that difficulties with suppliers had affected production, but these had been overcome after April and they had 'arranged an amicable settlement with the suppliers concerned'. Profits were down by more than £12,000, but they

The exaggerated lines had completely disappeared from this 1948 3½-litre Jaguar Drophead Coupe.

The three-quarter front view of the Jaguar 3½-litre Drophead Coupe show off its restrained lines extremely well.

still managed to make a net profit of £22,218, and pay a reduced dividend of five per cent. He was optimistic about the future, and with good reason: the new models were selling extremely well, and even the sceptics were having to take note of its competitive achievements. At this point William Lyons decided a holiday would be in order – the first for a long time – and he took himself and his family off to the south of France.

## The SS100

The SS100 captures the imagination of most enthusiasts today, but only about 300 were built, and they were not the easiest cars to drive quickly in their original form, but they added greatly to the image of the marque. In the last meeting at Brooklands in 1937, the Long Handicap race, Tommy Wisdom, at the wheel of a stripped down SS100, won the event at an average speed of 111.85mph (180kph), and put in the fastest lap of 118mph (190kph). The car had been well prepared, and it was pointing the direction of things to come; what could be achieved with the production engine and chassis of a modestly priced motor car.

The production version of the SS100 was the company's first genuine 100mph car, a figure that could be achieved by only a handful of cars at that time, all of which cost considerably more than the SS100. And the Harry Weslake designed engine was proving to be very reliable. It obviously had a personal appeal to William Lyons who drove one with great enthusiasm at the SS Car Club's Donington meeting in 1938, setting up fastest lap of the day at 68.81mph, and the best race average at 67.37mph. He was as determined behind the wheel of a motor car, as he was in everything else he attempted.

At this time, the leaping Jaguar emblem came on the scene. A company specializing in such things sent one to Bill Rankin for his approval. He approved of the idea, but not of the specimen sent to him, for among his many talents Bill was an amateur sculptor, and his idea of a Jaguar was rather different from the emaciated object sent to him. With the aid of F. Gordon Crosby, artist for *The Autocar* magazine, the leaping Jaguar, so familiar today, was created.

In May 1949 R.M.V. (Soapy) Sutton covered a flying mile at Jabbeke at 132.596mph (213.387kph) in an XK120 minus hood and screen, and fitted with an optional undershield.

The Jaguar Mk V was a stylish motor car, but in 1951 driven by Cecil Vard, it came third in the Monte Carlo, and surprised a lot of people.

They had not this sort of manoeuvre in mind when the Mk V was created, but this competitor in the Little Rally of 1953 had not been told.

## Boom Time

Those immediate pre-war summers were spectacularly sunny, and although the threat of war was heavy in the background, the baking beaches were packed with day trippers, for the worst of the unemployment was over. Charabancs loaded with excited and bewildered children carrying signs, 'First time to the Sea', trundled into the resorts, and barefoot children still scoured the meaner streets of our industrial cities. But generally, life was improving, and the middle classes, in particular, were enjoying a new era of prosperity, and these were SS Jaguar customers.

Certainly the sun was shining for William Lyons, his company, and the city of Coventry, for in the year beginning August 1938, he produced over 5,000 motor cars for the first time in the history of the company, of which a record 252 were exported. At the 1939 London Motor Show, which had now moved from Olympia to Earls Court, he showed a fixed head coupe version of the SS Jaguar 100, which rumour priced at £595. It was a beautiful car, but only one prototype was made.

In the sporting world he was also enjoying considerable success, a 3½-litre saloon entered by J.O.H. Willing winning the Grand Prix d'Honneur in the Concours de Confort at Monaco, while Jack Harrop from Manchester came first in the Open Cars over 15hp Class in the RAC Rally driving a 3½-litre SS Jaguar 100. Driving a 2½-litre version Tommy Wisdom came first in the 3-litre class in the Paris–Nice trial, and Sam Newsome, a Coventry Jaguar distributor and owner of the Coventry Hippodrome theatre, once again displayed his talents as a driver by roaring up the Shelsley Walsh Hill Climb in 42.95 seconds, an astonishing performance for an unsupercharged motor car.

Driving a works-prepared 3½-litre saloon in the Monte Carlo rally in January 1939, Jack Harrop (who was killed in the war) brought his car into equal tenth place, and won the Barclay Silver Cup for the best performance by a British car, the first important award claimed by an SS touring car. The car had been prepared by Walter Hassan, accepted by other engineers as one of the best engine engineers in the country.

Walter was working at Brooklands in 1938 when he was approached by Tommy Wisdom, motoring journalist and racing driver, who told him there was a job going at SS Jaguar for a chief experimental engineer. Walter was a Londoner, who affected a considerable

Possibly inspired by Cecil Vard's third place in the Monte Carlo Rally in the previous year, this Mk V is passing Buttermere in the Daily Express Rally.

**Walter Hassan OBE**

If you say that Walter Hassan is an old-fashioned engineer you are likely to be misunderstood, and what was intended as a compliment can be interpreted as a disparaging remark, but I believe it is the most apt way to describe him because he personifies all that was best in a breed of engineer who knew their theory, but were also intensely practical men who had the wisdom of a wide-ranging experience and the judgement born of oily hands.

In the motor industry today, where specialization is of paramount importance, it is almost impossible to gain the rounded engineering knowledge acquired by engineers of that generation. They worked for what were automotive boutiques by today's standards, where everything was happening almost within arm's length. It was in such surroundings that Walter T.F. Hassan started his engineering career.

More than seventy years later he is still designing engines; back to his first love – a vintage Bentley he has transformed with twin overhead camshafts.

Walter's father was the manager of a gentlemen's outfitters in Highgate – Walter says he sold socks – and he was the eldest of six children. He was educated at East Finchley Primary School, and then at the Northern Polytechnic.

'When I told my father that I was not interested in selling socks, it was decided to send me to Hackney Technical Institute, but at fifteen I had to start looking for a job', says Walter. He wanted to be a marine engineer, but in the land-locked regions of Upper Holloway, and East Finchley, the prospects were not bright, so he settled for automobile engineering, and with the diligent help of his father a well pressed and polished young Walter was taken to visit a number of prospective employers. In 1920 jobs were not easy to find.

His father knew someone at the Sunbeam works, so again they set off in search of employment, but with no success. On the way back, however, their luck changed.

'We were walking back through Cricklewood when my father noticed a new factory being built, which bore the name of the owner . . . W.O. Bentley.

'So he wrote to them, and asked for an interview for me; it was granted, and I started work as a boy learner aged fifteen, at ten shillings (50p) a week, as employee number fifteen. They had two prototype cars at the time, and I was the tea-boy, and generally making myself useful, but Frank Clements who was the experimental engineer, and also raced the cars, soon took me to Brooklands, and that I thoroughly enjoyed', he said. There he changed plugs, carburettor jets, and generally learned his way around an engine.

He was learning a lot about the practical side of automobile engineering, because he was surrounded by experts, but the theoretical side was not overlooked. 'A man at W.O. Bentley's called Dewhurst told me that I should become a member of the Institute of Automobile Engineers, so I attended the Regent Street Polytechnic for quite some time on a part-time basis, and eventually took the examinations for membership, which I passed.' Two years later he went over to the TT races in the Isle of Man where the Bentley's came 2nd, 4th and 5th, beaten only by the Sunbeam, and at the age of twenty-five he was virtually running the racing department and making annual trips to the Le Mans 24-Hour Race. 'Of course I had been there for ten years', he points out.

Walter also drove competitively himself, as the ground at Montlhery near Paris will testify. Driving a 3-litre Bentley in appalling conditions he spun off the track, hit a gate, and rolled the car over several times. His face was embedded in the ground so firmly he feels sure that the imprint must be still there today. As a result he spent three months in hospital, recovering and improving his French.

When Rolls Royce took over Bentley Motors in 1931 the wealthy sportsman, and successful Bentley driver Woolf Barnato, offered him a job looking after his racing Bentley, and through his association was born the famous Barnato Hassan Bentley, and later the Pacey Hassan. It came at a most fortuitous time for Walter who was about to be married, because with the job went a cottage on Barnato's Sussex estate.

Unfortunately a fire on the estate put an end to that, but it was only a temporary setback, and the omnipotent Barnato soon had him established in a flat above his garages in Belgrave Mews West. It was there that he built Old No. 1, a 6½-litre engined car in a 4-litre frame which went over the top of the banking at Brooklands in the 500-mile race, killing the driver. He re-built it as a coupe, but could never stop the exhaust fumes entering the body.

When Barnato decided that he was going to give up motor racing his paternalism continued, and Walter was summoned to his office, and told that he must consider his career. Barnato introduced him to Rolls Royce at Derby, which he did not like, and then to ERA at Bourne in Lincolnshire. For a few months he worked at Bourne.

'But my wife was then in Surrey, and I was drinking too much beer, so I arranged to join Thompson and Taylor at Brooklands, where I was employed on the Railton-designed record breaker to be driven by John Cobb', he said.

Here at Brooklands he first met Bill Heynes, chief engineer of SS Cars. Following Tommy Wisdom's successes at Brooklands in an SS100 Edgar Wadsworth, another wealthy motor racing enthusiast – as the majority had to be – asked Hassan to tune his car. 'I got a lot of help from Bill Heynes, who produced pistons and so on for me, and that was one of reasons why I went to SS

Cars in 1938', he added. He worked on aircraft carburettors and air transportable vehicles during the war, and afterwards played a leading role in the development of the XK120 engine.

Then he spent some years with Coventry Climax – headed by the delightful Leonard Lee – where they developed a fire pump that could produce twice the rate of water as a wartime pump at half the weight, and the engine from this soon became the backbone of our very successful Grand Prix cars. Thanks to Walter and Harry Munday Coventry Climax Racing Engines were producing new engines like peas out of a pod. Not all were successful, as Walter readily admits – the flat 16-cylinder was their principal failure – but the vast majority were.

When Jaguar Cars took over Coventry Climax they allowed the racing programme to continue until the formula changed, and then Walter Hassan, who was now part of Jaguar again, and Harry Munday produced the V12.

At eighty-five Walter Hassan is busy converting the single overhead camshaft Pacey Hassan Bentley, into a twin overhead camshaft version with the sparking plugs placed over the combustion chambers instead of at the side. He is almost boyishly enthusiastic. His hips and his knees are giving him a bit of trouble, but his mind is as sharp as ever.

In the 1950s a group of motoring journalists, of which I was one, were straining to appear very bright, and asked Walter why he had not tried such and such a technique on his engines. 'Ah, now we tried that in 1937, and it didn't work', he replied. Silence ensued.

Walter is known as an engine engineer, and he has a feel for and an intimacy with engines which is spellbinding, but this large man with his attentive, thinking eyes, is also an automobile engineer in the real sense of the word, in that he has designed suspensions, indeed, he has created complete motor cars from scratch.

I doubt if we will see the like of these 'old-fashioned' engineers again.

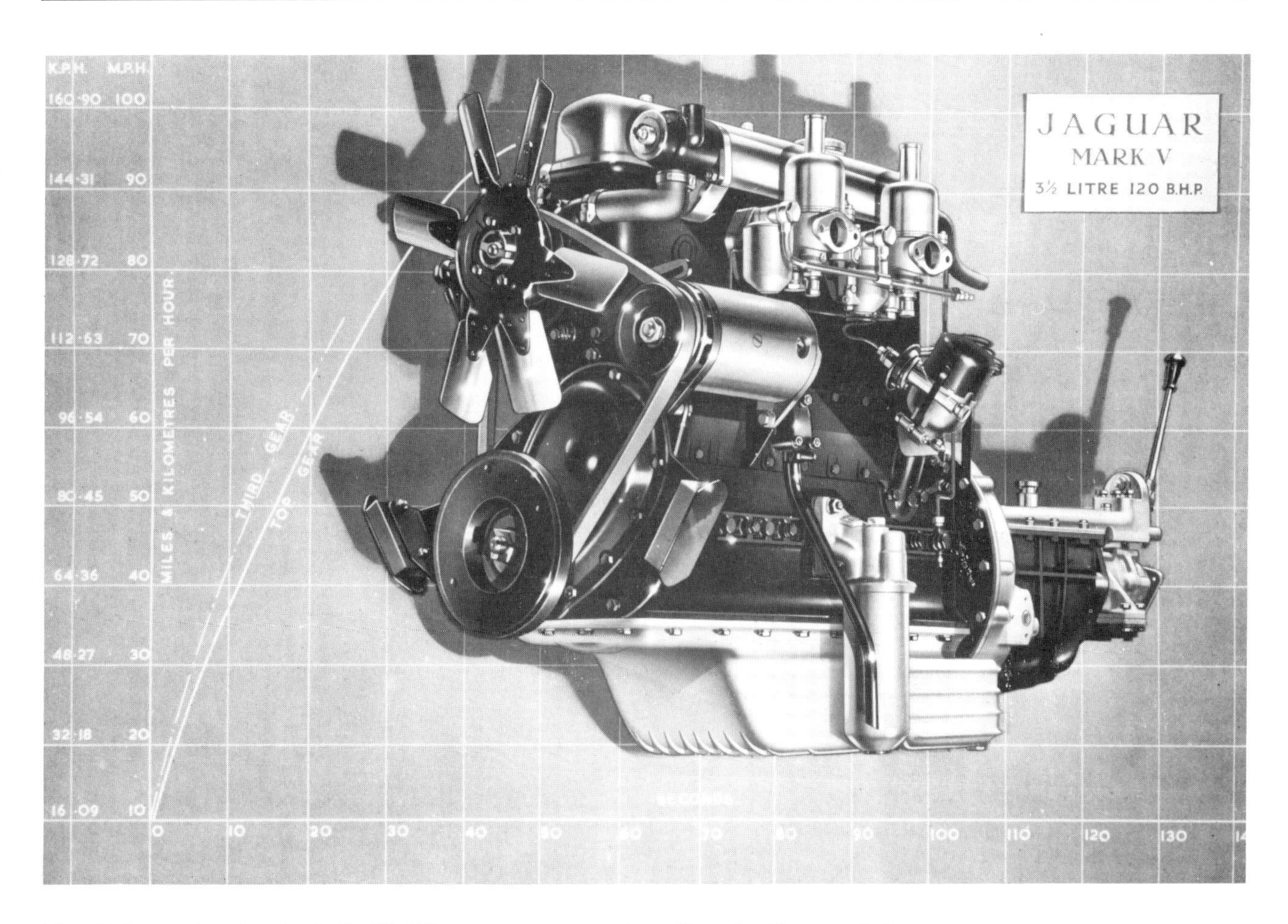


The 3½-litre push-rod engine in the Mk V Jaguar was a very workmanlike unit with many admirers.

It was very dashing to have models to assist in selling your cars.

This 2½-litre SS100 was rallying effectively in the Morecambe Car Rally of 1952.

distrust of anyone north of Watford, but he knew Bill Heynes, who was soon to become a director of the company, and he knew of William Lyons. He took himself to Coventry, was interviewed by Lyons, who approved, and late in 1938 he joined the company, and with Heynes, and later Harry Munday, was instrumental in producing the XK120 and the V12, the two most famous engines in the company's history.

At first he was involved in 'sorting out', as he says, the SS100 which Sam Newsome drove with such success at Shelsley Walsh by modifying the rear suspension. 'It was a pig of a car because there was no weight over the back axle', he says. He was also given the job of developing an independent front suspension system, but Walter and engines were inseparable, and soon he was producing more power from the 3½-litre engine, and did such effective work on the Harrop Monte Carlo car that on one special stage it produced the second fastest time of the rally, a very creditable performance for a big saloon complete with undertray, and spares. It was all the more remarkable because Hassan, like many others in SS Cars at the time, was operating on a shoestring, and their equipment in the experimental shop was derisory.

Nevertheless, Walter Hassan found Lyons 'an excellent boss'. 'He was mean, but we understood why he was mean; he was trying to build something up, and he treated us fairly'. Walter's association with the company lasted for many years, off and on.

Apart from the fixed head coupe the models were unchanged for 1939, and there was little change made to the 1940 models. The 3½-litre versions were given hydraulic piston style dampers, and heaters and an air conditioning system were offered as standard on the 2½- and 3½-litre models. On the 1½-litre saloon, which sold for £298, they were not available as standard equipment, but a special equipment model was available for £318, and for this the buyer did get

Many people thought that the Jaguar Mk V was the most attractive car produced by the company, and that the Coupe de Ville style model was the most attractive of the lot.

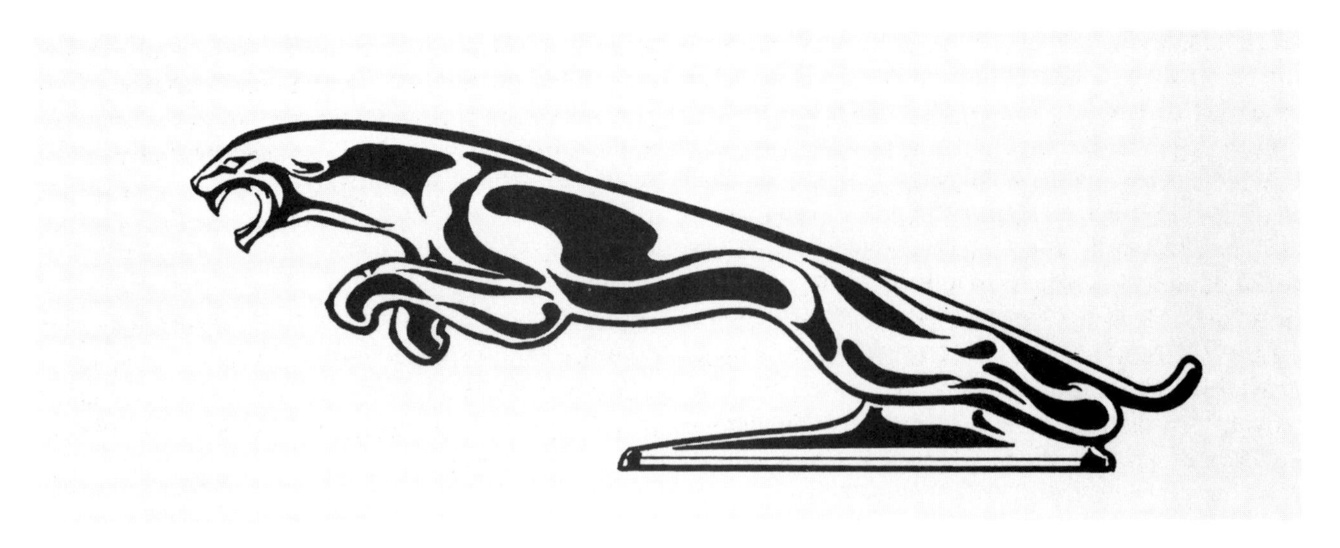

The famous leaping Jaguar emblem which is known throughout the world.

In the early 1980s the XJS nearly went out of production, but it is still going strong. This a Le Mans limited edition model.

air conditioning, plus bigger headlamps, fog lamps, and a smartly finished luggage locker. A Philco wireless had now come down to £15.15s, but the fitting charge remained the same at £3.

When the war came in September a new factory was built in Swallow Road with the aid of the war ministry, but with output approaching 200 a week before the war, building work at Swallow Road was in hand, and Motor Panels (Coventry) Ltd, whose factory was on the Whitmore Park estate had been bought by SS Cars Ltd.

Lyons and his directors were digesting this latest acquisition, and wrestling with the problems of expanding production when the country went to war. Although the company was immediately involved in war work car production did not stop overnight. A trickle of cars were being produced until about the middle of 1940, but by this time purchase tax had been imposed and customers required a permit from the Ministry of War Transport.

The company's contribution to the war effort was considerable, but with an eye forever searching the horizons, I am sure that the future of 'his company', was never far from the forefront of Lyons' mind. When the war ended six years later he was without doubt all ready to go.

# 6
# A New Engine – A New Era

## The War Years

In the British league of 'bombs dropped per square mile' Coventry was not at the top, but it suffered badly; the Coventry Blitz in the early years of the war was a tragic foretaste of things to come elsewhere in the country. Several factories suffered more than SS Cars – Daimler, Alvis and Rover – but in November 1940 six shops were destroyed, and many a morning Lyons arrived at his factory expecting to see a scene of devastation. In fact it only happened once.

They were trying times in more ways than one for William Lyons, who had just bought Motor Panels and suffered the effects of body supply problems. With car production fading his new bankers, Lloyds, insisted that he guarantee the SS account personally, which he did for some time.

War Department contracts were available and with his usual vigour he pursued them. During the war nearly 10,000 sidecars were produced as well as a great number of trailers, many specially designed to be used in the Far East campaign, and constructed so that they could be used on narrow tracks.

Aircraft contracts were the most important however, and it was thought that SS Cars would have a large slice of the manufacture of the Manchester bomber, but this was dropped. However, Lyons and his team were intent on getting their share of the available work, and before long contracts began to come their way. They became official repairers of the twin-engined Whitley bomber, and manufacturers, as well as fabricators of parts for the Stirling bomber, the Mosquito, the four-engined Lancaster and the Spitfire.

In the world of engines they became sub-contractors to Armstrong-Siddeleys' aircraft engine division making parts for the Cheetah, a massive radial engine which was very much in vogue at the time. Towards the end of the war the company also made complete centre sections for the first operational jet aircraft, the Meteor, and were honoured with a fly past over the Coventry factory.

## Acquisitions – Dispositions

Since there was nothing of interest for him to do in Coventry Walter Hassan went down to Bristol to work on aircraft carburettor development, but hurried back to SS Cars when he discovered that they were to develop an air-transportable, parachutable, lightweight vehicle. He was joined in Coventry by Claude Baily, who had worked for Anzani and Morris, and who became part of the engineering team as chief designer under Bill Heynes. It was a talented team and they produced two vehicles, one powered by a V-twin JAP engine mounted at the rear, known as the VA, and the other the VB which was powered by a Ford four-cylinder engine mounted at the front. Both had independent suspension, a good cross-country performance and were light. After tests the VB model was bought by the Ministry, and used for some years afterwards, but neither went into production.

Aircraft and parachute development overtook the vehicles, and transporting a normal jeep by air became commonplace. Lyons did quite a lot of recruiting during the war years, and apart from Baily others to join the team were a first-class production engineer John Silver, R.J. (Bob) Knight, who was a genius with suspensions, and was later in charge of engineering from 1972 to 1980, Cyril Crouch and Tom Jones, who became the chief body and chassis engineers respec-

The war time VB Jeep, like the VA, never went into production. Aircraft had become bigger and could cope with more conventional vehicles.

Walter Hassan demonstrates that the war time prototype vehicle codenamed VA was very light.

It could hardly be called a beautiful baby, but with independent suspension all round, a Ford engine at the front and lightweight it was designed as an air transportable jeep when twin-engined aeroplanes of limited capacity were all that was available. This was the VB, the VA had a big JAP engine driving the rear wheels. Aeroplanes became bigger and Jaguar's baby jeeps were not required.

During the Second World War Jaguar were very much involved in servicing aircraft, particularly for RAF Bomber Command, which were often shuttled to and from Coventry by women 'ferry' pilots.

tively, and a first-class accountant Arthur Thurstans, who joined the company from Lockheeds in 1943. Fred Gardner, always something of a law unto himself, could not be reconciled to someone snooping around his sawmill, accountant or not, and it needed the pacifying words of William Lyons to persuade him of the virtues of this new tool of industry.

One who had left was Harry Gill, that pillar of the early days, who had been moved over to Motor Panels, to work under the general manager, a man imported from Briggs at Dagenham. This was too much for the Yorkshireman and he left, but the story ends happily since he did well on his own account.

Another departure, this time at the end of the war, was Cyril Holland, who had been the original Swallow draughtsman, and the man who had created the jigs and tools in the company's earliest days. William Lyons had always needed someone to transform his ideas and sketches into reality, and in the early days it had been Cyril, but as a coachbuilder he found himself out of step in a steel-bodied age. He left for the joys of Bournemouth, and his own small works.

The acquisition of Motor Panels at the beginning of the war had not been a success. Lyons wanted to make his own bodies and not be dependent on outside manufacturers (something that was to feature largely in a major decision he made years later) but Motor Panels was not a success for SS Cars, and he sold it to Rubery Owen Ltd, a giant in the automotive engineering world. However, thanks to his War Department contracts Lyons had made some physical expansions, and built up his machine shop facilities, and he was soon to make another important acquisition.

## Good Buys

The first all new car to be produced after the war was the Standard Vanguard, and Sir John Black had decided on a one-model policy for his company; an arrangement which lasted for a limited amount of time – even Volkswagen could not survive on one model. He was soon to acquire Triumph as well, which Lyons had turned down in 1939 – having looked at the books he had been unimpressed – and on this front Sir John was to produce a number of models with varying degrees of

Another 'works' XK120 – not the easiest car in the world to drive quickly, particularly in the wet.

There were several attempts to produce the post-war Jaguar shape. The ones that were accepted were usually right.

It is easy to see why the Jaguar XK120 Roadster stifled the growth of many good sports cars that were around at the time.

success. The Triumph 1800, using the Standard four-cylinder 1.7-litre engine was the first to go into production in the late 1940s.

As the end of the war approached the minds of manufacturers were motivated once again by the production of cars, and at a meeting with Lyons, Sir John who had been in charge of the shadow factories which ringed Coventry, and had made a massive effort during the war years, explained that he would no longer be able to offer exclusive rights to the 2.7- and 3.5-litre overhead valve engines, as he had before the war.

Without hesitation Lyons offered to buy the production line, and when the offer was accepted he had the required cheque on Sir John's desk with almost indecent haste. Sir John was still the go-getter admired by Lyons, but he was now becoming slightly eccentric, and they had their altercations. When Sir John wanted to change his mind about the deal, it was flatly turned down, as was an offer by Sir John to merge the two companies. The proposition was ludicrous; no factory in Coventry was big enough to house both their egos, and when Sir John suggested that, with his acquisition of Triumph, he would put SS Cars out of business, their meetings became infrequent and strictly formal.

The opportunity to buy his own engine production facilities was heaven-sent, and Lyons grabbed it with both hands; it was another step along the route to becoming a complete manufacturer, but it was a route he never completed.

Walter Hassan was very much involved in the design and development of the XK engine and the V12 was very much his baby. In his time with Coventry Climax he also designed and developed their successful Grand Prix engines.

## Fire-Watching

Apart from coping with the day to day realities of a country at war Lyons, and some of his staff, allowed themselves the occasional luxury of dreaming, and Cyril Holland produced a number of models from William Lyons' sketches. A favourite time for informal discussions, and for thinking ahead, was when Lyons, Heynes, Baily and Hassan were fire-watching on Sunday evenings.

By 1944 these discussions had taken on a weight and urgency missing from earlier days, because even the most optimistic at the beginning of the war were literally dreaming of a time so distant and so obscure it was difficult to define. By 1944 however, victory was in sight, and the boss and the engineers got down to brass tacks; exactly what sort of an engine would produce the magic they needed in the post-war years to enhance their growing reputation, and fulfil William Lyons' dreams.

## Overhead Camshafts

He put it to the engineers that what was required was an engine of 2½-litre capacity (he did not believe that the public would be able to afford an engine of three litres or above), producing 120bhp, that was quiet, simple and therefore cheap to make. Then he added the rider that made them all blink; it must have twin overhead camshafts.

According to Walter Hassan he wanted the engine

In every small American town there is a drug store and a church, and in the 1950s in California there was often an XK120 as well. Ten thousand were exported to the USA.

to look like a grand prix engine of pre-war days, but to them this was an unnecessary complication, and they pointed out that his requirements could be met quite simply by developing the overhead-valve engines they had been using before the war with such success. The many disadvantages of such an engine for the purpose in hand were well thought out and detailed, and Lyons listened intently to their arguments. Then, the man with no engineering qualifications, but an abundance of flair, said that the new engine would have twin overhead camshafts. Discussions on the configuration of the engine ceased.

Walter Hassan points out that it was the right decision for the wrong reasons.

There is no doubt that it was at that fire-watching session that the fundamentals of the XK120 engine were decided, and although there were a few attempts at finding the right size, the principles remained.

There was nothing revolutionary about the XK120 engine; much more advanced engines had been made, but they were fitted to specialist cars, and owned by people who could afford to visit specialist garages and pay special prices. When the XK120 – a bronze-coloured one – was launched at the 1948 Earls Court Motor Show it cost £1,275 including purchase tax (£998 without), and was clearly about to open up a new market for twin overhead camshaft machines, and present new problems in servicing for mechanics who might have seen, but who were unlikely to have worked on, such engines.

No one person designed the XK120 engine; it was a team effort, but the principal players in that team were Bill Heynes, Walter Hassan, Claude Baily, Harry Weslake and Richard Oats, and they should be remembered as a remarkable combination, because they not only met Lyons' criteria, they exceeded it on every count.

When it first went into production it was producing 160bhp, it was quiet and easy to make, and it was so far ahead of its time as a production engine that it lasted for forty years in various forms.

As soon as the war finished work started on getting an engine into production, but which engine? The first one tried was a twin overhead camshaft unit of 1½-litre capacity, a very high revving unit called the XF, but this was abandoned because of crankshaft problems. Another 1½-litre unit was built following the pre-war BMW principles of overhead valve layout, but this proved to be too noisy, and eventually they built a four-cylinder 2-litre engine with twin overhead camshafts very similar to the XK120 engine. Always concerned that he might lose touch with the lower end of the market William Lyons had two engines in mind; one of two, and one of just over three litres.

## The Missing Engines

Walter Hassan says that they built five of the 2-litre engines, but they produced a 'sizzling' noise which did not please Lyons, who was, in any case, enamoured of six cylinders. But one of these engines had its moment of glory when it was used in a special record breaker driven by Colonel 'Goldie' Gardner on the Jabbeke motorway east of Ostend at over 176mph (283kph). The engine had been tuned by Walter Hassan to give 146bhp at 6,000rpm, with a maximum of 6,500rpm.

The decision was taken to go ahead with a six-cylinder engine of 3.2-litre capacity, and a decision on the 2-litre unit was put in abeyance, which is just as well because the remaining four engines went missing. Were they stolen? 'They just disappeared', says Walter Hassan.

## Leaks and Whines

Even with a talented team of engineers it is unusual if everything is right the first time round.

When the 3.2-litre was tested it was decided that there was not sufficient power, particularly at the bottom end, and to correct this the stroke was increased to 106mm, which coupled with a bore of 83mm were to be the dimensions of the original XK120 engine. But with production imminent, oil leaks were discovered around the crankshaft and the drive to the camshafts, and Hassan detected a whine in the camshaft drive mechanism, which was dismissed as a figment of his imagination by Bill Heynes. Convinced that it was not, and knowing of William Lyons' obsession with noise of any kind, he set about devising a system of camshaft drive that would eliminate the whine, and the oil leaks.

Although it was inconceiveable that anyone should fail to realize that Lyons was the boss, he reinforced his hands-on approach to the management of his company by spending a few minutes in every department each day.

On one such occasion Lyons was visiting the engineering department, and Hassan invited him over to listen to the engine running, and asked him if he could hear this particular whine. At first he said he could not, then he agreed that it was there, and Hassan explained how he could overcome the problem, although it would require parts of the engine to be re-designed. Heynes was called over, and on this occasion agreed that there was a whine.

Despite the fact that the introduction of the engine would have to be delayed Lyons gave instructions that the re-designing must be done, and in doing so made another major contribution to the success of the engine. When it appeared there were no whines, and no leaks, and it looked very exciting.

The XK120 engine will go down in motoring history

It was, of course, possible to over-cook things in an XK120, as this driver demonstrates at Goodwood.

as one of the great engines of all time, yet like so many things at that remarkable company, it was achieved on a shoestring, by dedicated, practical engineers, and a boss who was big enough to take the right decisions, unpleasant though they may have been.

The six-cylinder XK engines always had a long piston stroke, a characteristic which became unfashionable, but even the production models would rev comfortably up to 5,500rpm, and the competition versions much higher than that – the D-type Jaguar was exceeding 170mph (273kph) at Le Mans in 1954. More than anything the long piston stroke contributed to that effortless, silent power, which combined with the superb ride provided by Bob Knight, and his small team of chassis engineers, made the post-war Jaguars such outstanding cars.

In the 1960s I can recall talking to engineers from Daimler–Benz who could not believe the size of the engineering staff at Coventry. Though not in full flight themselves they were still employing thousands of engineers and technicians, and had more people designing door handles and accessories than Jaguar employed on the whole car.

## Jaguar Cars Ltd

While William Lyons had set in motion the new engine and new cars as soon as the war was over, there was the question of immediate sales, and the company's name. Clearly at that time the initials SS had unpleasant connotations for the majority of people, and as far as Lyons was concerned it also harked back to pre-war days and the company's association with the Standard Motor Company, which gave some people the impression they were an adjunct of that company.

So in March 1945 an Extraordinary General Meeting of the company was called, and at that meeting it was decided to re-name the company Jaguar Cars Ltd, and the SS Hexagon disappeared to be replaced by a monogrammed 'J'.

In the immediate post-war years there were still shortages of virtually everything including pool petrol (which had a low octane rating and was rationed) and ration cards for food, and everything from crockery to curtains was stamped utility. On the face of it, it was not an ideal climate for luxury cars, but there was an enormous pent up demand from people yearning to

A Jaguar XK120 Coupe similar to this averaged over 100mph (161kph) for seven days and nights at Montlhèry, near Paris, in August 1952. This is enjoying a more gentle time at the BARC Members meeting at Goodwood two years later.

Perhaps the only flaw with the head-on view of the 1955 XK140 Coupe was the headlamps, yet it was, and is, a very attractive motor car.

get away from WD Bedford 15cwts and the like, and it was soon apparent that Jaguar could sell all the cars it could produce.

The future programme was virtually in place, with the new engine powering a two-seater to be announced in three years time, alongside an interim saloon (the Mk V) and a new saloon in six years. In the meantime the pre-war range would be more than acceptable. Manufacturing started in July 1945, and by October of that year a trickle of cars were leaving the factory – all saloons with either the 1½-, 2½- or 3½-litre engines. The drophead versions were produced about eighteen months later and were for export only, and the 100 sports car never went back into production for obvious reasons.

Basically the cars were the same as those built before the war with semi-elliptic front springs, but some improvements were made such as hypoid final drive and modifications to the inlet manifold on the 1½-litre. The 3½-litre was fitted with a Metalastik crankshaft vibration damper, and a gearbox made by Moss – on which you could easily beat the synchromesh. All had the latest Girling brakes, but were still rod operated.

Prices increased because of higher production costs and purchase tax which had been introduced during the war, so the 1½-litre now cost £684, the Special Equipment version £729, the 2½-litre £889, while the 3½-litre came in at under four figures costing £991. Still remarkable value for money, but to the would-be buyer the price in many cases was academic, because it could be five years and more before the car was delivered.

There was virtually no choice of colour, but after six years of war customers were grateful for anything, and a very unhealthy sellers market came into being overnight. William Lyons realized that this lunatic situation would not last forever, and did his utmost to impress his staff and his workforce to prepare for the time when the going got tough.

## The Unions Appear

As time passed it would be true to say that Lyons' opinion of the trade union movement fell far short of idolatory, and in those post-war years he probably had a shrewd idea of what was in store. In 1946 there had only been a few unofficial stoppages, but the workforce had grown to around 1,500, and now included a host of different trades. People were pouring into the city from all parts of the country attracted by an abundance of work and high wages; it was fertile ground for the agitators, and there were plenty of them assiduously establishing a power base, and flourishing their communist allegiance.

In 1946 Bill Rankin's fertile mind had hit upon the idea of a Jaguar Sports and Social Club, and the *Jaguar Journal*, both of which had, of course, been approved by Lyons, and the *Jaguar Journal* of the time recorded a mass meeting of all employees in the main assembly shop when questions of industrial relations were discussed. Speaking for Jaguar Cars Ltd were William Lyons and Ted Orr, the works manager, while representing the workers were the shop stewards' committee chairman Charles Gallagher, the convenor P. Bentley, backed up by twenty-five shop stewards.

The meeting was lively, but not acrimonious, and at this time when thirty-five-hour weeks are under discussion it is interesting to note that in 1946 someone was asking 'What about the forty-hour week?' Lyons was on his feet instantly: 'It is something we would all like,' he said, 'but if we are to hold our own against the competition which is on the way we must get things done, and get things done now while the sun is shining for us.

'I am not condemning the forty-hour week, but it is no use living in a fool's paradise,' he added. Apparently the meeting ended on an optimistic note; in the future some meetings were not to end so happily.

## Export or Die

Britain had come out of the war on the winning side, but up to its neck in debt, and short of most basic commodities including coal and steel. Coal production, which had not been outstanding during the war, was even worse in the post-war years, and one of the ways Sir Stafford Cripps, a minister in Attlee's socialist

The first batch of Jaguar XK120s line up for export in 1949. It was some time before they were available on the home market.

At motor shows throughout the United States the XK120 was a great success, but what have they done to the Rolls Royce and Bentley.

government, decided to tackle the problem was to ban steel to all manufacturers unless they exported sixty per cent of their production . . . a figure which was to rise to over seventy per cent at one period.

It can be argued that this policy sowed some of the seeds which eventually lead to the demise of the British motor industry. Motor manufacturers, faced with a vacuum, were selling to every export market in sight regardless of whether they had a spares and service set up of any kind.

Very often they were exporting to places they had vaguely heard of, but of which they knew absolutely nothing. Alick Dick, who succeeded Sir John Black at the Standard and Triumph Motor Company, pointed out to me that in those days there was no MIRA testing ground at Nuneaton to check cars for their resistance to intense onslaughts of water or dust, and their experience of exporting to tropical, or desert-like countries was nil. Reports soon came back from South Africa that their cars filled with dust in a matter of minutes. Add to that the fact that there were very few spares, and it becomes apparent why the British motor industry did not always endear itself to its customers abroad.

There was no option however; you exported or you went out of business. William Lyons had dipped his toe into the export markets more than most of his contemporaries, but even so exports did not take off until 1948 when they exceeded home deliveries for the first time.

Jaguar had problems with spares in the United States (almost inevitable in a market of that size), and elsewhere, but far fewer than other manufacturers, and this was basically because Lyons was determined to conquer the problems, and because he had some first-class help.

None was better than a dynamic lady called Joska Bourgeois who was based in Belgium, and who, in no time at all was selling cars all over the Continent. Striking in appearance she was exceptionally shrewd and energetic, and as I recall a most impressive person to meet. She was soon the top seller of cars on mainland Europe, and possibly elsewhere. When the Belgian government put a clamp on imported luxury cars in 1948, at Madame Bourgeois' instigation Jaguars were assembled by Van den Plas in Belgium, who were no longer connected with Van den Plas of London. Happily the arrangement did not have to last for long, but it was the first time that Jaguars were assembled abroad.

A fire which destroyed 8,000 square feet of the factory in that bitterly cold winter of 1947, did not help production, but Lyons realized the potential of the American market, appreciated that they would have to build cars in left-hand drive to succeed, and was fortunate enough to meet someone who would give them a good start across the Atlantic.

Henlys still loomed large in the life of Jaguar, and on his return from a visit to America Bertie Henly told William Lyons of an Austrian called Max Hoffman, who would now be described as an entrepreneur, who was opening the American market for Volkswagen, and who could do the same for Jaguar. He had very good premises on the prestigious Park Avenue, and Lyons appointed him to handle Jaguar's business. Lyons left the east coast to Hoffman, but set off on a five-week tour mostly of Texas and the west coast, to inspect sales and service facilities, and appoint new distributors if possible.

Earlier in the year a friend of the Earl of Warwick, Charles H. Hornburg Junior, had called to see Lyons at the Jaguar factory after visiting Warwick Castle, and expressed an interest in selling Jaguars in the States. Lyons met him again on his latest visit, and with Hornburg's help set up a display of Jaguar cars in Hollywood, and one of their first customers was Clark Gable, who was to remain an ardent supporter of Jaguar for many years. As a result of his visit Lyons made several new appointments, and Hornburg was soon to have his own showroom on Sunset Boulevard, but Lyons realized there was still a lot to be done if America was to be as big a market as he intended. He also left with some doubts about Max Hoffman and his intentions.

The Motor Show at Earls Court was the first British motor show for ten years – there had been a motor show in Geneva – and for everyone it was very exciting, but for Jaguar it was particularly so. Although few if any at Jaguar appreciated it at the time, it marked the moment when Jaguar would climb to be Britain's top exporter; a remarkable feat for a company which compared with other British manufacturers such as Austin, Morris, Ford and Standard Triumph, was still small.

## Earls Court 1948

The first part of Jaguar's post-war revival, the introduction of the Mk V saloon and the XK120, known so far in the works as the Jaguar Super Sports Car, was about to be launched. The Mk V was introduced to the trade at the factory just before the Motor Show, with the Coventry Hippodrome Orchestra playing 'Lovely to Look At' in a lavish production master-minded by Bill Rankin for pennies as opposed to pounds. The mere fact that they were launching their first post-war cars did not mean that the Lyons maxim of 'look after the pennies and pounds will look after themselves' had to be forsaken. It went down extremely well.

The XK120 was shown to the press at the Grosvenor House on the Friday before the show opened, and this time there were no prizes for guessing the price, the weight or anything else. Quite rightly it was decided that no gimmickry was required with a car that was so stunningly beautiful. It received a tremendous press, and became the star of the show. Quite a number of visitors to that first post-war show went there solely to see the Jaguar XK120.

The show was opened by HRH The Duke of Gloucester, to a populace that was still immersed in austerity. For a few days the motor industry attempted to disperse the gloom. It has been said, and I think some believed it, that Jack Croft, the late Public Relations Officer for Standard Triumph introduced champagne to this country at the 1948 Motor Show.

Throughout the day, and a good deal of the night, he was surrounded by such vast quantities of the sparkling stuff, that the idea of his introducing it is not inconceivable. The Jaguars were not the only new cars on show; there was for instance, the new Morris Minor designed by Alec Issigonis, which was to set a new standard for small cars, the 'one-eyed' Austin Atlantic, a new Hillman Minx, and several others, but most would agree that the Jaguars stole the show.

Again the prices were exceptional, and left everyone still asking the question: 'How does he do it?' The price of the Mk V saloon with a 3½-litre engine was £1,263, and that of the XK120 £1,275. Both prices included purchase tax.

The two-seater stole the thunder at the Motor Show but the Mk V was not an undistinguished motor car and filled the gap nicely between the pre-war models and the Mk VII that was to come in 1951. Yes, there was a Mk V fitted with an XK engine, but it was done more for fun than anything else, and it was never intended to put such a version into production. Therefore, it was not planned as the Mk VI. In deference to

SALIENT FEATURES OF THE JAGUAR TYPE XK ENGINES

In this new range of Jaguar engines all compromise in design has been eliminated. Each engine can be truthfully stated to incorporate all the most advanced technical knowledge available to-day on naturally aspirated petrol engines. Tests carried out on the completed units have shown the wisdom of the decision taken by the Jaguar Company nearly nine years ago to develop an engine on these lines.

In addition to bench tests, totalling many thousands of hours, extensive road tests at home and abroad have been carried out and it is significant that the 2 litre engine, loaned to Colonel Gardner when he broke the world speed record in the 2 litre class at 176 miles per hour, is a completely standard unit with the exception of modified pistons to give a higher compression ratio.

From the following condensed resume of the more important features of the Type XK engine, it will be seen that no reliance has been placed upon the use of new or untried inventions. Instead, a blend of known and proved detail designs of the highest efficiency has resulted in the creation of a production engine of unparalleled quality and performance.

The following are some of the more important points :—(1) *Hemispherical head of high strength aluminium alloy.* (2) *Valve seatings of special high expansion cast iron alloy are shrunk into the combustion head.* (3) *Induction system, including the valve ports, were designed in collaboration with Mr. Harry Weslake, generally accepted as the foremost expert in this particular science.* (4) *Twin overhead camshafts, driven by a two-stage chain, act directly on the valves through floating tappets.* (5) *Oiling system—exceptionally large capacity oil pump with large diameter oil galleries, a feature which ensures an adequate supply of cool lubricant and eliminates frothing.* (6) *Exhaust valves of high grade austenetic steel immune from lead attack.* (7) *Water circulation—direct flow across the head from a high pressure pump. The head is fed by a gallery alongside the block which ensures equal distribution between all cylinders. The cooling to the block is controlled at a constant temperature by means of restricted circulation.* (8) *The crankshaft is a 65 ton steel forging, adequately counterweighted ; the main bearings in both four and six cylinder engines are 2¾" diameter. These bearings are larger than have ever been previously used on passenger car engines of similar capacity, and are responsible to a large degree for the exceptional smoothness with which these engines deliver their power, which is maintained up to the high maximum r.p.m. of which these engines are capable. The four cylinder has three bearings and the six cylinder has seven bearings. The bearings themselves are of the Vandervell thin shell type and have shown on test to have practically unlimited life.* (9) *Pistons—are Aerolite aluminium alloy, fitted with chromium plated top rings, which tests show give over 100 per cent. increase in life to the bores.*

This exploded version of the XK engine, produced by courtesy of *Motor* magazine, explained the virtues of this magnificent engine, which was first produced in 1949, and was still being used in the Limousine in 1990.

Bentley who already had a Mk VI it was not intended to produce a car with that numbering.

Although a 2½-litre version of the Mk V was produced its export success was reflected in the fact that of over 11,000 that were made, nearly 9,000 were with the bigger engine. A flat-rate tax had taken over in Britain from the RAC rating which had in the past penalized big engines, and undoubtedly that helped too, but the waiting list in Britain stretched for years, and so it was exports that made the impact. Mechanically the Mk V's were little changed from the previous model, but the body was elegant and distinctive, with its detachable rear wheel spats, and the chassis was completely new. It was a deep box-section frame, with side members arched over the rear axle, which not only gave it a better ground clearance, but that distinctive nose-down appearance.

It had independent front suspension with torsion bars and wishbones dampened by Girling telescopic shock absorbers, and Girling hydraulic brakes. Up until then Lyons had used his beloved wire wheels, but on the Mk V he used smaller 16in (40cm) disc wheels. It was not particularly quick, a top speed of just over 90mph appeared to be its maximum. It was heavy to drive, and hard work around corners, but for its day it was extremely comfortable, and above all it was very reliable. Although the police had taken a mild interest in SS cars before the war, the Mk V did attract the attention of a number of forces, some of which returned a colossal mileage in the service of the constabulary.

It was not an ideal rally car but an Irishman, Cecil Vard, confounded all the pundits in 1951 by taking third place in the Monte Carlo Rally in a 3½-litre version. It was soon to go out of production, so its success was not a great boost to that particular model, but in its three years it had sold well, and certainly not on the back of the XK120.

Bill Heynes, believed by many to be one of the most underrated engineers, led the teams that produced the XK engines and the twin camshaft racing version of the V12.

## An Instant Success

Not many people saw the 1940 BMW Mille Miglia, but those who did say that the Jaguar XK120 bore a striking resemblance to it, and it may have inspired Lyons, but whatever his inspiration the Jaguar XK120 was an eye-catcher to a degree that is almost unknown today. The traditional Jaguar radiator was abandoned for a narrow oval-shaped one, and the bonnet opened from the front in jaw-like fashion. There were detachable spats over the rear wheels, and a boot that was large for a sports car. It was possible to order a twenty-five gallon fuel tank, as opposed to the standard fifteen gallon unit, and this reduced the boot space, but not dramatically. It had a Vee windscreen, with a central pillar, but this was interchangeable with aero screens for competition work.

The XK engine and the striking body were mounted on a truly formidable frame, with large box-section cross members giving great torsional rigidity. Lyons kept the price down by using a similar suspension layout to the Mk V saloon, with torsion bars at the

Before the introduction of the MIRA test track near Nuneaton, the British motor industry had no proper testing facilities. Here an XK150 goes through the water splash in 1959.

front and semi-elliptics at the rear. The 12in drum brakes were Lockheed, hydraulically operated, and a fly-off handbrake was used, but it only operated on the rear wheels. Clearly Lyons thought this sufficient because he used a similar system on the Mk V saloon. The gearbox was built by Moss and had synchromesh on the top three gears, and was sweet but slow.

When I had beaten the synchromesh once or twice I recall mentioning this to Norman Dewis, Jaguar's chief test driver. He pointed out that I should 'pause for a second' before slipping it into gear. It had become second nature to Norman and he did not even notice that the synchromesh was a fraction slow. To William Lyons it did the job, and it came at a good price. The transmission was rounded off by a Borg and Beck single dry plate clutch, and the final drive was by hypoid bevel.

It was said that at that 1948 Motor Show about eighty per cent of the orders for the XK120 came from overseas buyers, mostly Americans, but it was almost a year before the first XK120 was delivered and no one on the home market saw one until March 1950. A friend of mine, who worked for Jaguar, bought one at about this time, and I can remember it attracting crowds where ever it was parked. Such a delay between announcement and delivery would certainly not be tolerated today, but in those post-war years, queuing was a part of life, and a luxury was always worth waiting for.

It had been intended to build only a limited number of the two-seaters, but demand was such that Lyons could see all those glorious dollars disappearing before his very eyes unless he stepped up production, and it was not until 1950 that he arranged for steel body panels to be shipped in, in volume from the Pressed Steel plant in Oxford, that production started in any appreciable numbers. Until then 240 cars had been literally built by hand.

It was a ploy of William Lyons to announce a new vehicle before it was ready for production, in order to give his staff and workforce something to go for. It must be stressed, however, that he was not alone in adopting a policy of announcing new models long before they were ready for production. Sir Leonard Lord, as he was then, and Sir John Black, were not above announcing motor cars which did not go into production for at least a year.

In retrospect it could be said that the launch of the XK120 was a close run thing, cushioned by the desirability of the car and the attitudes of the day.

This is the 1952 French Grand Prix at Rheims, which was for sports cars. Stirling Moss in a Jaguar won the race.

This is 1953 and the Jaguar team at the start of the Mulsanne straight. The famous bar and restaurant is just down on the left.

Same place, the start of the Mulsanne, but serious business this time, with Major A.P.R. Rolt in the winning car, hotly pursued by the bigger-engined Ferrari.

## A Real Impact

No modern car I can recall made such a stir, and such a prolonged stir, as the XK120; in price, performance and appearance it was almost symbolic of a new carefree, prosperous age. For those lucky enough to get their hands on one, it was a very exciting car to drive – the motoring magazines were fulsome in their praise.

Today there are almost as many motoring magazines as motor cars, but in those early post-war years, you could count them on the fingers of one hand; a full turn out of the motoring press amounted to about a dozen. Pillars of the motoring magazine world were *The Autocar* and *The Motor*, edited by gentlemen whose principle task was to exude the authority of their publications on all occasions. Professional journalists were not banned, but neither were they encouraged, since an amateur gentleman's approach was considered more suitable for magazines which considered themselves as publications of record, rather than story-tellers.

They were much sought after in public libraries by young men like myself, but by today's standards I imagine they would be considered rather dull.

*The Motor* in its road test of the XK120 attained a two-way maximum speed of 124.5mph (200kph), recording 90mph (145kph) in third gear and 62mph (100kph) in second. The car had the lower 3.64:1 back axle ratio and an 8:1 compression ratio, and weighed 25½cwt. Those sort of figures were quite remarkable at the time.

The magazine went on to say that it had good performance throughout the range and accelerated from a standing start to 30mph (48kph) in 3.2 seconds, to 50mph (80kph) in 7.3 seconds, and reached 60mph (96.5kph) in 10 seconds. It pointed out that the Light Sports Railton, powered by an American Hudson engine had fractionally beaten the 0–60mph (0–96.5kph) figure, but the Jaguar went on to accelerate to 100mph (161kph) in under 30 seconds, a feat beyond the Railton.

They described the ride as surprisingly good on even poor surfaces, but added that the flexible sus-

Norman Dewis, for many years test driver for Jaguar, is looking happy with the XKC at Jabbeke in Belgium. Norman usually did look happy.

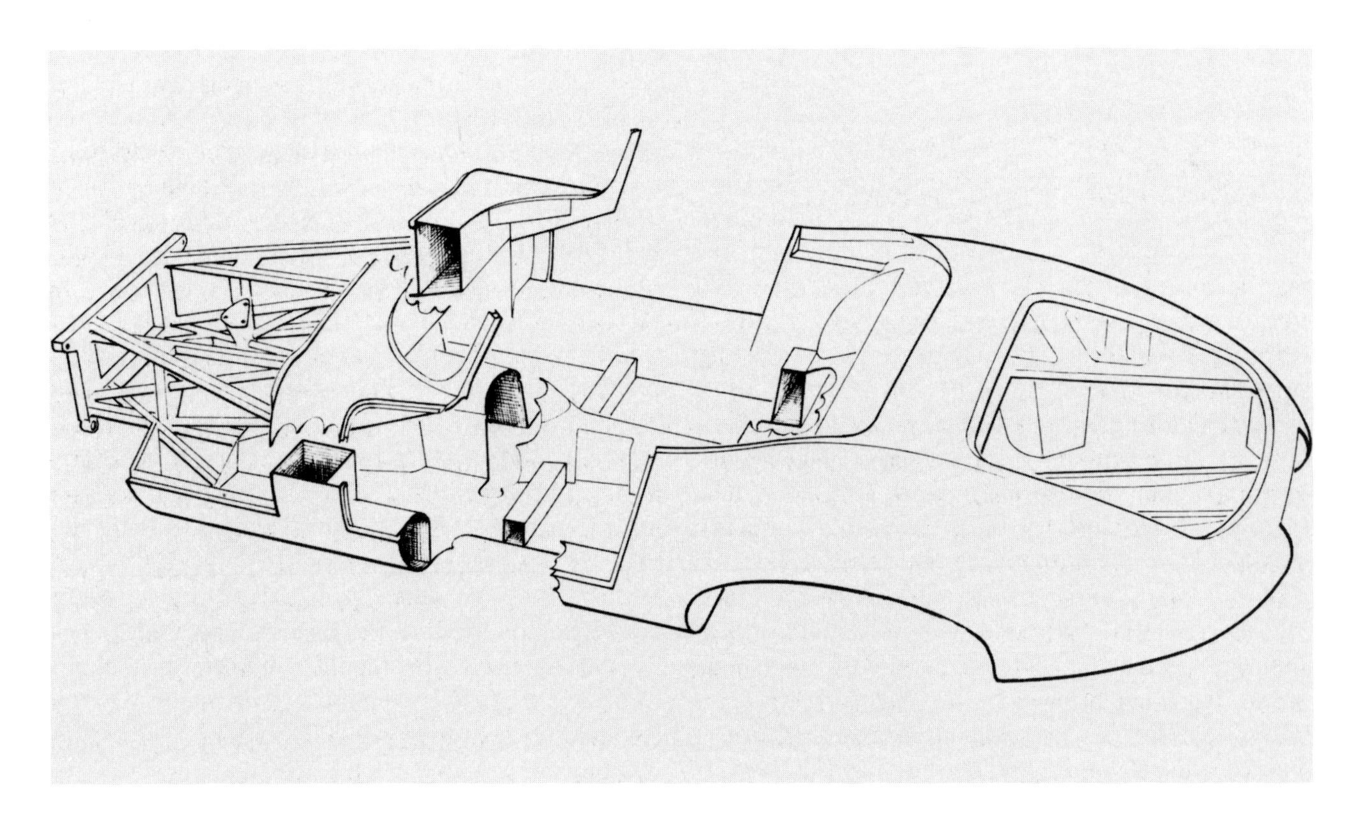

A cutaway drawing of the body shell of the XK120.

Colonel Gardner used a 2-litre version of the XK engine to set up new records in the 2-litre class, and here he is seen on the Jabbeke straight of the Ostend–Brussels autoroute.

pension allowed a trace of roll to be felt during really fast cornering, although the car had a precise controllability. They came to the conclusion that it handled better than it felt. With their test car they had no complaints about the brakes, but others did.

I first drove an XK120 in 1951, when they were still very rare, and one marvelled at the boulevard ride, the quietness (it still had a single exhaust), and the unbelievable acceleration to 100mph and beyond. In heavy rain the convertible hood leaked like a sieve, by today's standards the brakes were far from inspiring, and with a solid rear axle it needed to be set up properly for fast corners – it was unwise to take liberties. That said, it must be compared to other cars of the time, and it was magic.

The demand, both at home and from overseas, had taken them by surprise. Australia was then a big market for British cars, and Jack Bryson who had a small agency in Melbourne said he would take 2,000 cars in the first year. He expanded to Sydney, while others took up distributorships in Brisbane, Adelaide and Perth, and the problem was not selling the cars, but supplying them.

When William Lyons moved to Coventry in 1928 he had 40,000 square feet of factory space, and by 1950 it had expanded to 600,000 square feet, but it still was not enough. Every inch of that complex, convoluted factory was in use, and not only had he to expand production of the XK120, but a new saloon that the company had been working on since the end of the war was scheduled to be launched at the 1950 London Motor Show at Earls Court.

## The Move to Browns Lane

Every new car launched by the company was important, but to William Lyons the new Jaguar Mk VII saloon was very special, and he correctly assessed that this was going to be the big volume seller – by Jaguar standards – throughout the world. But what he needed was space.

There was room at Foleshill to add about fifty per cent to the work area, but Lyons could not get planning permission. Something else had to be found, and he found it at Browns Lane, about a couple of miles from the Foleshill factory. It has been the home of Jaguar Cars ever since. Coventry had been ringed by Shadow Factories during the war; some had been taken over by the Rootes Group, or by Standard Triumph and were fully used, but Lyons was aware that the huge Number Two Shadow Factory of Daimler in Browns Lane was being used less and less. He met Sir Archibald Rowland, permanent secretary to the Ministry of Supply, and a deal was arrived at by which Jaguar Cars was able to lease the million square foot factory, and in return they would supplement the Rover Company's work on the Meteor tank engine.

This they did, but no tears were shed when the contract came to an end and the company was able to concentrate on making motor cars.

The move from Foleshill to Browns Lane was completed in under two years, a truly remarkable feat in itself, but what made it even more outstanding was the fact that it was achieved without loss of production. The major domo for this operation was John Silver, assisted by all the departmental heads and, of course, the inevitable Harry Teather, boss of the stores, who had overseen that last major move from Blackpool to Coventry twenty-three years before, and who was invaluable in co-ordinating the movement of materials from every section of the works.

Another name that should be mentioned in the 'Big Move' is that of Ernest Holmes, a haulage contractor who by super-human effort could summon lorries from all over the Midlands to work at weekends, so that in between working hours at the weekend a whole department could be moved to Browns Lane.

It was an heroic exercise which produced its fair share of heroes, and in November 1952 Lyons called a gathering of distributors, dealers, suppliers and the press, and declared the new plant officially open. No doubt he felt it was time to renew acquaintance with a number of people who had been neglected over the past two years, for they had been hectic.

In 1950 William Lyons had been elected president of the Society of Motor Manufacturers and Traders, in recognition of his achievements in the industry, he had made the move, of course, and he had launched the car that was to make Jaguar the biggest exporter of motor cars in Britain.

# 7
# A Time of Glory

The 1950s must have been the most glorious decade in Jaguar's history; a time of near-infallibility, when their sporting successes, which are dealt with separately, captured the imagination not only of the enthusiast, but of those totally uninterested in motoring, a time of soaring exports and clamouring customers, and above all exciting new models that met the needs and mood of the times as though by magic.

It was a tight ship, with the skipper, William Lyons still very much in charge, and it sailed across a sea that could still be mastered with an enterprising, ingenious, and dedicated crew . . . the days of the super-ships, and mega-money investments were on their way, but they had not arrived yet. Because Lyons had literally created Jaguar Cars, and had watched every inch expand, he knew his company with an intimacy matched by hardly anyone in the motor industry, and because of this he was in a unique position among manufacturers above the level of the motoring boutique. Everyone I have spoken too who has ever worked for him has made this point: 'It was impossible to pull the wool over his eyes – whatever the department, whatever the job, he knew something about it, and possibly more than the chap he was talking to'.

He was an awesome leader, but by this time he was surrounded by a first-class team who could give him extremely accurate information on anything relating to his company and car production.

The London Rally was an event of considerable importance in the 1950s, and this is A.R. Eastwood about to take off in a 2½-litre SS100.

Great moments in a young man's life. Not as famous as NUB 120, Ian Appleyard used this car to win his last Coupe des Alpes, and I borrowed it as soon as it returned to England.

Ian and Pat Appleyard, in NUB 120, which is showing some signs of wear and tear after winning a Coupes des Alpes. The horse is fascinated.

Stirling Moss takes the flag in the 1950 TT at Dundrod at the wheel of an XK120.

The Mk VII saloon was a surprisingly quick competition car, and in this line up at Silverstone Stirling Moss is at the wheel of No. 4.

For instance, Arthur Whittaker, who had also grown up with the company, had his finger very firmly on the buying side, and drove some exceedingly hard bargains for a company that was not in the major league as far as numbers were concerned. Indeed when Jaguar became part of British Leyland it was discovered that they had often been paying less for components than BL who had, of course, been buying on a much larger scale, and should in the normal way of things, have had bigger discounts.

Again, he had only to summon someone like Tom Jones on the chassis side to get an exact appraisal of how much a job would cost. When it came to recruiting staff the 'Old Boy' network worked very effectively at Jaguar Cars. In 1946 the company was without a service manager, and Walter Hassan suggested a friend from his racing days, one Frank Raymond Wilton England, who for obvious reasons was always known as 'Lofty' England. He did a first-class job in that capacity, but as with many others at Jaguar he also had a second job, and when the company's motor racing programme got under way he was in charge of co-ordinating the project, a job he did with exemplary efficiency at a time when a number of sports car drivers were men of considerable background who had to be treated with care, and the racing team itself was mostly made up of men seconded from other jobs in the works.

Very different, in fact, from the polished professional organizations of today, where money appears to be of little consequence. We will hear more of Lofty England.

Tom Jones still lives not far from the Browns Lane factory, and was one of the small team of chassis engineers who created the Jaguar ride, that was envied by manufacturers throughout the world.

## The New Saloon

The XK120 made an enormous impact, but it was, of course, a two-seater convertible, and therefore had a limited appeal to the buying public despite its image, and morale-boosting lines. The Mk VII saloon which was launched at the 1950 Earls Court Motor Show, priced at £1,276 including purchase tax, was an entirely different proposition.

Clearly it was never going to reach the volumes of the Morris Minor or the Ford Anglia, but it was going to have a wider appeal both at home and abroad than any previous Jaguar model, and it was going to be profitable. For a company of Jaguar's size it was an ideal car to go for . . . but it had to be right.

It took about six years to produce the Mk VII, and like the XK engine which powered it, it was the result of team work. William Lyons had the ideas for the body shape, which were a continuing development of a theme, but they were gradually honed into the final shape following comments by the development team, and in particular Bill Heynes who, despite his engineering background and involvement, made many contributions to the styling of the Mk VII.

Some criticized it for being too bulbous, but fortunately the majority of the public and the press thought otherwise, and recognized it as a beautiful car. It was big – the wheelbase was 10ft (3m) and the overall

**Frank Raymond Wilton (Lofty) England**

Lofty England, who now lives in Austria, belongs to an age when all-rounders were not unknown. He was not only a first-class racing mechanic – he successfully raced both cars and motor cycles, and played a key role in Jaguar's racing successes of the 1950s, later becoming joint managing director, and eventually chief executive.

He joined Jaguar as service manager in 1946, and I first met him a few years later when, apart from his twenty-odd year stint in the motor industry and motor racing, he had flown Lancaster bombers during the war. He always looked at you as if he expected you to say something stupid, and was mildly surprised if you let him down. 'Comedians', was one of his favourite expressions, and he applied it with great relish to the press in general, and in the 1950s, to me in particular.

Despite his occasional acerbic manner, he was a man of great knowledge and experience, and if he liked you, he could not altogether hide a warm personality. I enjoyed his company.

Lofty had led the sort of life that would have fitted comfortably into the pages of *Boy's Own*, and after a five-year apprenticeship at the London depot of Daimler – a company of great standing at that time – he spent several years as a racing mechanic travelling around Europe. First he was with the racing driver Sir Henry Birkin, who had teamed up with Mike Coupar, to form a company which prepared racing cars, and after a spell with Alvis in London he and a friend called Charles Newcombe (who Lofty describes as the 'best welder/fitter/machinist I've ever known') worked for American sportsman Witney Straight, and spent a season in Italy preparing Maseratis with Giulio Ramponi, who was Straight's chief mechanic.

Later he and Newcombe worked for ERA, then he was with Richard Seaman, before the Englishman joined the Mercedes-Benz works Grand Prix team, only to be killed at Francorchamps in Belgium, just before the war. The next port of call, and a lengthy one by Lofty's standards of the day, was with the Chula 'Bira' White Mouse Stable, where he was in charge of three ERAs, an ex-Straight Maserati, a Delage and a Delahaye – he had plenty of experience as far as different cars were concerned. In 1938 he returned to the home of Alvis in Coventry, as service engineer, and was superintendent of the department before volunteering for the Royal Air Force in 1941.

Encouraged by his father to take part in motor sport, he owned a £10 Douglas motor cycle while still a Finchley schoolboy, and when he finished his apprenticeship at Daimler, he was allowed to drive a Double-Six Daimler in the 1932 RAC Rally, and came second. As a motor cyclist he rode at Brooklands, but his greatest achievements were at the Isle of Man, one of the great races in the world. Mechanical trouble put him out in 1935, but in the 1936 Lightweight event he rode his 249 Rudge Python-engined Cotton into second place being beaten by Yorkshireman Denis Parkinson on a 248 Excelsior. He was given a 'works' ride on a 248 Cotton-JAP in the following year, but retired on lap five with engine trouble.

Back at Alvis after the war, Lofty competed in the 1946 Brussels Grand Prix for 2-litre sports cars driving Gerry Dunham's special 12/70 Alvis, and was in third place behind an Aston Martin and a BMW when the float chamber came adrift, and the dashing old Alvis was reduced to a gallant sixth place.

This was the knowledge he brought to Jaguar's competition and service departments, which were probably the most fruitful, satisfying and enjoyable years in his career.

length 16ft 4½in (5m) – and it weighed in at 34½cwt, a monster by British volume car production standards of the time.

Like the XK120 it had a massive frame, similar suspension, but Girling hydraulic brakes with Dewandre vacuum servo-assistance in deference to the increased weight. The steering was also similar to that on the XK120, all of which made a contribution to cost cutting without losing any of the special Jaguar qualities.

The Mk VII was the first saloon to be powered by the XK engine, which was mounted 5in (12.5cm) further forward in the frame, and produced 160hp at 5,200rpm. The twin SU carburettors were supplied by two electric pumps, and in the boot were two saddle tanks of nine and eight-gallon capacity, and I can recall taking a Mk VII to France and asking the petrol pump attendant at Montreuil to 'fill it up'.

He had filled one tank and was putting the hose away when I pointed out the other filler cap. 'Two tanks-one car', he beamed, and topped up the second tank clearly convinced it was Christmas. The new saloon exemplified, taking into account the state of the art at the time, what William Lyons thought a saloon car should be like: It was quick – it would reach 100mph (161kph), and accelerate from 0–60mph (0–96.5kph) in 13.7 seconds – was exceptionally quiet in every way, and with a centrally-mounted short gear lever to operate the four-speed gearbox. It was a pleasure to drive, while the interior was redolent of leather and polished wood. It boasted a sliding roof, and a boot of pantechnicon proportions. As ever, Lyons knew just who he was aiming at.

The XK140 Roadster, with whitewall tyres virtually statutory for the US market, exported well, and had not lost the lithesome looks of the XK120.

Jaguar sales to the US started to boom with the introduction of the XK120, and this model carries the US Special Equipment.

Stopping astride the line was all important in driving tests, but this XK120 has made a good job of it. Even for a modest rally there was always a good turn out of spectators.

Perhaps the most famous XK120, the car in which Ian and Pat Appleyard won the Alpine Rally.

Oops. I do not think this lady has quite made it in the driving tests during the Eastbourne Rally. Driving tests were a great feature of rallies in 1952 when this photograph was taken.

The enthusiasm for rallying and racing in the 1950s and 1960s was exceptional, and this SS Jaguar saloon was taking part in the BARC members meeting at Goodwood in 1954.

Stirling Moss at the wheel of a very famous and hard worked XK120. Apart from competing successfully in many circuit events it also won the Liege–Rome–Liege rally, driven by Johnny Claes and Jacques Ickx.

Peter Walker racing an XK120 at a Silverstone circuit that was rather crude by today's standards.

To meet United States regulations the XK150 Drophead had lost some of its sylph-like looks.

Minus rear spats, and headlamps, this wire-wheeled version of the XK120 Drophead was probably heading for America.

Ian Appleyard's main claim to fame was his prowess at International Rallies such as the Alpine, but he was no mean performer on circuits, and here he is giving NUB 120 a whirl around Silverstone.

The XK140 Fixed-head Coupe still had extremely good lines.

A Jaguar XK engine being lowered into an Alvis light tank.

Walter Hassan and Colonel Gardner contemplate the 2-litre XK engine in the record-breaking car at Jabbeke.

The XK engine went into a wide variety of vehicles including this HCB Angus fire engine.

Something similar to Grace, Space and Pace was first used by MG before the war, but it is now part of Jaguar folklore.

Robert E. (Bob) Berry, who became public relations manager after Bill Rankin, but who later joined BL and then Alfa Romeo. He was not only a Jaguar man *par excellence*, but also a very fine driver of Jaguar cars.

The 1950 Earls Court Motor Show was not a resoundingly auspicious occasion; the Korean war was in full swing, and there was yet again another shortage of steel. Princess Elizabeth, who was to have opened the show was ill, and her place had to be taken by Princess Margaret. The printers were on strike so there was very little coverage of the event. On the bonus side petrol had been de-rationed in the spring.

But it was important to Lyons, not only because he was launching the Mk VII, but also because he was president of the SMMT, and as such the figurehead of the show. There was a dearth of new models, and the star was once again a Jaguar, but in his formal utterances Lyons was, as they say, quietly confident.

He pointed to the industry's growing exports, and emphasized that there were more new cars to come, and hopefully some would find their way on to the home market for the long suffering British public. Visitors to the 1950 Motor Show could well have been waiting for delivery of a Jaguar Mk V, which was then coming to the end of its three-year run.

## Instant Success

There was no chance of anyone buying a Mk VII on the home market; everything was for export, and the

A prototype of the Mk VII which was not too far from the production model. Again, note the rudimentary studio.

When the Mk VII was launched in 1951 it was generally regarded as a massive piece of machinery. When I see one now I think how compact it looks.

United States was the number one target. When the metallic blue Mk VII was removed from Earls Court it was immediately shipped to the Waldorf Astoria in New York for its American debut.

Orders were taken on the spot for 500 cars worth 7 million dollars, and this was for the eastern states only. Further orders worth 27 million dollars were taken by the end of the year. Jaguar were the top dollar earners of any exporters of cars into America, an accolade of which William Lyons was justly proud. Americans loved the Mk VII, it was their kind of car. It compared very favourably with Detroit-built products both in price and performance, and it scored heavily with its external and interior appearance . . . it had style.

It is worth noting that in 1946 Jaguar were exporting about twenty-six per cent of their production, but by 1951 that figure had risen to eighty-four per cent, and in three years – assisted enormously by the opening of the Browns Lane factory – production had risen by 118 per cent. In 1952 Jaguar sold 1,001 cars on the home market, and exported 7,978.

First advertising for the Mk VII described it as 'the car that turned the head of the world', but a little later this had given way to a classically simple version of the old MG advertisement: 'Grace . . . Space . . . Pace'.

The claim that it was a car that turned the head of the world was not extravagant, and in April 1951 the Jaguar Mk VII had reached Australia, and one was delivered to the Lord Mayor of Brisbane, Alderman J.B. Chandler. Six months later exports to South Africa began. The United States were the golden acres however, and Lyons decided that a new organization was required, and in 1954 Jaguar Cars North

In 1951 Jaguar again stole the limelight at the Earls Court Motor Show with the launch of the Mk VII, overshadowed here by two XK120s.

The Mk VII looked a very solid piece of equipment, but unfortunately many were subject to rather horrendous rust problems after about three years.

The Mk VII M was a particularly elegant motor car.

In the 1950s covering the Monte Carlo Rally meant following the competing cars from Glasgow to Monte Carlo. In 1954 Bob Berry and I went down to Monaco in this Mk VII. Afterwards we drove back to Dunkirk non-stop on the old N7.

Eastnor Castle in the Malvern Hills makes a suitable background for a two-tone Mk VIII.

By 1959 when this photograph was taken there were a few C-types about and with solid back axles they were interesting cars to drive on a circuit like Brands Hatch. This one has just climbed Druid's Hill.

America Corporation was formed with a Dutchman Johannes Eerdmans as president. The Netherlands had produced the 'economic miracle' of the seventeenth century, and Lyons was quick to appreciate that the talent for trading was still very strong in many Dutchmen.

Max Hoffman, who had been selling Volkswagens as well as Jaguars from New York had worried Lyons for a little time, but eventually incurred his wrath by announcing that he would continue his hiring and firing policy with dealers, regardless of their opinions. You did not take that attitude with William Lyons, and the relationship ended, but C.H. Hornburg continued to sell cars in the west.

In the United States Jaguar's home-produced competitors were fitted with automatic transmission, and it was clear that if Jaguar were to maintain their sales momentum they too would have to be equipped with automatic transmission. In 1953 the Mk VII was fitted with a Borg Warner 3-speed automatic transmission, for export markets only, and a few months later it was available with a Laycock de Normanville overdrive on both home and export models.

Within a few years automatic transmissions became almost *de rigueur* in the United States for most run of the mill motor cars, but apart from top of the range luxury cars they had been slow to catch on in Europe, despite the sophistication of modern units compared to those fitted to Jaguars in the 1950s. Although there was no gear shifting to be done the early automatic transmissions were, in my view, far from relaxing, with the engine revolutions soaring and subsiding as the gears changed . . . the frenetic movements on gradients were mildly alarming. By today's standards the change was not smooth, there was no over-riding control, and they suffered from 'creep' when you wanted to be stationary.

The steering ratio of the Mk VII became lower, no doubt to please American ladies, and although power steering was offered as an optional extra on Detroit-made motor cars it was to be a little time before it was offered on the Mk VII.

## Consolidation

Plenty was happening beneath the surface at Browns Lane, as we shall see, but outwardly the next few years were basically ones of consolidation when improved production techniques were introduced, sales

Pit lanes were wide open affairs when Major A.P.R. Rolt and Duncan Hamilton competed in the Goodwood Nine Hour race in 1952.

Worried that they needed more pace to win the race the C Type was given a droop snoop for 1952 with disastrous overheating problems resulting. In fact the 1951 cars would have probably been fast enough to win.

The famous Ecurie Ecosse Jaguars at Silverstone, with their almost equally famous converted coach transporter. Alongside is a Connaught.

and marketing were sharpened and additions made to a very successful range.

The 2-litre engine had been dropped at long last, not because they had all disappeared, but because it was considered noisy, and to introduce it at that time would have interrupted the production flow, and there was such a demand for the 3½-litre XK it was superfluous to requirements.

Earlier William Lyons had cast an acquisitive eye in the direction of Lagonda at Staines, and had sent Percy Shortley and John Witherall, the assistant secretary and costing specialist respectively, to have lunch with W.O. Bentley and Alan Good at Lagonda. This they did, and a most enjoyable time was had by all, but as a result of their report back to Lyons, he dropped the idea of acquiring the company.

Walter Hassan had also left Jaguar to join Leonard Lee at Coventry Climax, as chief engineer, having heard on the Coventry grapevine that the job was on offer. He enjoyed working for Jaguar, and was to return in a few years time, but the difference in age between Hassan and Heynes was small, and the opportunity to become chief engineer at Jaguar appeared remote at that time, so Walter moved on to fork-lift trucks at Coventry Climax.

Very soon, as every motor racing enthusiast knows, he was soon to be deeply involved with Coventry Climax racing engines, which powered four World Championship winning cars from 1959 to 1965, and in which Jim Clark won two World Championships. When he returned to Jaguar it was to design the V12 engine with Harry Munday, a unit which in 7-litre form powered the racing Jaguars which came first and second at Le Mans in 1990, and which had been introduced in the E-type in 1971.

It is interesting to speculate whether the original 5-litre double overhead camshaft V12, which was immensely powerful, could have competed successfully against the turbocharged engines recently competing in the World Sports Car Prototype Championship, especially when it is considered that it would have had almost twenty years of development behind it.

Sales throughout the world were soaring, but at home cars were in such short supply that Jaguar felt compelled to put out press notices saying 'Don't Blame your Dealer'. But William Lyons realized that they could not rest on their laurels, and there was an enormous untapped market for Jaguar with a car that was smaller than the Mk VII, and much more in the Grand Touring tradition.

# 8
# Motor Shows

In the immediate post-war period, and for much of the 1960s there was a great deal of theatre about the Earls Court Motor Show; it was the focal point of the year for the motor industry, and much still depended on the reception given to new models exhibited there. It was a magnificent stage for the then leaders of the British motor industry who liked nothing more than an occasional sortie into histrionics.

The vast halls of the National Exhibition Centre at Birmingham, the new home of the International Motor Show, are cathedrals consecrated to the sanctity of billion-pound turnovers, the omnipotence and omniscience of multi-nationals, and the devotion of the corporate man.

The products are within a grasp of perfection, the staging is spectacular, and the players are polished professionals, but you are conscious that the strings are being pulled elsewhere.

At Earls Court in those far off days there was still an arrogance; after all the British motor industry was second to the American, and it was the biggest exporter in the world, while the Germans were strugggling with a funny little car that looked like a beetle, the French were producing the basic Renault 2 CV, and later the more refined but still small Dauphine, while Fiat of Italy was producing a rather square, and uninteresting 1100 model.

Some British manufacturers believed, and others gave the impression, that we had the world at our feet, but by today's standards it was all on a small scale, and it was more amusing than offensive. And so were the brushes between the scions of our industry.

Sir William was the biggest exporter in the British motor industry, but in terms of size he was relatively small compared to Austin, Nuffield, Ford, and even Standard Triumph. His stature in the industry was high, and his achievements were fully recognized and appreciated. Yet in an industry containing so many bursting egos and powerful personalities there were bound to be conflicts, and although Sir William, forever upright and dignified, did not become involved in petty exhibitionism, it was interesting to note that he would avoid some people, like Sir John Black, if he could. Others were less inhibited.

During the Earls Court Show many of the leaders of the industry had an office installed at the show and stayed there for three or four days at the beginning of the show, and then came down from time to time for meetings with dealers and various social events. For them it was very much a hands-on event, a great deal of work, and socializing was done in and around Earls Court.

It was small enough to have an intimate atmosphere, and very little happened without the word getting around – at a time when characters abounded, there was always plenty to talk about in the pubs, clubs and restaurants. At that time any restaurateur, cab driver or night club owner would confirm that the Earls Court Motor Show just beat the Smithfield Show as a money-spinning event. Even on London itself it had a considerable impact.

## The Opening Day

The opening of the Earls Court Motor Show was always an exciting event because no one knew until the very last minute whether it would open or not, a situation that continued almost until the move to Birmingham. The stand fitters were a particularly militant lot and invariably opened negotiations on wage agreements at the time of the Earls Court Show, and if

This a Jaguar Ghia version of the XK140, seen at the Paris Motor Show in 1955. Perhaps not one of Ghia's better efforts.

they did not immediately get what they wanted, there was the threat of a strike. Since they did not immediately get what they wanted, I can hardly recall a Motor Show at Earls Court when there was not either the threat of, or an actual strike, on the eve of the show.

Fortunately Press Day intervened between the official opening of the show, and on many an occasion the stands were completed on Press Day. It was all rather typical of labour relations at the time.

Social mores have changed so much in the past forty years that the modern generation would have been astounded by the formality of the opening day of the Motor Show in the 1950s and 1960s. It cost £1 to get in which put an immediate limit on numbers, since a pound was considered a lot of money. Almost all the men wore bowler hats, and dark suits, and the women dressed as though they were visiting Ascot.

Sir Leonard Lord, the boss of the Austin Motor Company, who was to become Lord Lambury, was born in Coventry, the son of the superintendent of the public baths, and after an apprenticeship with Courtaulds, joined Hotchkiss and then Morris Engines, and rose to be the boss of the company at an early age. He

By 1956 Jaguar had quite a selection of cars at the Earls Court Motor Show. Here they are competing with the gas turbine-engined Rover.

Jaguar always produce a stand that is an eye-catcher, although problems with stand fitters have often made it a close run thing.

The power unit of Ian Appleyard's famous Alpine Rally winning NUB 120 after the application of a little elbow grease.

decided that he would retire when he was forty years old, and this he did, but Lord Austin enticed him out of retirement, and he joined the Birmingham manufacturer.

He subsequently became chairman and managing director of the British Motor Corporation, the most powerful man in the British motor industry. Although he was a Coventrian, in later life he developed a strong dislike of anything connected with Coventry, and I recall attending the Austin Motor Company Motor Show dinner which was held at the Grosvenor Hotel in Park Lane, and attended by over 1,000 guests. The whole affair was conducted like a military operation.

I was happily somnolent at a remote table when I heard my name being mentioned by Sir Leonard in his speech from the top table. Needless to say my euphoric state was shattered. Before the Motor Show I had written something to the effect that it was a poor performance to announce a car at one Motor Show and not have it in production by the next. I was referring to the Austin A30. With considerable vigour and venom Sir Leonard reminded me, and the other thousand guests, that this practice had started in Coventry and not Birmingham, and before criticizing others I should first look in my own backyard. Meaning Jaguar and Standard, for instance.

He was often moved to demonstrate that he set the

rules, and on one occasion he came to the opening day at Earls Court, minus bowler hat, and munching an apple. Pointing his prow-like nose at one of his competitor's stands he would move towards it followed by his Longbridge cohorts, pause for a moment, make some disparaging remark, which produced untold mirth among his followers, and then move on.

The apple had all but disappeared, yet he waited until he arrived at one of the immaculate Rootes Group stands – their factories were in Coventry – manned by equally immaculate salesmen, to dispense with his apple core.

Sir John Black was invariably accompanied by Lady Black on the opening day, at which he appeared, faultlessly groomed as ever, like a visiting general in civilian clothes, inspecting a rather entertaining unit. With furled umbrella and bowler hat at the right angle, he set a cracking pace, followed at a respectful distance by his wife, and his anxious retinue, all fervently hoping that they would not be asked a question, since providing the wrong answer was similar to being struck by lightning.

On one occasion I wanted to interview Sir John in his office at the Motor Show, but found my way blocked by a member of staff on the verge of nervous decline. Apparently someone had forgotten to change the flowers on his desk that morning, and these had been hurtled across the room. The atmosphere was as taught as terpsichorean tights. Yet when I was ushered in to see him at 11am he was all smiles and charm, and you would never have guessed that a cross thought had crossed his mind.

The Rootes family, and there were many of them, headed by Lord 'Billy' Rootes and his quieter, more calculating brother Sir Reginald, thoroughly enjoyed the Motor Show, because Lord Rootes was a salesman to his finger tips, and flourished in the buzzing, glass-tinkling atmosphere of Earls Court. The Rootes family came from Kent, but the Rootes Group had made their headquarters at Devonshire House, Piccadilly, and were slightly resented by other Midland manufacturers for this, and looked upon as rather frivolous and frothy.

## A Jaguar Supporter

In fact Lord Rootes was very astute, and realized that he had to concentrate on what he knew most about, and that was selling. The Rootes Group were a great

The cockpit layout was of great concern to Sir William, and the neat arrangement of this 1954 XK120 Roadster is a good example of the practical simplicity he liked to achieve.

The engine room of Colonel Gardner's Jaguar Mk VII looking slightly modified.

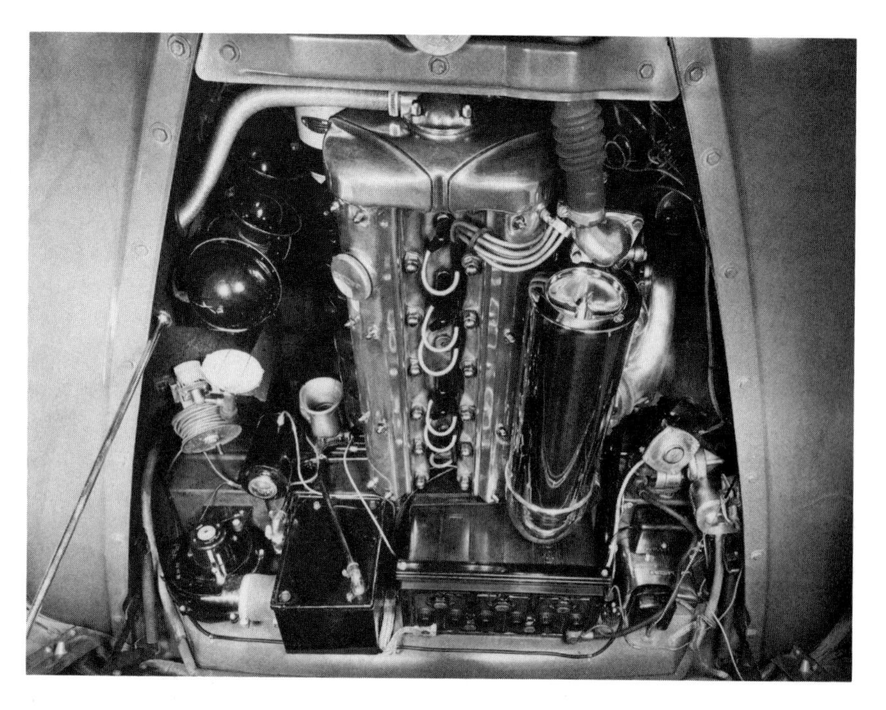

company for putting on a show, and entertaining, lead by such figures as the Hon. Brian Rootes and John Bullock, their almost irrepressible public relations manager.

Entertaining in London could be fun on occasions, but a sustained bout could be very wearing, but fortunately Trumpers hairdressers was not far from Devonshire House and many a Rootes Group man relied on that establishment to put his head back on before he could face the world with something approaching equanimity.

At that time the Ford Motor Company had not expanded across the country as it has today, and defended by the Thames and the Essex marshes, they were somewhat remote from the rest of the British motor industry, and this was exacerbated by the managing director Sir Patrick Hennessy, who had a faintly contemptuous attitude to any other car manufacturer but Ford.

In those days he did not smile a lot, and he treated the manufacture of Ford vehicles intensely seriously; an attitude that cannot be argued with because the company flourished under his leadership, and it is still there today, which is more than most can say.

For very good reasons he was also held in considerable awe by those who worked for him. In those days there was no lengthy procedure before anyone could be sacked . . . three words did it. Sir Patrick conducted a very efficient company, but he set the tempo, and there was nothing, that I could see, that was light-hearted about him. He did not, for instance, believe in public relations, and if he wanted something he would have a word with the right chaps, and tell them what he wanted, and only someone with a death-wish would suggest any form of gimmickry in his presence. It did not make for a jolly occasion.

But I do recall him saying, stern-faced but with a nod of the head as though he were making a great concession, that he thought Jaguar were doing quite well . . . perhaps he was a soothsayer.

Sir William had stolen the limelight at the Motor Show on sufficient occasions for it to have made an emotional as well as a practical impact. To him, and his generation, the Motor Show was an essential element in the success of a new model, and he liked the drama, and showmanship, because beneath his often austere appearance, he fully appreciated the value of a little sensationalism providing it was flattering to his products.

And, of course, his end-of-show party was his great indulgence, a moment when he did relax, and enjoy himself – he was holding court.

# 9
# Serious Racing

Like everyone else, Jaguar went into post-war motor sport with pre-war machinery, and while their performance was respectable, it gave no hint of things to come. The backbone of their success, particularly in hillclimbs and rallies, was the 3½-litre SS Jaguar, but it was not until the Alpine Rally of 1948 that Jaguar made an international impact, and the man at the wheel was Ian Appleyard, who was to make an even greater impression on motor rallying in the years to come.

John Ernest Appleyard had taken on the SS agency for Leeds in 1935, and his two sons Geoffrey and Ian were brought up in the motor trade. Geoffrey was killed in the war, but when the younger son returned home from the Forces, he decided to take up motor rallying as a sport and in 1947 entered the Alpine Rally – previously called the Alpine Trial – in a SS Jaguar 100, and managed to finish eighth, despite running out of tyres on several occasions, and road on one occasion.

The following year he managed to replace his car (EXT 207) with a similar 'works' car that had spent the war resting at Wappenbury Hall, the home of Sir William and Lady Lyons. He bought it, and it was prepared for the 1948 event, which he won. In the following year he drove the same car (LNW 100) to second place in the Tulip Rally, which was then an important event in the calendar, but this marked the end of the SS100's international competitive career, although it did compete in a number of national events, both at home and abroad, including the One-Hour Production Car Race at Silverstone in 1949.

Mortified by its low price, and the prospect of all sorts of extraordinary people coming into motor racing, it was originally looked upon with distaste by the *cognoscenti*, but it made its mark, and although I do not believe it was the most enjoyable car to drive quickly, in the hands of the right people it was a winner on many occasions, and now, of course, it is a most sought-after motor car.

## The Changing Point

A few months after Ian had come second in the Tulip Rally a new breed of Jaguar was to compete in its first race; the XK120 was to take part in the One-Hour Production Car Race at Silverstone, a meeting sponsored by the *Daily Express*, a newspaper which did so much to further motor racing in this country after the war.

In the spring of 1949 the XK120 was not in serious production, but an event was staged which greatly enhanced its already exceptional popularity. The XK120 had not been built with motor racing in mind, and neither had the XK engine, but because Sir William had insisted on twin overhead camshafts, it was built to a traditional racing formula, and clearly its potential was quite considerable.

The XK120 had proved that it was quick, and that it was silky smooth, but how quickly would it go in standard trim? It was decided to find out. In the spring HKV 500 was taken to the Jabbeke motorway which links Ostend to Brussels, the nearest stretch of motorway to Britain. At that time, if you spoke nicely to the Belgian Automobile Club, they could arrange, for a fee, for one lane over a few miles length, to be closed to normal traffic. No doubt the indefatigible Joska Bourgeois, the Belgian distributor, had a hand in these arrangements. It was a pattern set by Jaguar, and followed by Triumph and then Rover with Jet 1. It illustrates, however, the density of traffic on motor-

Duncan Hamilton in characteristic pose at Le Mans, after sharing the winning drive with Major A. P. R. Rolt.

ways at the time; one can imagine the furore that would be caused if a request was made to close a section of the M1 for testing.

The tester at Jaguar in 1949 was Ronald Manners Verney Sutton, a cousin of the Duke of Rutland, who had raced several makes of car in the heroic days of city to city racing, and had been tester for Lea Francis before joining Jaguar. He was generally known as 'Soapy' Sutton, and later joined Alvis, where his talents were used on military vehicles, with which he was quite familiar. Walter Hassan was supposed to accompany them, but was afflicted by influenza, so Sutton, and Jack Lea, a fitter who had been Soapy Sutton's riding mechanic in the 1930 Ards Tourist Trophy race, headed for Jabbeke, and soon proved that with the windscreen removed, and divested of number plates, the car would exceed 130mph (209kph) with ease.

Bill Rankin chartered a DC 3, and together with Sir William and Bill Heynes, the British motoring press (with the exception of one who missed the aircraft) were flown over to witness this dash down the motorway, when again several runs were made at over 130mph (209kph). Walter Hassan had by now recovered from influenza, but left the driving to Soapy Sutton. 'It didn't matter who was driving it', he commented. In 1989, to commemorate the 40th anniversary Jaguar took some journalists over to Jabbeke, and four of those who covered the original event are still alive today: Basil Cardew, Philip Turner, Courtenay Edwards and Gordon Wilkins.

When the figures were published in the press, it raised a number of eyebrows, because this was a car you could buy off the shelf – if you could possibly get one – yet it had set a speed record for un-supercharged production cars of 132.67mph (214kph), and still cost £1,275 including purchase tax. People were still asking: how does he do it for the price? When I look back on those days, and compare them to today, it becomes easier to understand how it was achieved. He never spent twopence when a penny would do.

The speed run at Jabbeke was a perfect example of how tight a rein he kept over expense of any sort. The tester and a mechanic took the car over, proved that they could meet the objectives, and a party of journalists was flown over for the day. The car was then driven back to Coventry, converted into right-hand drive, and prepared for the Silverstone race. Later it took part in the Liège–Rome–Liège Rally, and won in the hands of Johnny Claes and Jacques Ickx, and later was used in several other competitive events.

Everyone, and everything had to earn its money.

## Silverstone

The *Daily Express* had announced that there would be a one-hour production race at the main August meeting at Silverstone, and to the sporting-minded Hassan and England this seemed an ideal opportunity to go motor racing. The matter was obviously discussed with Sir William, and according to Walter Hassan he was quite keen, provided they could convince him that they had a good chance of winning. The race was being run over what was then the Club circuit, and Hassan and England hired the circuit, and as he explains 'set forth'.

They had a little difficulty in beating the lap record for the club circuit, indeed, before Hassan eventually beat it he had been through the straw bales on two or three occasions. They then went on to prove that the car would cover the distance at racing speeds, and it was then that Sir William said: 'Now I'll have a go', and indicated to Bill Rankin that he should accompany him. The outcome is mentioned in Chapter 1.

The job of selecting the drivers for the race fell to Lofty England, and because of his experience with Bira (who should, of course, have been called Prince Birabongse, but who preferred the simple B. Bira), he was his first choice. Then he selected a handsome young Englishman called Peter Walker, and an old adversary, with experience going back to pre-war days, Leslie Johnson.

In the tradition of the time they were all amateur drivers, and while they took their motor racing seriously, and always gave of their best, they all had other occupations, and I can well remember the Monte Carlo rally of, I think, 1951 when Leslie Johnson was driving a Sunbeam Talbot. Their motor sporting activities were very catholic in those days.

Johnson had just taken an interest in a laundrette

For more than one reason this was a famous XK120. It had been driven by many well-known drivers in circuit racing and in 1951 it won the Liège–Rome–Liège rally driven by Johnny Claes, and Jacques Ickx. The latter is the father of racing driver, Jacky Ickx. The spotlight were set in this unusual way to provide light on mountain hairpins.

In the 1950 Tourist Trophy race at Dundrod Stirling Moss and Peter Whitehead came first and second, and with Leslie Johnson they won the team prize.

business, and at the start clambered into his car still wearing a dark suit, in stark contrast to the other competitors who were swathed in sweaters and woolly hats. He arrived at Brussels in plenty of time – still in his dark suit – and was busy making telephone calls to England in an atttempt to tie up some more business details, whilst most other competitors were recounting tales of daring on the road. This continued down the route – there were no overnight stops on the five-day run – and I am sure he arrived in Monte Carlo still in his dark suit, but in a respectable position. Regrettably, he died from a heart attack at the end of an Alpine Rally in the 1950s.

For the race one car was painted red, the other white and the third blue, and it was a Le Mans-type start – in other words the cars were at one side of the track, the drivers at the other, and when the flag was dropped the drivers sped across the track to their cars and, hopefully, drove off. Stirling Moss was almost unbeatable at this performance, as he demonstrated at Le Mans on a number of occasions. The first away from this race at Silverstone was Len Potter in an Allard, but he was quickly overtaken by Bira, and from then on it looked at though it was going to be a Jaguar 1–2–3, despite the attentions of an exceptionally quick Frazer Nash driven by Norman Culpan.

However, with the race two-thirds gone Bira spun at Woodcote following a burst rear tyre, and although he attempted to change the wheel, the jack sank into the Silverstone turf, and that was that. So the white car driven by Leslie Johnson, the Jabbeke car, went into the lead and was followed home by Walker in the red car, having lapped the rest of the field at least once. Jaguars dominating the field at Silverstone were to become a common occurrence.

One way and another Tommy Wisdom, motoring journalist and competition driver, played a not insignificant part in the fortunes of SS and then Jaguar, and again he was to make a move which confirmed the virtues of motor racing to Jaguar. Wisdom owned an XK120, which he had bought from the firm (JWK 988), and he loaned this to the young Stirling Moss to take part in the Dundrod TT, in September 1950. Stirling was not the name he is today, and to loan the car was both a generous, and shrewd move on Wisdom's part.

The Dundrod circuit is tricky at the best of times, and on this occasion it was wet, but the young Moss beat the field hands down, demonstrating not only his ability, but that of the XK120. The Jaguar JWK 988 is fit and well in the hands of David Cottingham, of Chenies, Buckinghamshire.

In the United States in the same year Leslie Johnson had been driving an XK120, and had managed fourth place at Palm Beach in what could best be described as a Formula Libre event; the winner was a Duesenberg-Ford. However, it fanned the flames of interest at a time when even the Americans could not get their hands on XK120s.

Jaguar were, at this time, still feeling their way in competition motoring, and virtually having a go at anything to assess their virtues and vices. They wanted to make the biggest impact possible, but they had limited resources, and could not field limitless cars, in fact if a car was written off at any event it was a near catastrophe for the company, because very often there was nothing to replace it with.

## The Learning Curve

Lofty England does not regret this period, because he says they were attempting to get to grips with all sorts of racing conditions, and these proved of considerable value both for their future competition success, and for the improvement of production cars, since nothing showed up weaknesses quicker than competitive events. In the hands of Clemente Biondetti an XK120 – which Jack Lea had driven out from Coventry – took part in Sicily's Targa Florio, which is a particularly rough and rugged race, run over appalling road conditions, and for a while it led the race, but succumbed to a broken connecting rod; after which all connecting rods were crack tested.

The Mille Miglia is also a very special event, and few British drivers competed before the war, because an intimate knowledge of the thousand-mile route is a distinct advantage, and we did not produce motor cars that were particularly suitable. But in those post-war days we were trying anything, and five cars were prepared in 1950 for Biondetti, Johnson, Walker, Wisdom and Nick Haines, a motor trader. In the event Walker did not compete, and only Johnson finished – in fifth place.

The second post-war Le Mans was staged in 1950, and inevitably attracted three privately entered XK120s, or so the records say. In fact they were works-loaned cars, and it goes without saying that Leslie Johnson was one of the entrants, and together

Stripped down to the bare essentials this XK120 is put through its paces at Silverstone by Stirling Moss.

with H.L. Hadley he completed twenty-two hours before the clutch collapsed under the strain. The car had held second place for some of the race, but to ease the load on the brakes they had been using the gearbox rather more than would have been normal, and as a result the clutch centre pulled out. Jaguar were learning, and in future the standard Borgalite driven plate was removed, and a solid clutch plate was used instead, which solved the problem.

The Jaguar had whispered its way around the circuit, a fact not lost on many of the motoring writers at Le Mans, but they also noticed that despite its quiet ways it had put in one lap at 96.98mph (156kph). The second Jaguar finished twelfth, and the third fourteenth. The race was won by racing driver Louis Rosier, and Jean-Louis Rosier in a 4.5-litre Lago-Talbot, at an average speed of 89.71mph (144kph), although their fastest lap had been 102.84mph (166kph). Another Lago-Talbot was second – the last time this marque was to feature on the leader board at Le Mans was the following year – and in third place was the redoubtable Sydney Allard and Tom Cole in a 5.4-litre Allard J2.

The 1950 Le Mans saw the late E.R. (Eddie) Hall, a Huddersfield mill owner, competing in a 4½-litre Bentley in which he had finished second in the 1936 TT. He drove throughout the twenty-four hours on his own, the only time that feat has been achieved, although the Frenchman Pierre Levegh, who was killed at Le Mans in the crash of 1955, got near to it in 1952. He was leading the race in his own Lago-Talbot, well ahead of the Mercedes-Benz opposition, but he refused to hand over the car to his co-driver Rene Marchand, despite the pleas of his wife and his team.

A Le Mans type start at Silverstone. No safety belts or flame-proof overalls, but still plenty of photographers with a death wish.

This was F. R. W. (Lofty) England's invariable position at Le Mans; on the pit balcony overseeing operations. Things must have been going well because Sir William, in the white shirt, is smiling.

Winning Le Mans was his life ambition, and he was going to do it on his own, no one else was to have any of the glory. With just an hour and a quarter to go he missed a gear and blew the engine – Mercedes-Benz went on to finish first and second.

1950 also saw the first appearance of that legendary motor racing figure from America, Briggs Cunningham, who made a reconnaisance of the Sarthe circuit with two Cadillacs, one a more or less standard saloon, the other a monstrous two-seater with an all-enveloping body.

## NUB 120

The year 1950 saw the first appearance of a very famous rally car, NUB 120. Ian Appleyard, by now married to Sir William's daughter Patricia, had managed to obtain an XK120, and fitted with the optional low back axle ratio, slotted and strapped bonnet, he sallied forth for the Alpine Rally. That year five *Coupes des Alpes* were awarded for penalty-free runs, and four, would you believe, went to the 745cc flat-twin Dyna-Panhards, and the fifth to Appleyard, who also made Best Individual Performance, and collected just about every other trophy on offer.

There is nothing like the Alpine Rally now; it was totally different from today's international rallies. The rally was won or lost on the road, unlike rallies today when everything that matters happens on special off-road stages. The horrendous accident at Le Mans had not yet happened nor had the accident on the Mille

Miglia. Traffic was light compared to today, and up in the mountains you almost had the place to yourself. The road surfaces on some passes such as the Gavia were nothing more than loose stones, and there was nothing to stop a car going over the side – in most places it was a long way down.

In the Italian villages the crowds spilled on to the road, leaving only the narrowest of gaps for the cars to pass, and this inhibited many British newcomers to the event, for they instinctively slowed down. The experienced drivers kept going, and the crowd would open up in front of them like a wind-blown field of corn, with everyone gesticulating wildly, and screaming 'avanti, avanti'. At any motor sporting event the Italians are unique. It was, however, a civilized event, and the competitors went to bed at night, something I, and most other people missed on the Monte Carlo Rally. During the day it was quite simply a road race over the mountains.

The impact the name Jaguar made on continental crowds at that time was simply astonishing. In 1953 Jaguar had won Le Mans, and a month later Ian Appleyard was leading the Alpine Rally, and taking the driving tests on the water front at Cannes. Over the loudspeakers came the name . . . 'pilot Anglais Ian Appleyard . . . voiture Jagwaar', and there was a mighty roar of approval from the crowd, packed like dates in a box around the harbour. The fervour aroused by the Jaguar name was quite spine tingling, and even to be remotely connected produced a glow of pride. To those closely involved with Jaguar, and the Messianic presence of William Lyons, it was food and drink.

## The Target

Top teams in sports car racing in the 1950s were

Ian Appleyard had a great facility for finding appropriate number plates, and here he is in an XK140 in the 1956 RAC Rally.

Bob Berry, who was for several years publicity manager of Jaguar, owned some very special lightweight Jaguars, and here is a very special XK120 following Michael Head's C-type at Goodwood in 1954. Goodwood was the most attractive of all the circuits.

Ferrari, Mercedes-Benz and Aston Martin, and all of them won in turn the Sports Car Constructors' Championship, but despite Jaguar's success at Le Mans they did not win the Championship until 1987. The answer was that Sir William was not interested in it; in his view the only thing that mattered was Le Mans. (Today, I think that many people would still agree with him.) After their probes into various events, the distilled decision was that winning the Le Mans 24-Hour Race would be the most cost effective way of furthering their objectives; the one principle being to sell more production cars.

So a car had to be built that would win Le Mans. It was decided that not a great deal needed to be done to the XK engine, which retained its wet sump lubrication and twin SU carburettors, but Harry Weslake did modify the inlet ports and the exhaust sytem, and by using a lighter flywheel and high lift camshafts, power was increased to over 200bhp at 5,800rpm. A four-speed gearbox was used with ratios of 3.31, 4.41, 6.59 and 11.2:1. There were big changes to the body and the chassis, however, effected by Malcolm Sayer, an ex-Bristol expert in aerodynamics, and Bob Knight respectively, both of whom were to achieve wonders for the company in their particular fields.

The chassis was a tubular frame, with heavily drilled channel section side members to reduce weight. The car retained a solid rear axle, the casing being located by underslung longitudinal links, the fulcrums of which were attached to a transverse torsion bar. The standard Jaguar front suspension was employed but the steering was changed to rack and pinion from the standard re-circulating ball type, and 12in (30cm) drum brakes were used operated by Lockheed 2LS hydraulics, which included a form of automatic adjustment.

The car was known as the XK120 C, and Malcolm Sayer had produced a slippery shape which gave it a very distinctive appearance, and combined with the 200-plus bhp and a reasonably high back axle ratio,

With the exception of the C and D-types none of the XKs were intended for competition work, yet around the world they were entered for just about every type of motoring event, and this XK140 is competing at the Prescott Hill Climb in 1957.

The two Peters, Walker on the left and Whitehead on the right, after their 1951 win at Le Mans in the C-type.

gave it a speed of around 160mph (257kpg) on the famous Mulsanne Straight at Le Mans. With such refinements as a lighter battery it tipped the scales at 18½cwt, appreciably lighter than the touring model. The new car had been built with one object in mind – to win Le Mans, where the road surfaces were good, where there was only one sharp corner, and a four-mile straight, but to win you had to keep going quickly for twenty-four hours.

Bill Heynes stated that their plan was to run the fastest scheduled service over the Sarthe Circuit that could be envisaged.

The opposition was quite formidable: 4.1-litre Ferraris for Chinetti, Chiron and Spear, the 5.4-litre Chrysler-engined Cunninghams, the 4.5-litre Lago-Talbots, Cadillac Allards, DB2 Aston Martin saloons and a Nash Healey driven by Tony Rolt and Duncan Hamilton . . . among many others.

The drivers of the Jaguars were Leslie Johnson and Clemente Biondetti, a tough Italian of Mille Miglia and Targa Florio fame, farmer Peter Whitehead, the epitome of the calm, unruffled Englishman, and Peter Walker, Stirling Moss and Jack (Fearless) Fairman. William Lyons, now forty-nine, who was moving his factory into Browns Lane, still found time to watch the race.

## Le Mans Victory

With six hours of the Le Mans 24-Hour Race gone, the Jaguars, lights blazing, were running 1–2–3, and the inexperienced visitor to the race would have thought that they were well on their way to a sweeping victory, but at 10pm there is still three-quarters of the race to go, and no one at Jaguar was counting their chickens, which is just as well because very soon Biondetti was to come into the pits, point at the oil pressure gauge, and hold his hands up in despair.

On the pit counter Lofty England showed no emotion, exchanged a word with Bill Heynes, and kept a check on the remaining two cars. Stirling Moss had

Farmer Peter Whitehead in the winning C-type takes the flag at Le Mans in 1951.

Stirling Moss in a C-type won the 9-hour race at Goodwood in 1952 partnered by Peter Walker, but Peter Whitehead in a similar car ran out of road. His co-driver was Ian Stewart, brother of World Champion Jackie Stewart.

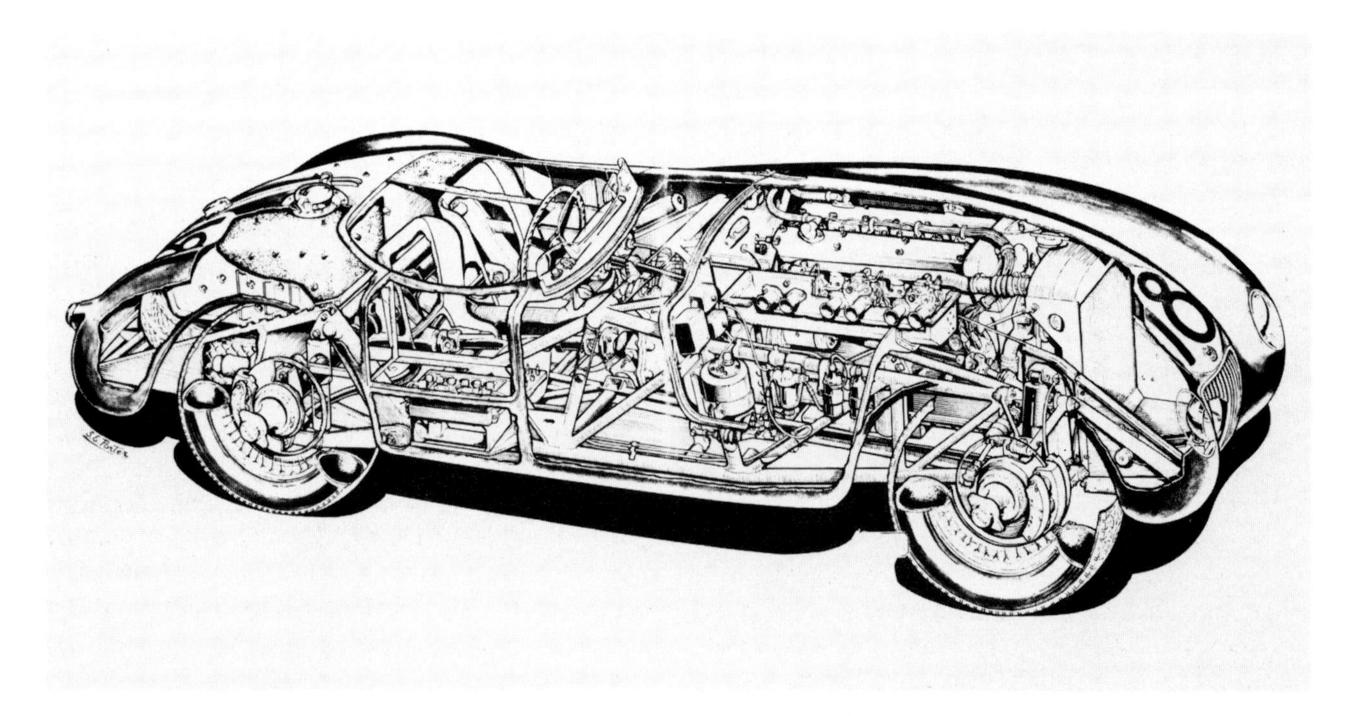

This cutaway drawing of the C-type shows its tubular chassis, and orthodox layout. It was, in fact, a very docile car, and could be taken on shopping expeditions.

Duncan Hamilton owned a C-type, and when he was not driving a 'works' car he was driving his own wherever he could.

set up a new lap record and was well in the lead. His car screamed good health as it flashed past the pits, under the Dunlop bridge and around the long bend, and on to Tertre Rouge. But Bill Heynes and Jack Emerson, the engine test boss, were concerned because the oil gauge on Biondetti's car had been working and there was plenty of oil in the sump. It was very worrying.

Then Lofty England, glancing yet again at his stop watch, looked worried. No Moss. At Arnage, at the southern end of the circuit, Moss was coming out of this, the tightest bend on the circuit when there was an almighty bang in front signalling only one thing – a broken connecting rod. He too had lost oil pressure with the inevitable result. Now there was only Whitehead and Walker left, but fortunately the Jaguars had built up such a lead in the early part of the race, that the English pair could afford to slow down and keep the engine running at its smoothest. Selected for their experience they did a superb job under wearing circumstances, and at 4 o'clock on Sunday afternoon Peter Whitehead crossed the line seventy-seven miles ahead of Pierre Meyret and Guy Mairesse in their 4.5-litre Lago-Talbot, the first Jaguar to win the Le Mans 24-Hour Race.

William Lyons granted himself the luxury of a number of smiles, congratulated the team, and then hurried back to Coventry and the move to Browns Lane.

## The Lightweights

Towards the end of 1950 the engineering staff were unsure whether the new competition model would be ready in time for the Le Mans race in June the following year, and the decision was made to build LT 1, 2 and 3, which outwardly looked very little different from a standard XK120, but the bodies were built of mangnesium alloy, and at 20cwt they were considerably lighter than a standard XK120, and as such they were extremely lively performers. Originally they had drum brakes, the boot was a dummy, the bonnet was a panel over the engine, and there were air intakes for the rear brakes. The whole body was strengthened to provide rigidity, and with an aero screen it looked very impressive.

But the C-types were prepared in time, so LT 1, 2 and 3 were relegated to the rear of the experimental shop. Bob Berry says that some years later he found

N.J. Scott-Wallace pressing on at Silverstone in his C-type in 1961.

Duncan Hamilton on the left, and beside him Major A. P. R. Rolt receive their garlands after their 1953 win at Le Mans. They are looking extremely well considering they had not been to bed for forty-eight hours.

The 1955 XK140 was the successor to the XK120, and was powered by a 190bhp version of the XK engine, giving it a top speed of 140mph (225kph). This two-seater version cost £1,598.

LT 3 looking very forlorn behind the experimental shop, and after a little negotiating bought the body and fitted it to an XK120 he already owned, and he raced the car (MWK 120) very successfully for sometime, but by then it had disc brakes, and a few other minor modifications.

It was owned after Bob Berry's racing days by David Cottingham, who sold it to a Canadian. It remained in Canada with the same owner until New Year's Day 1990, when David bought it back from him, and set about restoring it. LT 1 and 2 seem to have disappeared.

## Disc Brakes

The old Midland factories had a ring to their names, and a gravity which was a measure of their importance in the engineering world. Dunlop Rim and Wheel, one of the oldest in the Dunlop company, was such a factory, and it had an important role in Jaguar's racing successes, and the development of the disc brake.

The managing director at the time was the late Joe Wright, a man I admired, and to whom I am indebted for allowing me a rare and exciting moment in my life; a fleeting acquaintance with motoring history in the making. It was, I think, early 1952 when he telephoned

This drophead coupe version of the XK120 was a particularly attractive model.

Some additions had been made to the facia of the XK140, but fundamentally it remained the same.

Stripped of a few ancillaries the XK150S with its 3.8-litre 265bhp XK engine was a potent force in production car racing.

me at *The Coventry Evening Telegraph*, and asked me if I would like to go for a ride in a rather special motor car. Naturally, I agreed, and was rather disappointed to discover that he had arrived in an early model of the Standard Vanguard.

He asked me to take the wheel, and suggested we drove south towards Rugby. On the Coventry by-pass I was told, 'Put your foot down, and get it going as fast as you can, and then brake.' This I did, and the car stopped as I would have expected. Then I was told, 'Now I want you to repeat that operation as often as you like, and notice the results, and don't be shy, give it some stick'. Once again I did as I was told, charging up through the gears, then braking hard . . . time and time again.

'Noticed anything different?' I was asked. 'Yes', I replied, 'the brakes are not fading; they smell red hot but they are still working'. 'You are driving a car with disc brakes, one of the first people in Britain to do so,' said Joe Wright, 'and they are going to revolutionize motoring, mark my words'.

Younger generations of motorists know nothing of brake fade; they may have experienced brakes that did not work well because of wear, but since the advent of disc brakes, fade is almost unknown, yet it was a very common problem. It is claimed that drum brakes could be made to be as effective as disc brakes, but they would have had to be very big, very heavy, able to fit into the wheel, and also they would have been very expensive. For racing cars this was a very special problem, and it is said, apocryphally, no doubt, that the Bentleys went faster at Le Mans as the race progressed simply because their brakes began to fade, but since everyone had drum brakes, and although some might be better than others, no one had a distinct advantage. If you could provide a much better braking system then clearly you would have an advantage.

## Mille Miglia

There was nothing new in the principle of disc brakes, and Dr Frederick Lanchester, an engineer of genius, had developed a disc brake early in the century. He was short of the right sort of materials, and demand – no one appeared particularly interested – and Chrysler of America, a company with a great engineering tradition, produced a production saloon soon after the war with disc brakes offered as an option. Again they were not a roaring commercial success.

The engineers at Dunlop Rim and Wheel and Jaguar, were convinced that they had got it right, and after my demonstration I was convinced that they had too. They had had their problems: servo failures, boiling fluid, flexing calipers and so on but, hopefully, these were behind them. A 'secret weapon' would be immensely useful in Jaguar's tactics. Their strategy, as has been mentioned, was to be successful at Le Mans, and it was becoming clear in 1951 that Daimler-Benz were taking a very keen interest in sports car racing, and could well be entering their potent 300 SL Coupe. It was powered by a single overhead camshaft 3-litre engine, equipped with Bosch fuel injection, and clothed in a beautiful, and aerodynamic body which featured gull-wing doors. They took a very active part in racing throughout the year of 1952.

Jaguar decided to enter a C-type fitted with disc brakes for the Mille Miglia, and the driver was to be Stirling Moss who had done some of the development work on the disc brakes at Silverstone and airfields near Coventry. The disc brakes were working when the car went out after leaving the road and damaging the steering. It had also suffered from a leaking fuel tank, but at quarter distance it had been lying third. The race was won by a Ferrari, with the Mercedes 300 SL of Karl Kling taking second place. Jaguar had not covered themselves in glory at the Mille Miglia, and it was also to have an unfortunate impact on the 1952 Le Mans race.

Stirling Moss had been very impressed by the performance of the Mercedes-Benz cars on the Mille Miglia, and told Jaguar that in his view the cars would need more power, or have to be faster, if they were to win at Le Mans. This intelligence was taken seriously and rather late in the day they started to modify the bodies of the cars to give them less drag, and one of the results was a reduction in the size of the intake orifice for the radiator. This proved to be disastrous, with all three cars retired through overheating.

# 10
# Record Breaker

The 1952 Le Mans Rally was a disaster for Jaguar, and a missed opportunity of beating Mercedes-Benz. There is no doubt that if the cars had been kept in their 1951 specification, with appropriate modifications made to the oil pipes (vibration on two of the cars caused them to fracture in 1951) they were fast enough to have won the race.

That splendid motor racing character Duncan Hamilton was driving a Jaguar at Le Mans in 1952, and he points out that the Mercedes were not impressive that year; they were much slower on the straight than they had been led to believe, and there was no doubt that if Levegh had not been so stubborn he would have won the race in his Lago-Talbot.

They had had evidence of the overheating problem in practice, and Lofty England was concerned. Although the cars had been tested on the high speed circuit at Lindley, headquarters of the Motor Industry Research Association, it was only possible to attain speeds of 120mph (193kph), whereas at Le Mans 160mph (257kph) was the going rate for the Mulsanne Straight. None of the Jaguars lasted for more than three hours, but Duncan Hamilton points out that there was a wonderful spirit in the Jaguar team, despite their disappointment, and the feeling was, 'We will be back'. They were, and it was very different.

The year had not been a total disaster in sporting terms. Far from it, with Jaguar scoring in umpteen competitive events throughout the world, and the Ian and Pat Appleyard – NUB 120 combination winning the first Gold Coupe ever presented in the Alpine Rally for three penalty-free runs. In August the indefatigible Leslie Johnson took a Special Equipment XK120 fixed head coupe to Montlhéry on the outskirts of Paris and, with the aid of co-drivers Stirling Moss, Jack Fairman, and H.L. Hadley set up an astonishing collection of records. He also had the assistance of Mortimer Morris-Goodall and Desmond Scannall, secretary of the British Racing Drivers' Club, who looked after the logistics. Mortimer was soon to join Jaguar as assistant to Lofty England.

For a start they drove for seven days and nights at an average speed of 100.31mph (161kph) covering 16,852 miles (27,120 kilometres). They collected four world records and four class records, and a detailed examination of the engine by the Shell laboratories at the end of the marathon showed that: 'The crankshaft was still within production tolerances, and would have been passed by the inspection department for installation in a new car'.

Each success added to the mountain of magic being built by the Jaguar marque. No question then of shoddy workmanship, or poor materials.

## Civic Reception

Jaguar did not enter the Mille Miglia in an official capacity in 1953, but three C-types were entered, plus a Mk VII saloon, but the Italian road race did not suit the Jaguars which had, after all, been built with the smooth roads of Le Mans in mind. The C-types retired hurt, while the Mk VII was outpaced in the touring car section by a combination of a Chrysler with a huge engine, and driver Paul Frère.

In the meantime Norman Dewis, Jaguar's chief test driver, kept nipping over to Jabbeke with standard XK120's and, with undershield and aero screens, was timed at 141.846mph (228.272kph), while with the C-type – almost fifty 'production' models had been built – he achieved 148.435mph (238.876kph). It was another way of keeping their face in front of the public.

Stirling Moss came second at Le Mans in 1953 sharing the car with Peter Walker, but he won many other races in a C-type.

The 1953 race at Le Mans will always stand out in my mind because it was my first visit to the Sarthe circuit, and while in retrospect I have no doubt that my opinion over so many years is coloured with nostalgia, it was the most exciting race I have been to at Le Mans. The cars were C-types, still with wet sump lubrication, but the engines had been fitted with three Weber carburettors, and all were equipped with disc brakes all-round, as were all production Jaguars – no half measures for Bill Heynes. The twin-choke Webers increased the torque of the engines in the lower speed ranges giving them much better acceleration out of the slower corners. They were again the only cars with disc brakes, so in this department they had a considerable advantage.

The drivers were Stirling Moss and Peter Walker, Ian Stewart and Peter Whitehead, and Tony Rolt and Duncan Hamilton.

## A Different Outlook

Basically it was the same race as it is today, but in many ways it was different, even Le Mans was very different: the Hotel des'Ifs where the Jaguar mechanics and I used to stay, is now a block of flats; Grubers in the Place de la Republique, a monument to French bistros, is now an office block.

I believe that the cars and the race loomed larger in those days, because all the ancillaries, which dominate so much of the Le Mans 24-Hour Race today, were so much smaller. The paddock, for instance, hardly existed; there were a few tents and modest caravans, where the drivers could rest for a while, and eat and drink food prepared by wives and girlfriends.

There were hardly any transporters because almost all of the cars, including the Jaguars, had been driven to Le Mans from their base, and would be driven back after the race. There were some hospitality suites, crude by today's standards, above the pits, but none of the lavish establishments that abound today. And for the people of Le Mans, the race was not simply a money-spinning event to the south of the city. It was, for a weekend, part of the fabric of their lives, for the racing cars could be parked in garages next door to their flat, and during the two days of practice, and on race day, the cars were driven through the streets to the circuit in a cacophony of screaming engines and squealing tyres.

Jaguar's garage was not much more than a hole in the wall, up the road from our hotel. Little boys and girls hovered round the entrance and vied with each

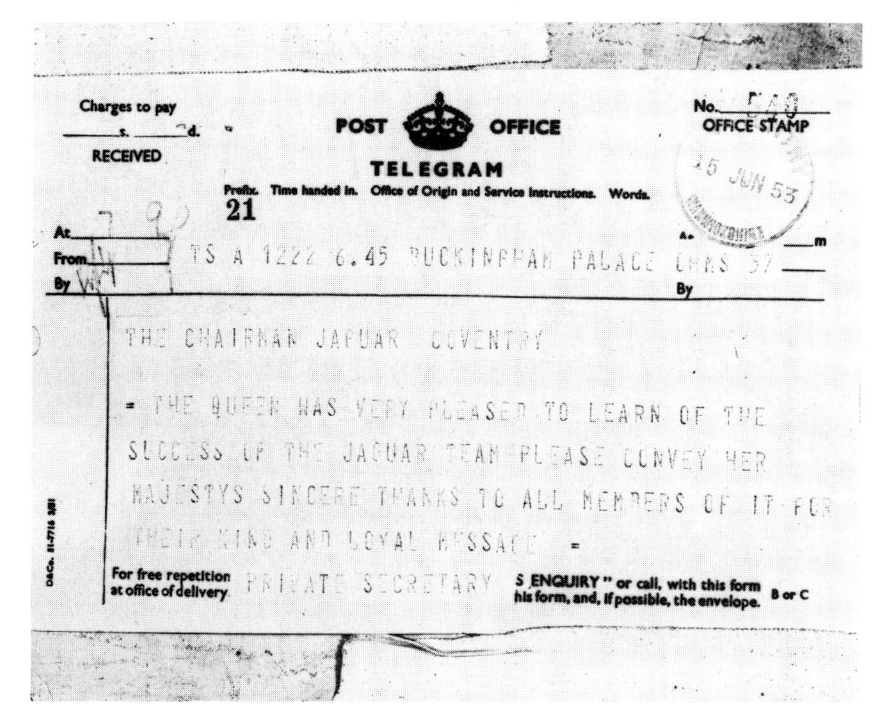

Charges to pay
s. d.
RECEIVED

POST OFFICE
TELEGRAM

Prefix. Time handed in. Office of Origin and Service Instructions. Words.
21

No.
OFFICE STAMP
15 JUN 53

At
From
By

TS A 1222 6.45 BUCKINGHAM PALACE CHAS 57

THE CHAIRMAN JAGUAR COVENTRY

= THE QUEEN WAS VERY PLEASED TO LEARN OF THE SUCCESS OF THE JAGUAR TEAM PLEASE CONVEY HER MAJESTYS SINCERE THANKS TO ALL MEMBERS OF IT FOR THEIR KIND AND LOYAL MESSAGE =

PRIVATE SECRETARY

For free repetition at office of delivery
"ENQUIRY" or call, with this form ... form, and, if possible, the envelope.
B or C

The telegram sent by the Queen when Jaguar won the 1953 Le Mans 24-Hour Race.

A bevy of brilliant engineers: (from left to right) Bill Heynes, Walter Hassan, Harry Munday and Claude Baily.

other to bring coffee and croissant to the toiling mechanics, and then looked bewildered yet painfully proud as they were profusely thanked in strong Coventrian accents. When the cars drove out to the circuit on Sunday there were almost as many people lining the route as there were at the circuit. And in 1953 the crowd was enormous, well over 200,000.

The greater part of the crowd were French, Lago-Talbots were still winning, and they were still arguing about Pierre Levegh, and his stubborn, wasted drive. The Reisen coaches from West Germany had not arrived, indeed German tourists were hard to find in France, and were not very popular. The British were there, of course, but not in their thousands. They arrived in their hundreds, adorned in cavalry twills and cravats, having just motored down in their Alvis or HRG, and took over hotels in Le Mans that knew their ways, and have now disappeared. *The Motor* had their suite on the pit balcony and it was the holy of holies, and strictly reserved for field rank and above.

James Tilling gave hourly commentaries on the race in English by courtesy of *The Motor*, and made regular sorties to their suite for sustenance, and it was fascinating to note how his commentary grew more relaxed as the night progressed.

The showground beyond the Dunlop bridge was as thriving then as it is today, but the entertainment was more bucolic, essentially rural French, with two-headed ladies topping the bill. The tented village heaved and sighed its way through the night, and open-air mass attracted the devout and the drunks. There was a Club des Pilotes which had never seen a racing driver, but it produced chicken and chips non-stop for twenty-four hours, and the social life centred around the minute caravans of BP, Ferodo and Dunlop. The late-lamented Gregor Grant, editor of *Autosport*, never moved except from one to the other, but he knew more about what was happening than people glued to the press box. Often he would never see a wheel turn, but his race reports were impeccable. He had a constant stream of visitors who kept him abreast of everything.

The Ecurie Belge D-type of Swaters and Rouselle came fourth at the 1956 Le Mans behind the winning Jaguar, an Aston Martin and a Ferrari.

In February 1957 a fire broke out in the tyre store which gutted large sections of the Browns Lane factory.

## A Different Breed

Jaguar came down to Le Mans in 1953 full of hope and not a little confidence, and this was fanned by the performance of the cars in practice; all went well, but No 18, the Rolt/Hamilton car, was just a little faster than the others, and on the Thursday evening Duncan Hamilton set up a new unofficial lap record for the circuit – then chicane-less – of 110mph (177kph), a full second quicker than Alberto Ascari in the 4.5-litre Ferrari.

Because it was so quick Stirling asked if he could drive the car, but Bill Lyons decided that he should take out the practice car with the lower axle ratio. This car, unfortunately, carried the same number as the Rolt/Hamilton car, No 18. Unknown to William Lyons the regulations had been changed and practice cars were not allowed. The pit staff knew, but in the general confusion the car, with the No 18 markings went out with Norman Dewis at the wheel to do a few warming up laps.

The Ferrari team protested immediately, and the protest was upheld by the race organizers. As a result Rolt and Hamilton were told that they had been disqualified. As soon as he knew what had happened William Lyons asked the organizers, the Automobile Club de L'Quest for a special enquiry, pointing out that it was the reserve car driven by the reserve driver, and although it had the same No 18 number, it was not the Rolt/Hamilton car.

His request was granted, and he was told they would hear his protest on the following morning . . . the day of the race. It need hardly be said that both Tony Rolt and Duncan Hamilton were bitterly disappointed, and felt that the hearing on the following day would be little more than a ritual since the rules at Le Mans were rigidly enforced. They did not believe they had a chance of driving, and as Duncan Hamilton later explained in his book, *Touch Wood*, 'We decided to drown our sorrows in the usual way'.

Tony and Duncan were true amateur motor racing drivers, but no one could have described them as amateurs when it came to drinking, and with their wives moving in together, and giving them up as a bad job, they spent the night steadily imbibing.

On Saturday morning they were sipping coffee in Gruber's, and feeling ghastly, when a Mk VII Jaguar pulled up, and the immaculate figure of William Lyons appeared. He told them that he had paid a 25,000 franc fine, and they were back in the race. It was 10am and

The XK150 Drophead Coupe began to look a little more bulbous than its predecessors, but it was a very luxurious car and in 'S' Type form with a 265bhp engine available in 1959 it was very quick. It also featured Dunlop disc brakes on all four wheels.

the race started at 4pm. Neither had had a wink of sleep for twenty-four hours, and twenty-four hours of racing lay ahead.

Le Mans did not boast a Turkish bath, so they returned to their chateau, had hot baths and drank more black coffee, but by 2pm they still felt dreadful. There was only one thing for it: a little hair of the dog.

Both had a large brandy, 'purely for medicinal purposes', as Duncan pointed out. By the start they were feeling fine, and Tony Rolt took the first stint, while Duncan watched anxiously lap after lap the progress of his team mate, sipping, once again purely for medicinal purposes, a large brandy.

The start at Le Mans in those days was spectacular. Sixty cars lined up against the pits, with their noses at a slight angle towards the Dunlop bridge. The drivers stood in their own individual white circle painted on the ground, at the opposite side of the track, and when the flag was dropped they raced over to their car, jumped in, switched on the ignition and were off. No seat belts in those days. Clearly some drivers were a little more adept than others at this performance, and with typical Moss thoroughness, he practised the manoeuvre, and was always one of the first away.

From an almost tangible silence there was an explosion of sound as sixty highly-tuned engines burst into life, and tyres screamed their annoyance at being brought so brutally into use. For about half a minute there was pandemonium as the cars disappeared under the Dunlop bridge, then a buzz of intense conversation broken only by the engine screams of a late starter, then silence again as everyone waited to see who would be leading the pack from White House and on to the pit straight.

The crowd was enormous in 1953, and it would have been difficult to find room for a pin in the stands opposite the pits. All heads were turned towards the White House, and there was then a roar of excitement as the cars came into sight. It was Sidney Allard in the lead in one of his own cars, followed by the 4½-litre Ferrari of Villoresi, then Stirling, and in seventh place going well was the Rolt Jaguar. Allard did not last long, retiring with no brakes, and by the fourth lap Stirling had taken the lead and the order was: Moss, Jaguar; Villoresi, Ferrari; Cole, Ferrari; and Rolt, Jaguar. With little over an hour gone Stirling was in the pits with fuel-feed problems, but Rolt overtook Villoresi – no mean achievement when the Ferrari was going well – and again it was Jaguar back in the lead.

Stirling had another pit stop which put him back to

21st place, but neither he nor Peter Walker had trouble again, and Stirling was driving like the wind. During the night the lead changed occasionally at pit stops, but it was mostly the Rolt/Hamilton Jaguar in the lead, and the crowd, which seemed to me as dense at 4am on Sunday morning as it had been for the start, roared their support each time the Jaguar left the pit.

The two Englishmen were big fellows, they had flamboyant personalities which appeared to transmit to the crowd. Hamilton came back with the windscreen shattered, and his nose in only slightly better condition having hit a bird at 150mph (240kph) on the Mulsanne Straight. They took off from the pits with the back end snaking, wrestling with the wheel as they piled on the power. In short they looked like the sort of chaps who should have been winning Le Mans, and the crowd loved it.

The advantages of disc brakes were beginning to make their mark. The two Alfa Romeos dropped out, Cole very sadly crashed at the White House and was killed, and the leading Ferrari had clutch trouble, and eventually stopped out on the circuit, but not before it had been overtaken by Stirling Moss. So with only a few hours to go it was Jaguar first and second, with the Cunningham of Walters and Fitch third, running a very consistent race, but well behind Moss, and thirty miles behind the leading Jaguar, so it needed a catastrophe for Jaguar to lose the race. In fourth place was the third Jaguar of Whitehead and Stewart.

The Jaguars and the Cunninghams were the only two teams to finish intact, and there can be no doubt that the Jaguars shattered the opposition, because although the Ferraris were potentially the fastest cars on the circuit, they had not had the benefit of disc brakes. Duncan Hamilton said that he could reduce his speed by 120mph (193kph) in 300yd (274m) on the approach to Mulsanne Corner, an enormous advantage particularly in the early hours when mist is such a problem at Le Mans. To compensate for the Jaguar's superior brakes the opposition had to drive excessively hard, and the cars would not take it – certainly not for the sustained period necessary at Le Mans.

## Disbelief

One commentator pointed out rather obviously that the race had been won by a combination of speed, endurance and stopping power. Duncan Hamilton added a more pertinent rider, 'The will to fulfil an ambition and good cognac'.

They had averaged 105.85mph, the first to exceed the magic 100mph (161kph), and by 2pm on Sunday they had covered 278 laps, one more than the winners of the race in 1952. No wonder William Lyons allowed himself a smile. During the race Frank Rainbow had dropped a battery on his foot, and had been taken to hospital in Le Mans. Naturally, after the race his fellow mechanics went to see him, and were they envious; broken toes not withstanding.

'He was sitting up in bed, surrounded by beautiful nurses, fruit, chocolate and flowers looking really pleased with himself. You would have thought he had won the race', said one of his colleagues.

Jochen Rindt, the German racing driver was, in my opinion, a particularly good fellow, and I recall telling him the story of the Rolt/Hamilton episode at the 1953 Le Mans race. Jochen was no stranger to Le Mans, having shared the winning Ferrari in 1965 with American Masten Gregory, but the medicinal brandy was more than he would accept. He shook his head in disbelief and said 'It is just another of your stories'. Such was the gulf between the drivers of the fifties and the sixties.

# 11
# The D-Type

## The Rise of Ecurie Ecosse

The Jaguar C-type had achieved what it had set out to do – win the Le Mans 24-Hour Race. In 1953 it went on to win the Rheims 12-Hour Race – always a good one for Jaguar – and in the Belgian 24-Hour Race, Ecurie Ecosse entered three C-types and did well to finish second behind a 'works' Ferrari. Again Ecurie Ecosse sent James Stewart and Roy Salvadori to the Nurburgring in a C-type, and again the Jaguar finished second to a Ferrari driven by Mike Hawthorn and Guiseppe Farina, while at the Goodwood 9-Hour Race two Jaguars driven by Moss/Walker, and Rolt/Hamilton, were doing well until lubrication problems began because of oil surge; they had, of course, wet sump lubrication.

It would be appropriate here to mention Ecurie Ecosse, a team that played a considerable part in the racing history of Jaguar, and when Jaguar retired from racing in 1957, they took over the mantle, and apart from anything else won two Le Mans 24-Hour races. The relationship with Jaguar was very close – they always had first offer on the previous year's 'works' cars, and took over the 1953 C-types *en bloc*, but there were no other links either financially or in direction.

Ecurie Ecosse is a famous name in motor racing, and the Automobile Club de L'Quest were even moved to playing pipe music over the tannoy system at Le Mans when they were racing. But it started in Edinburgh, in a very modest way.

Inhabitants of that delightful city would no doubt proclaim that most things of any worth originate there, but David Murray, a keen motor racing enthusiast started the team from a small mews headquarters, enlisting the help of Bill Dobson, Ian Stewart, and Sir James Scott Douglas Bt., plus that redoubtable engine-tuner W.E. (Wilky) Wilkinson.

A good deal of information passed between Ecurie Ecosse and Jaguar, and it certainly was not all one way – the Scottish team produced some very quick cars – but they flew the flag for Jaguar at many meetings throughout the world at which Jaguar, with its limited resources, would have been unable to compete.

## Epitome of a Racing Sports Car

In 1953 the company revealed a prototype that was in fact, something in between the C-type and the new model that was to take its place. It had a very aerodynamic body of monocoque structure, but the C-type's wet sump lubrication XK engine. It was not until May 1954 that the D-type was announced. In the experimental shop it had been known as the D-type for sometime, and the name stuck, but there was no logical reason, since there had been no A or B-type, and C had stood for competition, however, D-type it was.

Malcolm Sayer worked out the body shapes mathematically to produce the least drag, and it was a happy coincidence that it also turned out to be exceptionally beautiful. It was the first car built by Jaguar with monocoque construction, and it was Sayer's *tour de force*. In the eyes of many enthusiasts today it is the very epitome of a racing sports car. The engine was mounted within a tubular frame in front of the monocoque centre section, which was of immense strength, and the tail assembly was bolted to the centre section.

The front suspension was conventional Jaguar with upper and lower wishbones, and longitudinal torsion bars, while the rear suspension retained a live axle,

In 1954 the D-type was tested at Hendricks Field, near Sebring, before the Sports Car G.P. on 13 March that year. From left to right are: Fred Heacock, chairman of the race committee, Briggs Cunningham, the entrant and a great supporter of American motor racing, and Mr William Lyons, as he then was.

trailing arms and torsion bars. Later Bob Knight fitted a de Dion rear axle, which he thought improved the handling, but it was not used because, as he points out 'we did not have time to develop it properly'. The suspension was conventional, but very finely tuned, and again it must not be forgotten that the object was to win Le Mans, and the road surface there had been improved since 1953; anything else was a bonus. (Incidentally, HWM of Walton-on-Thames, Surrey, built a Jaguar-engined sports car, and that did have a de Dion rear suspension.)

Dry sump lubrication had been contemplated for some time, but the oil churning incident at Goodwood, hurried the decision along. Three Weber carburettors were retained, so was the 9:1 compression ratio, and bhp was said to be 250 at 6,000rpm. A four-speed synchromesh gearbox was employed using very high ratios: 2.79, 3.57 and 5.98:1, which varied from circuit to circuit. At Le Mans Stirling Moss was timed at 172.6mph (277.8kph) on the Mulsanne Straight, a remarkably high speed for a car which still used a lot of basic Jaguar components, such as propellor shaft and rear axle. Although the factory had experimented with fuel injection in 1954, a mechanical fuel injection system was first used at Sebring on a factory-entered car in 1956, and then a fuel injected 3.8-litre engined car, prepared at Coventry, was entered by Ecurie Ecosse in the 1957 Le Mans.

However, while the C-type did look like a sports car, albeit a special one, the D-type with its fairing behind the driver, its oval-shaped air intake, and Perspex windscreen which curled around the driver, did give more than a hint of things to come. Yet this very quick motor car could still be driven on the roads, and was driven to Le Mans for tests where, in the hands of Tony Rolt, it covered a standing lap at 107mph (172kph), and a flying lap at 115.6mph (186kph) – quicker than Ascari's fastest lap in the previous year.

The Mille Miglia was missed in 1954, which was probably very wise, and soon it was June, and another Le Mans. The entry list was impressive with Ferraris of 4.9, 4½ and 3 litres – the 4.9-litre V12 was said to produce nearly 350bhp – Cunninghams, Aston Martins, including a supercharged coupe, Maserati, Gordini, and the Lago-Talbots, but no Alfa Romeos, the Disco Volante having been retired. The three Jaguars were entrusted to Rolt and Hamilton, Moss and Walker, and Whitehead and Ken Wharton, a Midland driver entering the Le Mans team for the first time.

## A Close Run Thing

The sun did not shine on anyone at Le Mans in 1954. It rained for a good deal of the time (and in the wet Le Mans is a very miserable place), but the Jaguar team were in trouble early in the race with misfiring, which was later traced to fuel filter blockage. Maurice Trintignant and Froilan Gonzalez (euphemistically known as the Bull of the Pampas) were in the lead in the 4.9-litre Ferrari, Maglioli and Marzotto were out in the 4½-litre Ferrari after holding second place, which was now held by Whitehead and Wharton, ahead of Rosier and Manzon in a third Ferrari.

On a rain-soaked Sunday first Moss went out when

Mike Hawthorn was timed at 192mph (309kph) on the Mulsanne Straight in a D-type in 1956, and in the same year race winner Ron Flockhart said of the D-type that the faster it went the more stable it became.

Silverstone in 1988, when Jaguar won the Championship and Le Mans.

The Jaguar XJR-9, not at Le Mans, but in Le Mans trim with the lower fin etc.

Sir John found motor racing a slight strain, and here Jan Lammers cheers him up.

Good pit work is essential at Le Mans, and the pit crews are the unsung heroes, many of whom labour through the race with hardly a break.

Le Mans at night has a very special atmosphere, and is quite unique.

The Jaguars in full flight in the 1990 Le Mans 24-Hour race.

This particular D-type is particularly famous, and is here in road-going trim.

The hood on the XJS V12 Convertible can be raised or lowered with the minimum of fuss.

Few things are more redolent of luxury than the XJS V12 Convertible.

The Jaguar XJSC V 12, which followed the 3.6 version, had a very hefty price tag, and not a very long life.

The early Jaguar SS100 was powered by a 2½-litre Standard built engine, but in 1938 they were equipped with a 3½ litre unit, although bodywork remained virtually unchanged.

The XK140 Drophead Coupe which in special equipment form had a 210bhp engine still sold for under £2,000.

The driver's view in the SS100.

This is a 3½-litre version of SS100.

The 3.5 litre SS Jaguar Drophead Coupe was a far cry from the exaggerated lines of the earlier SS models.

Before the end of the war the line for 2½ and 3½-litre engines had been transferred from the Standard works, and this 1947 Jaguar was powered by a 3½-litre engine built in-house.

In March 1945 Jaguar Cars Ltd., was formed, and the famous Jaguar motif came into its own, although it had been used on SS Jaguars before the war. It was, however, an optional extra (two guineas) until 1957 and the Mk VIII.

The Jaguar 1.5-litre saloon was the last Jaguar with a Standard-built engine.

This 1947 version of the 3½-litre saloon was wider, and had a bigger boot than its predecessors. In that year it sold for £1,099.

The Drophead Coupe version of the XK150 was a particular favourite in the US market.

Although the Jaguar Mk V had a new body, the Mk VII was the first new Jaguar saloon after the war.

There was in my mind a great deal of substance and dignity attached to the 1958 Mk IX.

The big Jaguar saloon was a very thirsty car and unsuitable for the austerity of the late 1940s, but most were shipped abroad, and you could wait years for one on the home market, so it was an academic problem for most people.

In 1948 every motor car was in demand but there was a special demand for the Jaguar Drophead Coupe and the SS100. The SS100 never went into production after the war, and Dropheads were scarcer than pineapples.

When launched in 1961 the Roadster, powered by a 3.8-litre engine, cost £2,098. I thought it was the best looking of the lot.

The rocker type switches very much in evidence on the dashboard of the V12 E-type. Air conditioning was available.

From the front end the V12 E-Type had lost some of the refined looks of the original model.

The 2+2 was particularly attractive to those who enjoyed the joys of an E-Type but also appreciated a little more luggage space.

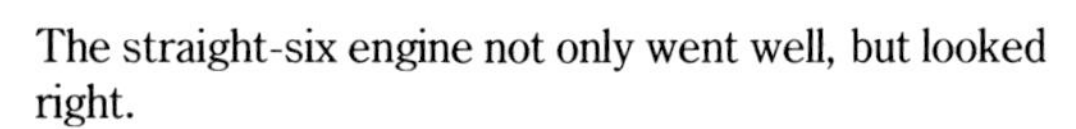

The straight-six engine not only went well, but looked right.

Wire wheels were an intrinsic part of a Jaguar to many enthusiasts, but the knock on hubs did have a tin opening effect in an accident.

The headlamps had been recessed in the Series II to meet US safety regulations, but the looks had not been lost.

Nautical men might say the Jaguar Piranna had a rather heavy transom.

When the XJS was produced in 1976 it was fitted with a four-speed manual gearbox, and automatic was optional. It became standard in 1979.

With electronic fuel injection – it originally had four carburettors – the XJ12 produced an effortless 285bhp, and was and still is, one of the most enjoyable means of travelling from A to B.

Surrey Jaguar dealer Guy Salmon was steeped in the motor trade, and a lover of motor cars. He produced this version of the XJS HE for Jaguar's Golden Jubilee.

If the D-type was the ultimate in sports cars, which many believe, the C-type ran it a very close second.

his brakes totally disappeared, and he was lucky to find an escape road, then Whitehead's car retired with cylinder-head trouble, and it was left to the old alliance of Rolt and Hamilton in the remaining D-type. Their car was going well now, and so were they; Hamilton lapping at 117mph (188kph), but had they enough time to catch the giant Ferrari? The answer was no, but it was a close run thing, and when Gonzalez crossed the line he was only three miles ahead of the Jaguar, and the race average for the Ferrari was 105.1mph (169kph), and that for the Jaguar 105mph (168kph). A Cunningham driven by Spear and Johnston was third, and a privately entered C-type driven by Belgians Swaters and Laurent was fourth.

Once again the sun shone on the Jaguar team at Rheims, where they finished 1–2–3. But the rest of the year was quite quiet, with a little excitement at the TT on the Dundrod Circuit in Ulster, where there was an exceptionally good field. Jaguar entered three cars, Rolt and Hamilton, and Whitehead and Wharton in standard D-types, but Moss and Walker had a 2½-litre engined car, for this 'index of performance' race, which invariably ensures that a smaller-engined car wins.

Two years later Jaguar were to produce a 2.4-litre engined car, and they had been developing experimental engines, but at Dundrod all three retired, and to add a final note of gloom when the cars were being unloaded at Belfast a crate had been dropped on William Lyon's personal Mk VII with disastrous effect.

## Mercedes are Back

In 1955 Mercedes-Benz had produced the 300 SLR's, eight-cylinder 'silver arrows' complete with a new innovation, air-brake flaps that rose behind the driver, and were to be driven by Moss and Fangio, Fitch and Kling and Levegh and Simon. The Jaguars were the long-nose models, with modified rear suspension, an extra oil pump, an engine producing 285bhp, and an even higher rear axle ratio of 2.53:1.

The year had started appallingly for William Lyons and his wife. Driving to Le Mans earlier in the year, on business connected with the race, their son John had been killed in a road accident. But William Lyons hid his grief, and carried on.

The hope was that it would be a monumental battle for supremacy between the Jaguars and the

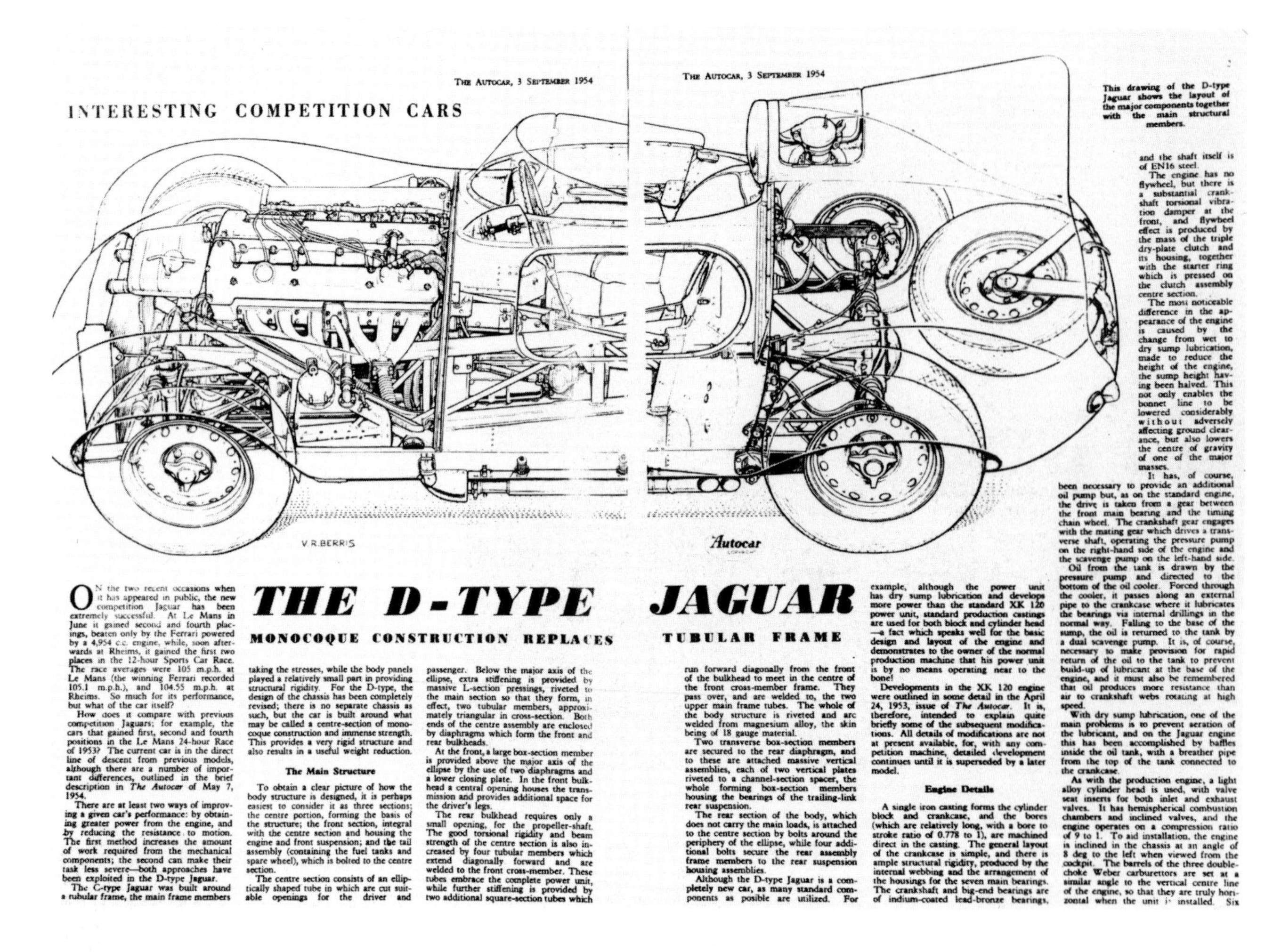

The Autocar, 3 September 1954

INTERESTING COMPETITION CARS

The Autocar, 3 September 1954

This drawing of the D-type Jaguar shows the layout of the major components together with the main structural members.

V.R.BERRIS

Autocar

# THE D-TYPE JAGUAR

## MONOCOQUE CONSTRUCTION REPLACES TUBULAR FRAME

On the two recent occasions when it has appeared in public, the new competition Jaguar has been extremely successful. At Le Mans in June it gained second and fourth placings, beaten only by the Ferrari powered by a 4,954 c.c. engine, while, soon afterwards at Rheims, it gained the first two places in the 12-hour Sports Car Race. The race averages were 105 m.p.h. at Le Mans (the winning Ferrari recorded 105.1 m.p.h.), and 104.55 m.p.h. at Rheims. So much for its performance, but what of the car itself?

How does it compare with previous competition Jaguars; for example, the cars that gained first, second and fourth positions in the Le Mans 24-hour Race of 1953? The current car is in the direct line of descent from previous models, although there are a number of important differences, outlined in the brief description in *The Autocar* of May 7, 1954.

There are at least two ways of improving a given car's performance: by obtaining greater power from the engine, and by reducing the resistance to motion. The first method increases the amount of work required from the mechanical components; the second can make their task less severe—both approaches have been exploited in the D-type Jaguar.

The C-type Jaguar was built around a tubular frame, the main frame members taking the stresses, while the body panels played a relatively small part in providing structural rigidity. For the D-type, the design of the chassis has been completely revised; there is no separate chassis as such, but the car is built around what may be called a centre-section of monocoque construction and immense strength. This provides a very rigid structure and also results in a useful weight reduction.

### The Main Structure

To obtain a clear picture of how the body structure is designed, it is perhaps easiest to consider it as three sections; the centre portion, forming the basis of the structure; the front section, integral with the centre section and housing the engine and front suspension; and the tail assembly (containing the fuel tanks and spare wheel), which is bolted to the centre section.

The centre section consists of an elliptically shaped tube in which are cut suitable openings for the driver and passenger. Below the major axis of the ellipse, extra stiffening is provided by massive L-section pressings, riveted to the main section so that they form, in effect, two tubular members, approximately triangular in cross-section. Both ends of the centre assembly are enclosed by diaphragms which form the front and rear bulkheads.

At the front, a large box-section member is provided above the major axis of the ellipse by the use of two diaphragms and a lower closing plate. In the front bulkhead a central opening houses the transmission and provides additional space for the driver's legs.

The rear bulkhead requires only a small opening, for the propeller-shaft. The good torsional rigidity and beam strength of the centre section is also increased by four tubular members which extend diagonally forward and are welded to the front cross-member. These tubes embrace the complete power unit, while further stiffening is provided by two additional square-section tubes which run forward diagonally from the front of the bulkhead to meet in the centre of the front cross-member frame. They pass over, and are welded to, the two upper main frame tubes. The whole of the body structure is riveted and arc welded from magnesium alloy, the skin being of 18 gauge material.

Two transverse box-section members are secured to the rear diaphragm, and to these are attached massive vertical assemblies, each of two vertical plates riveted to a channel-section spacer, the whole forming box-section members housing the bearings of the trailing-link rear suspension.

The rear section of the body, which does not carry the main loads, is attached to the centre section by bolts around the periphery of the ellipse, while four additional bolts secure the rear assembly frame members to the rear suspension housing assemblies.

Although the D-type Jaguar is a completely new car, as many standard components as posible are utilized. For example, although the power unit has dry sump lubrication and develops more power than the standard XK 120 power unit, standard production castings are used for both block and cylinder head—a fact which speaks well for the basic design and layout of the engine and demonstrates to the owner of the normal production machine that his power unit is by no means operating near to the bone!

Developments in the XK 120 engine were outlined in some detail in the April 24, 1953, issue of *The Autocar*. It is, therefore, intended to explain quite briefly some of the subsequent modifications. All details of modifications are not at present available, for, with any competition machine, detailed development continues until it is superseded by a later model.

### Engine Details

A single iron casting forms the cylinder block and crankcase, and the bores (which are relatively long, with a bore to stroke ratio of 0.778 to 1), are machined direct in the casting. The general layout of the crankcase is simple, and there is ample structural rigidity, produced by the internal webbing and the arrangement of the housings for the seven main bearings. The crankshaft and big-end bearings are of indium-coated lead-bronze bearings, and the shaft itself is of EN16 steel.

The engine has no flywheel, but there is a substantial crankshaft torsional vibration damper at the front, and flywheel effect is produced by the mass of the triple dry-plate clutch and its housing, together with the starter ring which is pressed on the clutch assembly centre section.

The most noticeable difference in the appearance of the engine is caused by the change from wet to dry sump lubrication, made to reduce the height of the engine, the sump height having been halved. This not only enables the bonnet line to be lowered considerably without adversely affecting ground clearance, but also lowers the centre of gravity of one of the major masses.

It has, of course, been necessary to provide an additional oil pump but, as on the standard engine, the drive is taken from a gear between the front main bearing and the timing chain wheel. The crankshaft gear engages with the mating gear which drives a transverse shaft, operating the pressure pump on the right-hand side of the engine and the scavenge pump on the left-hand side.

Oil from the tank is drawn by the pressure pump and directed to the bottom of the oil cooler. Forced through the cooler, it passes along an external pipe to the crankcase where it lubricates the bearings via internal drillings in the normal way. Falling to the base of the sump, the oil is returned to the tank by a dual scavenge pump. It is, of course, necessary to make provision for rapid return of the oil to the tank to prevent build-up of lubricant at the base of the engine, and it must also be remembered that oil produces more resistance than air to crankshaft webs rotating at high speed.

With dry sump lubrication, one of the main problems is to prevent aeration of the lubricant, and on the Jaguar engine this has been accomplished by baffles inside the oil tank, with a breather pipe from the top of the tank connected to the crankcase.

As with the production engine, a light alloy cylinder head is used, with valve seat inserts for both inlet and exhaust valves. It has hemispherical combustion chambers and inclined valves, and the engine operates on a compression ratio of 9 to 1. To aid installation, the engine is inclined in the chassis at an angle of 8 deg to the left when viewed from the cockpit. The barrels of the three double-choke Weber carburettors are set at a similar angle to the vertical centre line of the engine, so that they are truly horizontal when the unit is installed. Six

This cutaway drawing of the D-type appeared in *The Autocar* in 1954, the year it first took part in the Le Mans 24-Hour Race.

Mercedes-Benz; in fact the race was more than overshadowed by the horrendous crash in front of the pits, two-and-a-half hours after the race started. I was there and I must say that most of the race passed in a blur of telephone calls, and a taxi ride to Paris with photographs I had bought from someone who turned out to be a professional Welsh protographer. Only one was used, the remainder were considered too horrific for publication in 1955. I doubt if that would be true today.

Pierre Levegh was an enigmatic man, whose real name was Pierre Bouillon. He had taken his uncle's name, Veghle, and produced an anagram – no one appears to know why, because there were no obvious reasons. He had earned a reputation as a tuner of motor cars, and also as a driver, but he was not considered to be a 'great' driver, and his preference was for endurance events. Comfortably cushioned against the vicissitudes of life, he was an all-round sportsman; a first-class tennis player, yachtsman and an international ice-hockey player. But his burning passion was to win Le Mans. He could have won in 1952 but for his stubbornness.

After this race the Mercedes-Benz team manager, Alfred Neubauer told Levegh 'The next time Mercedes comes to Le Mans you will drive one of their cars'. True to his word Neubauer gave him a drive in 1955 when Levegh was fifty years old; too old, many

This D-type is being hurried along by M. Salmon at Silverstone in 1961.

The beautiful lines created by Malcolm Sayer are very evident in this shot of a JCB sponsored D-type approaching Druids Corner at Brands Hatch.

thought, to be driving in a twenty-four hour race in such a potent machine. In practice he was the slowest of all the Mercedes drivers, and it was clear to some that the car was too much for him. Neubauer was asked to drop him, but he refused; he would not go back on his word.

Hawthorn, in the Jaguar, was leading Fangio by a few seconds, and both were driving as though they were in a Grand Prix, not a twenty-four hour race. Levegh was about to be lapped by Fangio after just two-and-a-half hours. Ahead of him Hawthorn had been told two laps earlier to come into the pits, and he thundered past the much slower Lance Macklin Austin-Healey, braked hard and pulled into the pits. Macklin, slamming on his brakes was not stopping quickly enough and pulled over to his left to miss the Jaguar. He was hit by Levegh whose Mercedes flew into the air and into the crowd, a disintegrating mass of flaming magnesium alloy. Fangio in the second Mercedes got through the narrow gap between Hawthorn and Macklin.

There was, of course, chaos at the circuit, particularly in the area around the stands opposite the pits. Makeshift first-aid stations were created, ambulances struggled to get through the crowd, and spectators thronged to the scene to gawp, or search for friends. Past the Dunlop bridge, and beyond, no one knew there had been an accident, and the organizers wanted to keep it that way, so they did not stop the race. No announcement that there had been an accident was made until the early hours of Sunday morning. The problem of getting ambulances out was bad enough; if the 200,000 plus crowd suddenly moved to the exits thinking the race was over, it would have brought everything to a standstill. That was the thinking.

With the Mercedes team at Le Mans opinions on whether to retire or not were divided. They were in the heat of battle, and were being urged by Charles Faroux to continue. He explained that if the Mercedes team retired they would have to give an explanation, and everyone around the circuit would know what had happened. They wanted to avoid this at all costs.

The XKSS was a road-going version of the D-type, and under twenty were made. No price was quoted for the home market for this motor car which would accelerate from 0–100mph (0–161kph) in 14.4 seconds. The price quoted in New York was the equivalent of £1,570 in 1957 – enough to make one weep.

Some memorable representatives of a great marque. From left to right: 1950 XK120, 1951 C-type, 1955 road equipped D-type and a 1966 4.2 E-type Roadster.

In Stuttgart, the headquarters of Mercedes-Benz, they knew more about the accident than most people at the circuit, thanks to German television coverage. About 9.30pm Dr Fritz Nallinger, the chief engineer, telephoned Neubauer to stop, but Artur Keser, chief of public affairs at Mercedes, was fighting to keep the team in the race, and appealing to higher authority, the boss, Dr Fritz Koenecke.

Artur Keser explained that the race was now continuing, they had been asked by the race organizers not to retire, and he felt that the Jaguars were going too fast, and would not finish.

At about 11.30pm he managed to get in touch with Dr Koenecke – trying to make telephone calls was appallingly difficult – and the managing director told Keser that he would not give him an instruction, but try to convince him, and they spoke for half an hour. Dr Koenecke said that they were not involved in the battle, they were at headquarters, the general staff and they could see that there was no virtue in winning the race; it was a Mercedes car that had killed over eighty people, and they must retire. Eventually Keser agreed and after telling Jaguar that they were to retire, at 1.45am the Mercedes team withdrew with the Fangio/Moss car in the lead.

Seven hours after the accident Lofty England could see no point in retiring, and as the man on the spot, and the man in charge, kept the team racing. Like a shroud the rain, soft and thin, began to fall at dawn with the Hawthorn/Bueb Jaguar still in the lead followed by a Maserati, Aston Martin and the Rolt/Hamilton Jaguar. There were only twenty-five cars racing, and by this time everyone knew what had happened. Most of the crowd appeared numb from the shock although pockets carried on as though nothing had happened; eating, drinking, bidding at a mock auction.

At 4pm a sad, but unbowed Charles Faroux drop-

A room with a magnificent view. The practical cockpit of the Jaguar XKSS.

ped the flag on the winning Jaguar of Hawthorn and Bueb, and the seventeen other cars still running. It was still raining, as though the Heavens also disapproved.

The traditional champagne was there, but no one was sure what to do with it, with the exception of Mike Hawthorn. He took it, and had a mighty swallow before passing it on, laughing and smiling. It had been a hard drive, and he had won with the help of Ivor Bueb, but regrettably no one had told him that this was not just another race. The following day a French newspaper carried a photograph of Hawthorn and Bueb with the caption: 'Cheers Mr Hawthorn.'

## Mike Hawthorn

After twenty-four hours of intense racing the judgement of people in the front line can be distorted, and it is unfortunate that Jaguar had no one at the circuit, detached from the front line, who could have profered advice on their approach to victory.

Mike Hawthorn, was not a callous man, but he made a number of mistakes in his public life from the lack of what would now be called 'good public relations'. In my view Peter Collins, who was killed at Nurburgring in 1956, was a better natural driver, but for 120 per cent effort, no one could improve on Mike Hawthorn.

Immediately after the accident at Le Mans in 1955 I recall seeing him, even whiter-faced than normal, running around the caravans in a daze, but when Lofty England told him to get back in the car and drive, he did. Hawthorn's attitude was that the team he was driving for would give him the best car possible, and in return he would drive it as hard as possible. He was not a whinger, and as a result he was held in considerable affection by everyone in his team, and he was particularly admired at Jaguar.

Many thought that the Le Mans 24-Hour Race would be cancelled in 1956, but it was not, it was delayed until August so that alterations could be made to the circuit to prevent any recurrence of the debâcle of the previous year. The Le Mans 24-Hour Race is the biggest annual money-spinner in the Sarthe region, and as the latest battles with FISA demonstrate, it is something they would abandon with the greatest reluctance.

The Jaguar 'works' team and two cars from Ecurie Ecosse competed at Rheims, which this year was staged before Le Mans, and against a not very impressive field the two 'works' cars came first and second, followed in third and fourth places by the two Ecurie Ecosse cars of Titterington and Fairman, and

Flockhart and Sanderson. The winning car was fitted with Lucas fuel injection, while the remainder used three Weber carburettors, but for Le Mans the three 'works' cars driven by Hawthorn and Bueb, Frère and Titterington, and Fairman and Wharton were equipped with fuel injection. The sole Ecurie Ecosse car driven by Flockhart and Sanderson retained the three Webers.

To meet the new regulations they had wraparound windscreens, and smaller fuel tanks of 29-gallon capacity, and the odd weight-saving modification such as smaller diameter frame tubes. Opposition consisted of two Aston Martin DB.3S models, a new Aston Martin DBR.1 2½-litre prototype, Ferrari Testa Rossa 2½-litre cars which were equally new, a couple of Gordini 2½-litre cars, one powered by a six, the other an eight-cylinder engine, and two 'works' Lagos with 2½-litre Maserati engines; not a particularly formidable field.

This was just as well because in the second lap, with rain falling, Paul Frère skidded in Le Esses, Fairman managed to avoid him, but was smote in the rear by Portago's Ferrari, and the upshot was that two Jaguars were out. The third, driven by Hawthorn was in big trouble with a hair-line split in a fuel pipe, and he was in and out of the pits in the early stages of the race with horrifying frequency, and before the trouble was rectified he was twenty laps down. Fortunately the Ecurie Ecosse Jaguar was going well, and took the lead from the Moss/Collins Aston Martin at dawn when Moss came into the pits to re-fuel, and never lost the lead, although the Aston Martin was challenging hard when they crossed the finishing line, and the Ecurie Ecosse car averaged 104.46mph (168.10kph) to the Aston Martin's 104.04mph (167.43kph) – another close run thing. Trintignant and Gendebien finished third in a Ferrari, while a D-type driven by Swaters and Rousselle, and entered by Ecurie Nationale Belge, finished fourth.

Hawthorn was having another blinding drive, and

The exhaust fitted to this XKSS is non-standard, and it has a rather special registration number.

Hawthorn at full flight in a D-type was a memorable sight. He was gaining four seconds a lap on the leaders, and it was an astonishing display of tenacity and skill for him to finish sixth, but after the ill-fated race the previous year, one wished that the gods had smiled more favourably, and he could have won a less controversial race.

Yorkshireman Peter Bolton, and his colleague Bob Walshaw had entered a special equipment XK140 fixed head coupe for the race, and after a modest amount of preparation at the Coventry factory, headed for Le Mans with tools etc., fixed to the roof. At one point in the race it had moved up to twelfth place, well ahead of much more exotic machinery, when it was called in by officials who promptly disqualified it for refuelling a lap earlier than was allowed under the new regulations. Later they discovered they had made a mistake, apologized and offered their sincerest regrets. They had, apparently, confused the Bolton Jaguar with another Jaguar – could it possibly have been the winning car?

Mike finished racing with the Jaguar sports car that year, but gave some exciting performances with the 3.4-litre Jaguar, winning the first race for that model at Silverstone in 1957, and then went on to win the Driver's World Championship, the first Briton to do so. He was killed in 1959 while driving his own rather special Jaguar 3.4 on the Hoggs Back in Surrey. It is often inferred that Hawthorn died because he was racing with R.R.C. (Rob) Walker, who then owned a gull-winged Mercedes-Benz. This is not so – Mike Hawthorn died because he was travelling quickly when something went wrong, with either him, or the car.

A significant result in the 1956 Le Mans race was the fifth place of Von Frankenberg and Von Trips in a 1,498cc Porsche, which just kept going – at a fair old lick – as the others fell out. In a few years Porsche would dominate Le Mans.

## Jaguar Retire from Racing

In October 1956 Jaguar announced that they were to retire from motor racing. It had been known for sometime that the formula at Le Mans was to change, that smaller engines would be required and if Jaguar were to be competitive they would need to build an entirely new car. Again, it must be remembered that Le Mans was the only race that Sir William was interested in, and they had now won it four times, so he could be forgiven for believing that they had proved their point.

Lofty England loved motor racing, Bill Heynes had grown to love it, and so had many others at Jaguar, but to Sir William it was a means to an end, and nothing more.

A statement put out by Jaguar said: 'The information gained as a result of the highly successful racing programme which the company has undertaken over the past five years has been of the utmost value, and much of the knowledge derived from racing experience has been applied to the development of the company's products.

'Nevertheless, an annual racing programme imposes a very heavy burden on the technical and research branch of the engineering division, which is already fully extended in implementing plans for the further development of Jaguar cars'.

The statement went on to say that development work on competition cars would not be abandoned, but a decision when to return to racing would be made when circumstances were right. It was to be a long time.

Oddly enough 1957 was the most successful year that Jaguar had at Le Mans, the five D-types entered finishing in first, second, fourth and sixth places. The winner was again an Ecurie Ecosse car driven by Flockhart and Bueb, with the second in the hands of Sanderson and Lawrence. Lucas and Mary, a French pair, were third, Belgians Frère and Rouselle fourth, and the old war horse Hamilton and American Masten Gregory sixth in what was the fastest car, but they had lost time when an exhaust pipe burnt a hole in the floor.

It must be recorded that Bill Heynes, the director of engineering, was not in favour of Jaguar pulling out of motor racing, and he made it quite clear that he thought racing had been a considerable asset to his department; attracting talent, and providing inspiration, and a team spirit that was difficult to replace. I suspect, also, that Bill Heynes enjoyed the excitement of motor racing; something that could not be replaced by a new car launch at Browns Lane.

## Monza

In 1957 the D-type took part in its last serious international event; a rather wild, imaginative – some would say mad – race at Monza in Northern Italy, called the Race of Two Worlds or, alternatively, Monzanapol. The idea was a 500-mile race – à la Indianapolis – between Indy single-seaters, and European sports cars. It all proved a bit too much for the racing establishment, who had an attack of the vapours, and it was ostracized by most of the drivers, but the rebellious Scots were true to tradition and entered a team.

It got there thanks to the ingenuity of a French blacksmith, because on the route from Le Mans, a converted coach carrying a couple of cars broke a rear spring, and the nearest garage sought out the local blacksmith who, after a few moment's contemplation, decided he could make some replacements. Alas, such people appear to have disappeared in Europe.

Offenhausers and the like were designed for banked circuits, and the banked circuit at Monza suited them, but it was not exactly ideal for the D-types; for a start it was bumpy – unlike Le Mans – and they had problems with tyre temperatures. Jack Fairman, who was not christened 'Fearless' for nothing, explains how he was approaching the banking at about 165mph (265kph) when a rear tyre lost its tread, so speeds were kept down to 160mph (257kph) on the D-types and the race was run in three heats of 166 miles (267

This XKSS was owned by Campbell McLaren when it appeared at a rally at Beaulieu in 1977.

kilometres) each, with an hour between each heat.

The only three Indy cars running at the end came in one, two and three, followed by the three D-types which had run with hardly a hitch driven by Fairman, John Lawrence and Ninian Sanderson.

Jaguar D-types did continue racing, Jim Clark – perhaps the greatest driver of them all – drove one, and was the first driver to lap at over 100mph (161kph) in a sports car, on an unbanked British circuit, but their day was effectively over, and Brian Lister, who had put many engine and chassis combinations together, produced a Lister-Jaguar, which was to dominate sports car racing until Cooper, and then Lotus came along with mid-engined cars.

## Born to Blush Unseen

Sir William had instincts about engineering, but he had no fundamental knowledge, and he was always a little wary of engineers, whereas in other departments he had no doubts. Bob Knight recalls that he always had prototype models built in sheet metal, and together with his ally Fred Gardner, who was in charge of the sawmill, he would disappear and produce prototypes unaided, apart from Fred Gardner.

Great industrial leaders such as Sir William Lyons are often clothed in an aura of infallibility, so it is comforting to lesser mortals to know that when left to their own devices they could often come up with some horrendous results. One or two of the Sir William–Fred Gardner projects got as far as being made into runners by the experimental shop, but they progressed no further. In the 1950s Sir William even contemplated building a single-seater using a 2½-litre XK engine, and went so far as to cannibalize a C-type, but in the end the project was dropped because the sports cars were succeeding, and the link between Grand Prix cars and their production cars was tenuous to say the least.

# 12
# The Jaguar 2.4-Litre Saloon

Meanwhile, back at the factory William Lyons and his well-honed team were making the most of their motor racing success, boosting production and exports, and incorporating many of the lessons learned from racing. In the decade of the 1950s production was to rise from 6,647 in 1950 to 20,876 in 1959, and in the same period exports rose from 3,926 to 10,476 – this last figure represents seventy-six more than were sold on the home market, an incredible feat. As early as 1952 the XK120 had benefited from the company's racing experience with a special equipment version that produced 180bhp at 5,750rpm, and by 1955 the power of the Mk VII M had been increased to 190bhp at 5,600rpm.

Waiting lists of two years for Jaguars were commonplace, and Jaguar dealers were not involved in anything so tiresome as selling cars – they allocated them. Although the Browns Lane factory had produced the C- and D-types, and some production models had been modified, there had been no new models since the launch of the Mk VII in 1951, and every motor manufacturer knows that long runs are the way to make money, and in those days when tooling costs were derisory compared to today, it was even more true.

The first 2.4-litre Jaguars never looked quite like this, but this prototype was almost there. The studio was somewhat fundamental, but it was astonishing what Jaguar achieved with such rudimentary facilities.

One of the original 2.4-litre Jaguars which were noticeable for their narrow rear track and small rear window.

The United States was still far and away the best market for Jaguar, and only Volkswagen, a relatively inexpensive car, outsold them, and so William Lyons tended this fertile garden with particular care. Service schools were set up for all Jaguar agents, and in 1954 the whole distribution system was overhauled, and an American subsidiary company was created called Jaguar Cars North American Inc.

## Rumours are Rife

On the strength of booming sales, rumours of new models to come, and a rumour that Chrysler was to bid for Jaguar, the five shilling ordinary share soared in the autumn from fifty to seventy shillings. (Chrysler was a favourite bogeyman at the time – they were also rumoured to be bidding for Standard Triumph.) None, however, were true.

But the rumours about new models were correct, although somewhat colourful in detail. About 12,000 XK120s had been built, with a fixed-head version joining the ranks in 1951, but it was clear that this sporting two-seater needed a little face-lifting to maintain its image. So, in the autumn of 1954, the XK140 was announced, and went on sale in the following year first as a two-seater, and then as a fixed-head, and later a drophead coupe. In standard form the engine gave 190bhp at 5,600rpm, and was more refined mechanically. The body on the standard model retained disc wheels and rear wheel spats, plus rather big bumpers for the benefit of the American market. An important change was to rack and pinion steering as used on the competition cars, and Laycock de Normanville overdrive was available on top gear as an option.

The cockpit space in the coupes was increased to provide room for two children, or extra baggage, and later models were offered with automatic transmission. The XK140 roadster cost £1,598 and the most expensive model was the drophead coupe at £1,644 including purchase tax. A Special Equipment version was produced which had wire wheels, twin exhaust and a 210bhp engine. This car would reach a fraction under 130mph (209kph), but because its weight had increased by about 3½cwt over the XK120 with a similar body, the acceleration was marginally worse. The handling had improved, and so had the gearbox; it was no longer easy to beat the syncromesh.

The XKs had not been built with competitions in mind, yet the XK120 did have an illustrious career in the sporting field. The XK140's career was more modest; it was getting a little overweight.

William Lyons had realized for many years that he needed something between a big saloon and a two-seater sports car, and as in the SS days when he insisted that they should always produce something for the lower end of their particular market, so he knew what was wanted for the 1950s and 1960s; a more compact motor car, but one which was still a Jaguar from bumper to bumper. Together with Bill Heynes, Bob Knight and their teams he had, for several years been working up the idea of a unitary construction compact car, a complete break with tradition for the company, for although the D-type was of monocoque construction, it could hardly be called a volume production model.

As was so often the case he showed great perception in reading the market, because it was the right car at the right time, and although it cost over £1 million to tool up for the new model – a vast amount of money at the time – thanks to Lyon's good husbandry, the money was available.

Recently, Sir John Egan had a similar problem: He knew that they needed a compact model to slot between the XJ40 and the XJS, but in the 1980s it was going to cost around £200 million, and they just did not have that kind of money.

## The Launch

In September 1955 the great and the good were summoned to Browns Lane for the launch. What were they going to see? A new four-cylinder engine, the 2½-litre that made a brief appearance at Dundrod, or would they follow fashion and go for a V8? It was rumoured that a V8 engine was being built at Browns Lane, and it was true, but this was a massive tank

The Jaguar Mk II was a big improvement on its predecessor, and a modern equivalent is much needed by Jaguar today – something they are aware of, and are planning to put right.

engine, and it would be some years before a V8 car engine was built. What they saw was a short stroke version of the XK engine, which had been brought to fruition by Bill Heynes.

As usual William Lyons had insisted that the new engine be almost silent and smooth, and there was no way in which they could make a four-cylinder match his criteria, so the stroke of the six-cylinder XK engine was reduced to 76.5mm, giving it oversquare characteristics (the bore was 83mm), and a capacity of 2,483cc. Like the 3.4-litre it had a seven bearing crankshaft, twin overhead camshafts, and an output of 112bhp at 5,750rpm. It also followed normal Jaguar practice in having a Borg and Beck single dry-plate clutch, four-speed synchromesh gearbox and recirculating ball steering gear, but having said that, in every other respect it did not follow Jaguar practice.

Until now all production Jaguars had been built with a separate frame, usually built by Rubery Owen, and then the body panels were assembled and fitted to the frame. The new 2.4-litre was of unitary construction (the body and frame was one piece), with special stiffening at each end to provide the strength and rigidity required. There are many benefits in this type of construction including a considerable weight saving. These bodies were supplied by Pressed Steel at Oxford, and were trucked to Coventry unpainted, and untrimmed – in other words 'in the white'.

For the body styling William Lyons had not quite rung the bell this time, and the rear end was severely tapered, and the glass area was restricted. The track at the front was 4in (10cm) wider than that at the rear. The suspension was also different with coils and wishbones at the front, and a rear suspension of cantilever semi-elliptic springs, trailing links, and radius arms located by a Panhard rod, the whole lot being insulated with rubber blocks to obviate any tendency towards the drumming noises sometimes found on motor cars of unitary construction.

No disc brakes yet, which was a pity, but Lockheed hydraulic, servo-assisted brakes were standard equipment. As usual it came with a set of tools but these were now housed under the boot along with the spare wheel. The price of the basic model was £895, but the Special Equipment model, which was the most popular by far, cost £1,299 including purchase tax, and included a heater, electric clock, arm rest for the rear seat, and the leaping Jaguar mascot. Overdrive oper-

You would imagine that wire wheels had been designed with the Mk II Jaguar in mind.

This shows the equipment the police packed into the boot of a Jaguar Mark II.

ating on top gear only was an optional extra. Apart from the D-type which went to rather rarified customers, prepared to pay £3,633 for an off-the-shelf racing sports car, all the Jaguar range still sold for under £2,000.

A 2.4-litre model fitted with overdrive was tested by *The Motor*. They gave it a top speed of 101.5mph (163kph) in overdrive, 93mph (150kph) in fourth gear, and 68mph (109kph) in third gear. It took 14.4 seconds to reach 60mph (96.5kph). Today you could do better with a Ford Escort, but it must be remembered that this was thirty-five years ago in a motor car that still weighed 27cwt despite its unitary construction.

I recall driving one soon after they were announced, and the only criticism I had was with the handling, the back end being a little 'tweaky' in my view. The public liked it, however, and more cars were finding their way on to the home market, although it would be 1963 before home sales overtook exports, and that was temporary, and by only a small number of vehicles. Production was increasing and would top 20,000 by 1959. Employment was rising too, to almost the 4,000 mark.

It is interesting to note that in 1959 it took a workforce of almost 4,000 to produce 20,000 vehicles, and thirty years later a workforce treble the size was producing treble the number of vehicles; productivity had clearly not increased a great deal.

## Knighthood

In the New Year's Honour List of 1956 William Lyons was made a Knight Bachelor in recognition of his remarkable achievements in the export markets, and in building his company from such humble beginnings into one that was recognized throughout the world for its exceptional products.

I must say that the title rested comfortably on the shoulders of this naturally formal man, and the accolade 'Sir William' slipped off the tongue with such ease that there must have been a natural affinity between the two. William he would tolerate from a cherished few, Bill he could not abide, Mr Lyons sounded too much like the quarter deck of a clipper ship; Sir William was just right.

In March of 1956, the year that the 2.4-litre and the XK140 went on sale, Sir William and Lady Lyons, and

This C-type is seen in the Silverstone pits in 1956. The Jaguar 'works' C-type team was driven to and from Le Mans.

the board of Jaguar Cars Ltd, greeted Her Majesty the Queen, and Prince Philip, who toured the Browns Lane plant, saw the Le Mans winning D-type, and met many of the workforce. Prince Philip took a particular interest in the drawing office. It was the first state visit by Royalty, but not Jaguar's first connection with the Royal family since both Queen Elizabeth the Queen Mother, and the Duke of Kent were Jaguar owners, and the Duke of Kent had visited Browns Lane. To mark the occasion the City of Coventry presented Prince Charles with a one-tenth scale model of a D-type executed by the consummate artist Rex Hays.

When Her Majesty the Queen arrived at Browns Lane, Sir William had a distinguished reception area in which to greet her, something he had lacked for many years, and dearly wanted. The move from Swallow Road gave him the opportunity, and in 1952 they had been able to build offices on to the old social facilities block, which apart from a works canteen included a ballroom which Sir William immediately envisaged as a company showroom, and by the time of the Royal visit, it was. The Browns Lane factory was a rambling place, and soon they were able to take over the part that had been used by the General Electric Company for various government projects, but even so they were running out of space. It was sad that it had to be a monumental fire in the plant in February 1957, which gutted a third of the works, that gave them another opportunity to expand.

## The Fire

At the end of 1956, because of the Suez Crisis, petrol coupons returned to a motoring public that was still well versed in their use, but it depressed the market for big, thirsty cars, and it was not a good time to sell a used Jaguar. It could have had a serious effect on Jaguar Cars if it had stretched on beyond May 1957, but fortunately for everyone it did not, and the worst that happened was a cut in the backlog of home orders.

In January of 1957 the first photographs were released of a new sports model, the XKSS, which were in effect road-going versions of the D-type, with no fairing and two seats. They were built from D-types that were in store and near completion, so it is unlikely that there would have been a long run, but any hopes of making more than a handful were dispelled on the evening of 12 February, when a blaze started in the tyre store and in no time at all had spread to the assembly lines.

This gives some idea of the devastation caused by the fire at the Browns Lane factory in 1957. Every damaged car was scrapped on the orders of Sir William.

Despite the damage done by the fire in February 1957, within thirty-six hours cars were coming off the line, in very small numbers. But by the beginning of April Jaguar announced they were back to normal, and the 3.4-litre engine was put in the compact saloon.

Despite the often heroic efforts of everyone who was available – the Public Relations staff were pulling or driving blistered cars out of the factory – hundreds of cars were damaged beyond repair, and damage estimated at £3½ million was done before the Coventry Fire Brigade halted the fire. If there was a bright side to such a disaster, it was that the fire had not affected the machine and engine assembly shops, for it would have taken months to get them back into operation, and the future of Jaguar Cars would have looked very bleak indeed.

The fire was another opportunity for Sir William to demonstrate his resilience and determination. He told Harold Hastings of *The Motor* 'We'll do the job . . . the fire makes it just a little harder that's all.' The minute the firemen had left the factory bulldozers moved in to clear paths through the factory, burnt out cars were brought out by fork-lift trucks, or manhandled out by the workforce, and temporary walls were built to seal off ruined parts of the works.

The Queen sent a telegram of sympathy, and encouraged by suppliers, dealers, other motor manufacturers, and owners, an amazing clearing up operation got under way. Within two days a shortened production line was in operation, and thanks to the co-operation of Dunlop Rim and Wheel now at Jaguar's old Swallow Road factory, a temporary testing and rectification bay was set up.

Such was the spirit at Browns Lane that by the end of April over 1,000 cars had been built, of which seventy per cent had been exported, and the company proudly announced that they were back to normal. They had been inundated with offers for the wrecked cars, but Sir William took the decision that every one of them should be destroyed. The danger to the reputation of the company if bodged-up Jaguars had appeared on the market was too great.

## The 3.4-litre Model and XK150

As if to emphasize that it was business as usual, on 26 February the company announced another new model – the 3.4-litre. This was the same body as the 2.4-litre saloon but with the 3.4-litre engine fitted with a different head, high lift cams and two SU HD.6 carburettors and a dual exhaust system. It was, they announced with some pride, their first 120mph (193kph) saloon. Outwardly it differed from the 2.4-litre with a bigger radiator grille, and smaller rear wheel spats, but to cope with the 210bhp it was given stiffer suspension, and other modifications were made to cope with the extra weight. It still employed drum brakes, and the three usual forms of transmission were offered – manual, Borg Warner automatic or manual plus overdrive. The basic price was £1,672, which was again magical for a car which various motor magazines declared had a genuine 120mph (193kph) performance, with 97mph (156kph) in third gear and acceleration from 0–60mph (0–96.5kph) in 9.1 seconds and to 100mph (161kph) in 26 seconds.

These were breath-taking figures for a car costing well under £2,000, and this model, and later derivatives were to dominate saloon car racing for some years to come, with the odd modification to the suspension which included strengthening the location points of the Panhard rod.

In May of 1957, with the factory back in full swing – it turned out to be a record year for production with 12,952 vehicles built – yet another version of the sports car was announced, this was the XK150, a rather bulbous motor car in my view, but the Special Equipment model, and that was the one that most people bought, came with disc brakes as standard equipment. It was a great step forward because the improvement in braking enhanced the car no end, and very soon disc brakes were available on the 2.4-litre and 3.4-litre saloons with the same effect. There was some disappointment when it was revealed that only coupes would be available at first, and it was a year before the two-seater convertible was available, and by then the horse power of the XK engine had gone up to 250bhp.

At the time of the announcement two engines that had been in production for some time were on offer, the 190 and 210bhp versions. The standard fixed-head coupe, which few people bought, cost £1,764, but the popular Special Equipment version of the drophead coupe, with automatic transmission had, inevitably, topped the £2,000 mark by £161. Sir William was a man of many parts, but a sizeable slice had never stopped being the salesman of his youth, and he was

The Mk II Jaguar 3.8-litres produced some very exciting and close racing, and here Jack Sears leads Mike Parkes at the British Grand Prix in 1962.

constantly attempting to anticipate market demands, and doing it very successfully most of the time.

In the 1950s and 1960s American motor manufacturers had become rather concerned at the level of European imports, just as they are worried today about Japanese imports, and they had started to produce models to face up to the European opposition. They were not proper sports cars; but they had a sporty appearance, and great stress was laid on the power they produced. They were not outstandingly successful, but I think they hurried Sir William's decision to put a bigger engine in the 2.4-litre body, and produce the XK150, which was very much aimed at the United States.

Because most of the XK150s built were Special Equipment models with disc brakes I think Jaguar can claim to be the first manufacturer to produce a volume car with four-wheel disc brakes. The Triumph TR3 had beaten Jaguar to the gun, but it had discs on the front wheels only, a practice that was followed by most manufacturers when disc brakes became popular, but Bill Heynes had insisted right from the start that his cars would have disc brakes all round; there were to be no half measures. When in 1958 the XK150s became available it was offered with a 250bhp engine that incorporated a Harry Weslake designed head, and for this car disc brakes were essential.

The big Jaguar saloons were now established, and becoming more and more accepted as boardroom cars, but playing tunes on the body styling was difficult. In 1957 the Mk VIII was produced for £1,830, powered by the 210bhp engine, but still equipped with drum brakes, and it was not until the Mk IX was produced in 1959 that a big saloon was offered with disc brakes, power-steering, and a 3.8-litre engine. With a top speed of around 113mph (182kph) this was a very quick and comfortable saloon, and more agile than its appearance would indicate.

As has been mentioned when the design of the original XK engine was conceived in the 1940s, unimaginable potential was built into it; the stroke had been shortened to turn it into a 2½-litre, and now the bore was increased to 87mm and it was raised in capacity to 3.8-litres, and by 1965 the bore was to be increased again to raise it to 4.2-litres. It had been fitted with SU carburettors of various sizes, with three Weber carburettors, and eventually it was to have fuel injection. It had powered motor cars, racing cars, speed boats and tanks – a truly remarkable engine.

But which was the best? For the racing version the 3.4-litre with the three Webers did exceptionally well, and the 3.8-litre with fuel injection was also very successful with Ecurie Ecosse at Le Mans, but for a road car my favourite was the 3.8-litre engine. It was flexible, very quick, as smooth as silk, and it gave the impression that it would go on for ever.

## The Mk II Series

The second version of a model is not always a noticeable improvement on the first, but this was not so with the Mk II versions of the 2.4-litre and 3.4-litre saloons. At the end of 1959 these compact saloons were given a face-lift that improved their appearance enormously in my opinion. The tapered stern was dispensed with, a bigger glass area was introduced, and 2.4, 3.4 or 3.8-litre engines were now available. Disc brakes were standard equipment, and many detailed improvements had been made to the suspension. They were now very desirable cars, docile in traffic, but extremely long-legged motor cars on the open road, with the 3.8-litre version giving a top speed of 125mph (201kph).

The popularity of Jaguars among the constabulary had been growing steadily, but the advent of the Mk II models made them the most popular traffic patrol cars in the country; they had the performance, the space to carry all the equipment then used by the police, and they were offered at the right price. The car's sheer versatility was hard to match.

# 13
# Empire Building

It could be said as the new decade moved into place that Sir William, and the whole hierarchy of Jaguar Cars, had a great deal on their plate. Two major new models were imminent; the E-type and Mk X, and the XJ6 was more than just a faraway dream. Bill Heynes' engineering department was developing a V12 engine, and a V8, and they were running out of production space.

Room to develop had been a problem for Sir William for years, and the extensions made after the fire were quickly full to overflowing. He could not create a new site in Coventry, and was being urged by the Government to move to depressed areas such as Merseyside, and Scotland, the prospects of which filled him with considerable gloom. He sent out reconnaissance parties, but their reports only confirmed his worst fears.

Sniffing the air Sir William believed that an answer to his problem might be found nearer home, as it was in the move from Foleshill to Browns Lane, and indeed it was; on 26 May 1960 it was announced that Jaguar Cars was to buy the famous, but ailing Daimler factory at Radford from the Birmingham Small Arms Company, or BSA, and for an outlay of £3,400,000 Jaguar Cars doubled in size overnight.

Daimler had lost its way, and although it had produced some first-class military vehicles during both the First and Second World Wars, and many fine cars over a number of years, it was no longer the name it

Sir William had recently been knighted when Queen Elizabeth II visited the Coventry plant in 1956, and is seen here admiring the D-type.

had been – for Daimler had been the premier manufacturer of motor cars in Coventry both before and after the First World War. If you worked at Daimler you were a rather superior being and, of course, Daimler had been suppliers of vehicles to three Kings, and manufacturers of the famous 'Silent' Knight sleeve valve engine, and the memorable V12s, or Double Sixes.

They had started producing motor cars at a refurbished cotton mill between Sandy Lane and the Coventry Canal in 1897, but moved to Radford in 1908. In 1910 they were acquired by BSA, an industrial giant at the time, and in 1931 they absorbed Lanchester, but in the post-war years they were building buses, mainly double-deckers, and a wide if not very successful array of saloons, limousines and sports cars, powered by a variety of push-rod engines ranging from 2½ to 4.6-litre capacity. When Jaguar took them over they were producing the fibre glass Daimler SP 250 sports car, and the V8 Majestic Major, which was quick with a top speed of 114mph (183kph). This splendid engine, and others, had been designed by Edward Turner, who had also designed the Triumph Twin motor cycle engine.

In March 1963 Coventry Climax became part of the Jaguar group, and this is an aerial shot of the Climax factories.

An aerial view of Guy Motors at Wolverhampton.

Not too bad for someone who had started his life as a wireless operator in the Merchant Navy.

## Problems of Size

In the 1960s the commercial vehicle business was good for both buses and trucks, so good in fact that Leyland used to boast that other manufacturers only kept going because they could not produce enough; a rather unnecessary remark which proved to be quite untrue. There were good export markets in Africa, South America, Ceylon, Hong Kong and Australia as well as a very good home market. But, significantly, only Bedford had made any impact on the continental markets; with an empire on which the sun never set, British commercial vehicle manufacturers had not concerned themselves with this overcrowded market. When they did it was too late. The Leyland Atlantean had set the pattern for double-deckers with a rear engine, and low loading at the front and in the centre, and the Daimler Fleetline followed the pattern with a few modifications, and soon they were producing thirty chassis a week – good for a big commercial vehicle. Not surprisingly, one of their best customers was Coventry Corporation Transport.

Sir William set about modernizing both Browns Lane and Radford, moving all engine production to the Radford plant, and bringing in 'nearly new' paint equipment – he never lost his feeling for economy. In his current mood of expansion he looked at Lotus, but decided against it, but in 1961 he bought Guy Motors of Wolverhampton from the receiver for an extremely modest £800,000. A family concern, which for a short period had made motor cars, Guy Motors were not able to cope despite the comfortable climate, and had lost £300,000 in the previous years.

There were quite a few personnel moves, and Sir William decided to give them a new image, and created the 'Big J' – or big Jaguar – and a new range went on display at the 1964 Commercial Vehicle Show. In the world of trucks Sir William also demonstrated his perception, and realized that the slogging Gardner engines, which had been the backbone of the British commercial vehicle industry for years, were not powerful enough for the new motorway, trans-continental vehicles that were being created.

Gardner were, and still are, an engineering firm of

The roadster version of the XK150, with whitewall tyres and destined for the USA.

When Jaguar took over Guy Motors in 1961 the commercial vehicle was flourishing, and the company was successful with their Big Js and medium-sized trucks.

considerable repute, based in Manchester, and controlled for years by Frank Gardner in a manner as autocratic as Sir William. When Sir William said that he wanted a more powerful engine he was told – like the man who asked about the brake horse power of a Rolls Royce – that it was sufficient. This, of course, did not please Sir William, and he went off in search of another engine manufacturer, and a preliminary arrangement was made with the American engine specialist Cummins, that they would assemble engines in Britain for Guy, but then it was discovered that their V6 and V8 engines, available at the time, would not be suitable, and the arrangement was dropped. But it is interesting to note that Gardner went on to produce a straight-eight engine, as opposed to their straight-sixes, and Cummins now produce engines in Darlington. However, the 'Big J' was in production for fifteen years, until 1979, and the company became a very profitable business. With engines still in mind Jaguar acquired Harry Meadows Ltd, an engine manufacturer next to the Guy works in Wolverhampton, but this proved to be an error, and it was soon sold.

A more beneficial acquisition took place in March 1963 when Coventry Climax became part of the Jaguar Group, under an amicable arrangement between Leonard Lee of Coventry Climax and Sir William, and Walter Hassan returned to Jaguar as Director, Power Units, and was soon joined by Harry Mundy, a talented engineer of considerable character.

Between 1955 and 1964 Jaguar's profits quadrupled to almost £2½m, and by 1966 production of Jaguar cars had risen to 25,000 a year. It was a great success story, but Sir William had his problems; he was approaching seventy years of age with no natural successor, and his top management was ageing too – Arthur Whittaker, Bill Heynes and Ernest (Bill) Rankin, to name but a few, all pillars of the company were near to retiring. He was also becoming extremely nervous about his supply of bodies, for Pressed Steel was now part of the British Motor Corporation, and Sir William had seen what had happened to Jowett Cars of Idle, Bradford, when Briggs Bodies, their suppliers, had been taken over by Ford . . . they had gone out of business.

He was also taking note of amalgamations abroad, and appreciated the strength that an association with another company would bring, but he wanted Jaguar to remain autonomous, and more than anything he wanted his body supplies guaranteed. Jaguar had never been short of suitors, even from the days of Sir John Black, and one of the most persistent over the years had been Sir Henry Spurrier, the boss of Leyland, and a fellow Lancastrian. Even after Sir Henry's death he was again approached by Leyland, and was offered a deal in which he would be in charge of the whole car business – which then included Standard Triumph – but it meant losing the autonomy of Jaguar, and Sir William turned the deal down.

Few people knew of the machinations that were going on behind the scenes in the British motor industry as the gestation period of British Leyland started, so it came as a surprise when on 11 July 1966 Sir George Harriman, chairman of British Motor Corporation, and Sir William, announced that the two companies were to merge, but Sir William would remain in charge of an autonomous Jaguar. That, at least, was the arrangement at the time.

Sir William firmly believed that the merger would safeguard Jaguar's future, and it would operate as a separate entity.

Bob Berry was one of the few people who knew that the merger was imminent since he had been asked by Sir William to write a rationale on the merger which was to be presented to Sir George, and which he accepted. With 260,000 of the 480,000 voting shares Sir William had always taken the major decisions on his own, and this, of all decisions, was to be no exception to the rule.

# 14
# Launch of a Legend

Sir William had less impact on the E-type than any other car he produced, yet if any model symbolizes all that Jaguar represents, it is the E-type.

Clearly Sir William approved of the car, nothing happened at Jaguar Cars unless he did approve, but the instigators of the concept of a lightweight two-seater based on the D-type were Bill Heynes – by now Vice Chairman, Engineering – and Malcolm Sayer, the gifted aerodynamicist. At first Sir William was lukewarm towards the project, but in the end the persistence of Heynes and Sayer convinced him, and while he contributed to the sweeping lines with his own inimitable flourish, the basic styling was very much the work of Malcolm Sayer. He, after all, had produced the D-type, and there are few cars more beautiful.

As 1961 approached the production engineers at Jaguar were having a frantic time; not only were they to produce the E-type, but later in the year the big Mk X saloon was to be launched, using monocoque construction, independent rear suspension, Powr Lok limited slip differential, a new coil-spring front suspension and the 3.8-litre engine with three SU HD.8 carburettors. The Mk X did not go on to become a legend, as did the E-type, but it required just as much effort to get into production.

There were many rumours about an E-type in the previous year, and these were fuelled at the April practice session for the 1960 Le Mans 24-Hour Race, when a Jaguar entered by American Briggs Cunningham, and driven by Dan Gurney and Walter Hansgen, appeared on the scene. It bore the registration number VKV 752, and bore a strong resemblance to the D-type with its body shape and rear fin. If anyone had known, it also bore a strong resemblance to the E-type that was to be launched in the following year.

Known in the factory as E2A it was bigger than the first prototype, and was powered by a fuel-injected racing engine, and in the practice session it was quick enough to lap at over 120mph (193kph), making it second fastest. In the race it was fastest in practice sessions, but once the flag had dropped it did not do so well spending a long time in the pits after holding a brief third place, and finally retired in the early hours of the morning.

Minus its fin, and with a hump on the bonnet to accommodate the 3.8-litre engine it went to the United States and was raced by Hansgen for a year with some success, before being returned to Coventry. However, the activity at Le Mans was sufficient to prompt Bill Rankin to put out a statement saying that they had prepared a 3-litre car for Mr Cunningham, but it did not mean they were returning to motor racing – nor was the car new.

## A Beautiful Compromise

Some might argue that the E-type was not new, in that it owed a great deal to the D-type, but although this beautiful racing sports car had inspired the new model, the E-type was clearly very different in many respects. The basic similarity was in the construction of the body, in that both had a monocoque centre section of 20 gauge sheet steel, braced by box-section members consisting of the door sills, propellor shaft tunnel, scuttle assembly and cross members. To this were attached sub-frames front and rear, and on which adhered the engine, steering and front suspension, and at the rear the independent suspension and differential.

The engine was basically the same as that used in the XK150 S, a triple carburettor version of the 3.8-

The 4.2-litre Jaguar E-type with a hard top, before it had been modified to meet US regulations.

litre XK engine developing 265bhp at 5,500rpm. For the first time the three SU HD.8 carburettors were fed by a Lucas electric pump fitted in the fuel tank, and an electrically-driven radiator fan was also used for the first time by Jaguar. Steering was by rack and pinion, and the gearbox was four-speed, but amazingly there was synchromesh on only the top three gears. No automatic or overdrive was offered, on the grounds that there was no room to fit them in. Brakes, of course, were Dunlop discs all round, the rear ones being fitted inboard.

## Independent Rear Suspension

The body was different to anything we had seen before, and in my view breath-takingly original, and attractive. It came in two forms, as an open two-seater – with detachable hard top as an option, and this I thought was the most attractive E-type of all – or as a fixed head coupe.

British manufacturers in general had been slow to adopt independent rear suspension, maintaining that the extra cost outweighed the virtues, and the Triumph Herald demonstrated that an inexpensive form of independent suspension did have its drawbacks. Jaguar had been thinking about it for several years, and it was tried on the prototype E2A, but the E-type was the first production Jaguar to have independent rear suspension. It used twin coil springs each side, incorporating Girling telescopic dampers, and the wheels were located by parallel transverse links of unequal length and longitudinal radius arms.

For ease of assembly and servicing, the whole of the rear suspension, including the inboard disc brakes, were mounted on a detachable bridge piece. Alternative rear axle ratios of 2.93, 3.07 and 3.54:1 were offered to complement gear ratios of 3.31, 4.246, 6.156 and 11.177:1. The clutch was a Borg and Beck single dry plate unit, while the Salisbury hypoid final drive incorporated a Powr Lok limited slip differential.

Keeping the curved windscreen clean presented a problem, and this was overcome by using triple blade wipers. Standard tyres for the wire wheels were 6.40 x 15 Dunlop RS5s, but racing R5 tyres could be specified, and they were among the few optional extras such as a radio, chromium-plated wire wheels, and the detachable hard top for the open model. Prices were again amazing: £2,098 for the roadster, and £2,197 for the fixed-head coupe, both inclusive of purchase tax.

## The Launch

Weighing only 24cwt, and with 265bhp available, the performance of the E-type left everyone gasping with amazement in 1961, and it is still a hard act to follow in the 1990s. The coupe, which was slightly faster through the performance range, produced a top speed of 150.4mph (242kph) when tested by *Autocar*, a figure that was not repeated by subsequent production cars, but the difference was marginal, and they could all approach 150mph (241kph).

It was in acceleration where they excelled, even the open car reaching 60mph (96.5kph) in 7.1 seconds and 100mph (161kph) in 15.9 seconds, and 130mph (209kph) in a fraction over half a minute. It would accelerate to 78mph (125kph) in second gear and 116mph (187kph) in third. Fuel consumption was between 16–18mpg (26–8kpg), not very different from the XK120 of 1949. In 1961 these figures were electrifying and once again the perennial question was asked: how does he do it?

The launch of the E-type was at the Geneva International Motor Show in March 1961, and staged in the Parc des Eaux Vives on the west side of Lac Leman, and Sir William was there at the head of his team. Several reasons have been offered on why he chose Geneva for the launch, and it has been suggested that he selected Switzerland because of the flagging fortunes of the British motor industry in that country, believing that the introduction of the glamorous E-type might boost our image. It certainly did that, but the Swiss are too pragmatic to believe it was going to affect the reliability of more popular makes.

The fact that Geneva was neutral territory, and that everyone in the world of motoring who mattered would be there, and that by launching it in Geneva, he would save himself the expense of separate launches must have weighed very heavily with a man who disliked parting with a penny unnecessarily. The

A longer wheelbase was given to the 2+2 version of the E-type, which became standard with the V12 engine.

To my mind the windscreen was too high on this fixed-head coupe version of the Series II E-type.

casual way in which money is spent in the motor industry nowadays would have appalled him; after all it was his money that was being spent.

As we have seen Sir William had a flair for publicity, and when it was suggested that it would be a splendid idea to take potential customers for a demonstration run in the E-type, up a hillclimb route not far from the Parc des Eaux Vives, Sir William readily agreed. Two drivers were delegated to do this job, Norman Dewis, who was the chief test driver, and Bob Berry, public relations manager, and no mean performer on the race tracks.

Bob had already had some experience of driving the E-type quickly. He had had to bring one of the demonstration cars over to Geneva, and it was essential that it was there for the opening press day. As often happens on these occasions there had been problems in preparing the car on time, and instead of leaving Coventry early on the previous day as planned, Bob found himself driving down to catch the midnight ferry from Dover to Dunkirk. When he disembarked at dawn there was thick fog which lasted for miles, but by averaging over 70mph (112kph) he still got the car to Geneva in time to be cleaned, tanked up and ready for action shortly after midday. There were, of course, no autoroutes in 1961.

## A Unique Experience

The idea of taking prospective customers up the hillclimb, quickly expanded from a cosy idea for the chosen few to an exercise so big that the police had to be called in to control the crowds. For Geneva society it became the 'in' thing to do, and the clientèle was insatiable if not very knowledgeable.

When passengers settled themselves in the car, they were asked by either Bob or Norman whether they would like to go up the hill very quickly, normally, or gently. Bob recalls one woman passenger who was outraged that there should be any question of how she would like to be driven up the hill. 'Very quickly, of course', she exclaimed. Nevertheless Bob put it to her just once more, 'You are quite sure you want to go

**Ride to Monza**

In my view, the best looking E-type made was the 1961 model with the detachable hard top. And there it was in all its British racing green glory, sitting outside the main office at Browns Lane, Coventry, waiting to take me to Monza and the Italian Grand Prix. It was a superb looking car.

Inside the cockpit I almost glowed with excitement; the big, practical array of instruments, the snug seats, slim steering wheel and ahead, acres of arching bonnet. A mental reminder: don't forget there is three feet or more of motor car ahead of the furthest point you can see.

The 3.8-litres came to life with a modest crack, and I was on my way. No 70mph (112kph) speed limit, no safety belts, no motorways, but still lorries nose to tail on the A5. But what a joy the E-type was on that crowded road. Down a gear, a blip on the accelerator, all 265 horse power started banging away together, and you were away. With disc brakes all round and a limited slip differential it was a very modern car even by today's standards.

I travelled across the Channel on the *Free Enterprise 1*, the first of the purpose-built car ferries, which was tiny in comparison to modern ferries, but luxurious against its Townsend predecessor, a converted frigate called the *Halladale*.

When you drove across France in 1961 you were not isolated by autoroutes from the intimacies and pave of French towns and villages; you passed through hundreds, but on the open roads the traffic was sparse, and the gendarmerie noticeable by its absence, so with a good car a 50mph (80kph) average could be maintained with reasonable ease.

It was wise to check the oil whenever you filled the fuel tank, because the 3.8-litre was thirsty on oil, and as soon as the bonnet was raised a crowd assembled. I recall at Vitry Le Francois there were so many people crowded round the car that I had the greatest difficulty in persuading them that I was the current owner and please could I get in. Langres, a delightful walled town, was my overnight stop and then on to Lausanne, the 6,500ft Simplon Pass and down to Domodossola, and along the shores of Lake Maggiore to the two-lane autostrada to Milan.

On this I had a rather amusing incident. Soon after I arrived on the autostrada a Swiss-registered Maserati tucked in behind me, and the driver and his female companion seemed to find it very amusing that I was sticking, more or less, to the speed limit despite the total lack of traffic. Through the mirror I could see them coming within inches of my rear bumper, and making what they thought were suitable grimaces.

It seemed to me that the honour of Britain and Jaguar were now at stake. The speedometer was showing 145mph (233kph) when I passed the two motor cycle policemen parked at the side of the road. The Maserati had dropped out of sight, but through the mirror I saw the policemen pull out on their Moto Guzzi machines, pursue me for a while, before they gave it up as a bad job. Radio communications were not as sophisticated as they are today, and I was very pleased to get off the autostrada unscathed.

It is not an exaggeration to say that in Italy the E-type was a sensation. If I parked outside a restaurant it emptied, with the restaurateur often in the lead. And, of course, it was a challenge to every motorized Italian, which did become trying.

The Italian Grand Prix is the most colourful and intense in the world, and in those days it was also one of the fastest. Wolfgang von Trips, who was a German Count, was always known as Taffy, came to Monza after two or three unlucky seasons leading the World Championship, and continued the good work by setting up the fastest time in his Ferrari in practice.

The Italian crowd visit Monza to see a Ferrari win – the driver is something of an irrelevance – and with three Ferraris entered and two on the front line of the starting grid, their enthusiasm was at boiling point, and they were swarming up the safety netting even more than usual. Approaching the South Curve von Trips and Jim Clark touched each other, and von Trips' car hurtled into the crowd. He was killed and so were thirteen spectators.

The Italian authorities said that Jim Clark had caused the accident and were threatening to put him in gaol. He was whisked away by Sir Jack Brabham in his private aeroplane. The telephone lines between Italy and Britain broke down, and it was after 2am when my night news desk eventually called it a day. Louis Stanley, the boss of the BRM team came into the hotel with Graham Hill, ordered a bottle of champagne, purely for medicinal purposes, and we sat and talked through the day's events.

By then there seemed no point in going to bed so I bathed, paid my bill, and at 5am pointed the E-type in the direction of Calais. The drive over the deserted Simplon was one of the most exhilarating in my life; I had never driven anything that flattened a mountain so effectively.

Over the summit and the sun was bathing Lac Leman and, it seemed, the whole of Switzerland, in a brilliant glowing light. I re-fuelled and had breakfast in Lausanne, then headed over the Jura mountains and into France, to Besancon, Chaumont, St. Dizier, with the rev counter flickering at 4,000rpm and the speedometer rarely below 100mph (161kph). Often I sat on 120mph (193kph) for mile after mile.

An omelette outside Rheims, more fuel, more oil, then off again. By sheer coincidence I passed the Calais sign at exactly 5pm. Including all stops my average speed worked out at 63.9mph (102.8kph). I waited two hours for the *Free Enterprise 1* – with only one boat the service was somewhat less frequent in those days – and was home in Buckinghamshire by 11.20pm. I had covered 876miles (1,410 kilometres) in the day, and I could not think of a better car in which to make the journey. Indeed, I have driven to Milan many times since, but nothing has been as enjoyable as the E-type.

An E-type in Red Square, Moscow attracts the crowds.

The prospects of sales were not good in the USSR, but it could be considered an investment for the future.

up very quickly'. Again he received the outraged, 'Of course'.

She was so rigid with fear when they arrived at the top of the hill that it took Bob and some sympathetic helpers quite a time to get her out of the car.

The impact the E-type made was greater than I have seen for any other motor car, yet it was then a two-seater, had limited appeal, and was not going to be one of the world's top sellers, but it appealed to the Walter Mitty in everyone. And at Geneva 500 were sold at the Show, and in the following month when it was taken to New York for the Importers' Exhibition six were sold within half an hour of the doors being opened. Subsequently orders worth £22½ million were taken for Jaguar cars in North America, and this reflected the impact of the E-type and Mk X, because it represented a doubling of demand for Jaguars in North America.

It did not take long to record its first racing success either. In April T.E.B. (Tommy) Sopwith, who ran the Equipe Endeavour, entered an E-type for the 25-lap Trophy race for grand touring cars at Oulton Park, and in the hands of Graham Hill it beat Ferraris and Aston Martins, to win at an average speed of 83.22mph (134kph). Its victory was all the more remarkable because it had only been collected from the factory on the day before the race.

In 1964 the E-type was offered with a 4.2-litre engine (4235cc), which was not simply a bored-out 3.8-litre, but the possessor of a completely re-designed engine block, with the middle four cylinders closer together and the outer two more widely spaced. It was also provided with an alternator, revised ancillary drives and a new one-piece cast aluminium manifold. With a 9:1 compression ratio it produced 265bhp as did the 3.8-litre, but it improved the torque at the bottom end and in the middle ranges to provide that silent power, and effortless acceleration that were now accepted characteristics of the Jaguar engine.

## Even Bigger

The four-speed manual gearbox now had synchromesh throughout the range, and the single plate Borg and Beck clutch had given way to a Laycock-Hausserman diaphragm spring clutch, and a Lockheed vacuum booster had been fitted to the brake system, which put the price up to £2,033.

Two years later the E-type was extended by 9in (22.5cm), and the roofline raised by 2in (5cm), the overall frontal area increased by 5 per cent and the weight by 2cwt, and the 2+2 was born. With more space there was now room for an automatic transmission, a great boon to the Americans, but otherwise the only mechanical changes were to cope with the extra weight. The extra weight did affect the performance and the automatic version had a top speed of 136mph (218kph), while the acceleration to 60mph (96.5kph) took 1.6 seconds longer.

In my view the E-types started to go downhill as far as appearance was concerned with the introduction of the 2+2, because the extra 2in (5cm) on the roofline spoilt those amazing lines. US regulations did not help and all three models in the 1968 Series Two range suffered. They were afflicted with headlamps that were higher and positioned further forward, spoiling the bonnet line of the car; and heavy lamp clusters both behind and in front did not help appearances. Neither did the larger orifice on the bonnet to cope with optional air conditioning, and the wraparound bumpers front and rear added too much chrome to a proper British sports car. Rocker switches became obligatory on the dashboard, but one slight improvement was the windscreen on the 2+2 which was moved forward at the base to give a less severe angle.

Power steering was now optional, and to meet US emission control regulations Stromberg carburettors were fitted which, together with the extra weight, had an horrific effect on the performance. However, as that was going down the braking was improving with the use of a Girling system with three pistons at the front and two at the rear. The price had gone up marginally to £2,245.

The next big move in the E-type saga came in 1971 when the V12 engine was fitted to the car as a production test bed, because its real home was the yet-to-be-announced XJ saloon. They were called the Series Three, and both the 2+2 and the two-seater roadster used the long wheelbase, so in the two-seater there was plenty of space. Power steering was now standard – rather necessary with the extra weight

A drophead coupe version of the E-type.

of the V12 – and the automatic transmission was available on the two-seater.

Brakes were constantly being improved and ventilated front discs were fitted, while the structure had been stiffened, and a collapsible-type steering column fitted. The body looked quite a bit different, and the open orifice was replaced with a lattice grille, and to accommodate the bigger tyres the wheel arches had been flared. The V12 was heavier than the six-cylinder XK engines, but only by 80lbs, and it was not giving very much more horse power at 272bhp using four dual-choke Zenith downdraught carburettors.

Compared to the de-toxed 'sixes' performance was back – almost – to E-type standards, with a top speed of over 140mph (225kph) and a 0–120mph (0–193kph) figure of 26.5 seconds. The handling was virtually unaffected, and it was a motor car of immense character; almost silent, and deceptively quick. It was also very thirsty, with a fuel consumption of around 14–15mpg (22–4kpg). Prices? Well, they were still very competitive, but they had gone up rather more dramatically than had usually been the case, and the new roadster was listed at £3,123, and the coupe at £3,369, which meant that in ten years the two-seater had increased in price by £1,293; still trifling by today's standards. The last E-type was built in 1974, but sales went on until well into the following year, yet the price of a new E-type never rose above £4,000, something to bear in mind when you note the prices of them today.

In the late 1960s and early 1970s Jaguar's exports to North America relied heavily on the E-type, because they were not exporting many saloons, and since its launch in 1961 72,520 were built, of which around 60,000 were exported. A little over 30,000 XKs were built, and the XK120 was the biggest seller.

## Competition

Although the E-type looked like a racer, it had been built as a grand touring car, and was no match for the all-out racing sports cars competing in its era, and although E1A and E2A were built (the A stood for

A Series II E-type.

aluminium), the factory were not really interested in racing at this time; they had far too many other things on their plate. However, in 1962 about a dozen lightweight versions were built at the factory, using aluminium for the monocoque and body panels, and also for the engine block, and this resulted in a weight saving of about 500lbs, and these were raced in many places – Briggs Cunningham had three – but without any real success. They needed more development.

With the advent of the V12 American Bob Tullius, a dedicated sports car racer of long standing – I recall him racing Triumph TR2s – persuaded British Leyland, who were then in charge, that the V12 E-type, with some massaging from his Group 44 Team, could be successful in Category B sports car events, and so give a boost to Jaguar's flagging fortunes in the US market. It was agreed that Tullius would look after racing on the east coast and Huffaker Engineering of California, would look after the west coast. Group 44 was a very professional organization, and in their own field they did extremely well; in the first season they finished as Northeast Division Champions, with five victories and seven track records from seven starts.

In the following year they did even better with seven victories and eight track records out of ten starts, making Bob Tullius the Sports Car Club of America (SCCA) National Champion. Even with support from Jaguar they were not quite so successful when playing away at Le Mans, but that is a later story, and at least they pointed the way.

# 15
# More and More Saloons

The 1960s were stirring times, and Sir William had a lot of balls in the air; the E-type had been very successfully launched, and the Mk X was to come, although a worrying factor was that tooling for the Mk X had cost £4 million, whereas tooling for the integral-bodied 2.4-litre just five years before had cost £1 million.

There had been strikes, ultimately about money, and Sir William, along with the Chancellor, Selwyn Lloyd, was warning about the dangers of excessive wage demands and their effect on inflation. For us a *déjà vu* situation, but at the time economic lectures were, if not unknown, a rarity. Jaguar were still selling at competitive prices at home and abroad. In 1963 Sir William was able to announce at the annual meeting that a third of the cars made went to the United States, and that sales in Europe generally were up by forty per cent, although by more in certain markets such as France which did not produce a competitive car.

In Italy the Jaguar 3.4-litre sold for the equivalent of £2,114, or £69 less than the Mercedes 220SE. In West Germany, as it was then, distributor Peter Linder had given sales a considerable boost with his successful racing programme, but even so it was impossible to compete with Mercedes on price, or servicing facilities, and the Jaguar Mk II sold for £1,940, while the Mercedes-Benz 220 was offered for a little over £1,000. Then as now, it was the graciousness and exclusivity of the Jaguar that were its main selling points in Germany.

The American motor industry was fighting back against the growing number of European imports with cars like the General Motors Stingray, and the Ford Mustang, which were sporting cars if not sports cars, and were very quick, and not simply in a straight line. Indeed cars like the Ford Galaxie, with engines the size of Battersea Power Station (6.9-litre V8s), were pushing Jaguars, and other makes, off the leader board in saloon car racing in Britain.

Production at Jaguar was going up; it reached 24,018 in 1961, and by 1966, its last year of independence it had reached 25,936. It was virtually impossible to buy an E-type on the home market in 1961, but other models were more easily available, and the split between sales at home and abroad was roughly half. Motorists at home were beginning to get the feel of what it must be like in a buyers' market. In 1961 some elevations were made to key figures, particularly in view of their extra responsibilities within the growth of the company.

Arthur Whittaker became Deputy Chairman, Bill Heynes Vice Chairman (Engineering), John Silver and Robert Grice became members of the board, retaining their production and works directorships, and Lofty England became Assistant Managing Director, an appointment of some significance in view of later moves. Edward Huckvale continued to serve on the board as company secretary.

By now, however, the British motor industry had no longer got the field to itself, the German industry was winding up to full song, the French had almost passed through their utility phase and were moving more up market, and although Giovanni Agnelli had not yet sorted out the Italian motor industry – he was still going through his playboy stage – it was producing some very interesting motor cars. And, of course, the Japanese were to put a tentative foot into the market at the end of the decade. Regrettably, the significance was lost on most people.

It was into this much tougher background that Sir William introduced his Mk X and a whole string of saloon cars, both Jaguar and Daimler, during the coming decade.

## The Mark X

The Mk X Jaguar was the biggest car that the company had produced, and it was big in every sense of the word: it would carry five people in comfort, it had an enormous boot (27cu ft), and it looked big. Yet for a car of its size it weighed only 35cwt, just ½cwt more than the original Mk VII. It was, of course, the first big car they had made of integral construction, all its predecessors having a separate frame, and it incorporated a lot of the features of the E-type, including the independent rear suspension. The front suspension was also independent, incorporating double wishbones and coil springs with telescopic shock absorbers. A hefty anti-roll bar was located between the lower wishbones, and the complete assembly, which included the steering, was mounted on a separate sub-frame, which was located in the body with rubber mountings. Rubber mountings were used extensively both in the front and rear suspensions, and gave some trouble with the early models, along with the radiator, but neither lasted for long.

The engine was the 3.8-litre again as used in the 150S and E-type, producing 265bhp, and an average fuel consumption was 16–18mpg (26–8kpg), though an enthusiastic driver could produce much lower figures. Dunlop disc brakes, with quick change pads were fitted all round, and the handbrake was self-adjusting working on the rear wheels. Borg Warner automatic transmission with intermediate hold was the most popular transmission, but it was also offered with a four-speed manual gearbox with an optional overdrive, and a Powr Lok limited slip differential.

Because of the strength of the body the door pillars were slimmer than was usual on Jaguar saloons, giving a better all round view for the driver, and the body had a very rounded appearance, much in vogue today, and looked particularly attractive from the front with its twin headlamps, and neat, uncluttered grille. The interior was up to their usual luxurious standards, with a

It looks quite real, but it is a wooden prototype of the Mk X.

They were not quite sure which sort of headlamps they would use on this wooden prototype of the Mk X.

comprehensive heating, cooling and de-misting system, and an added touch of luxury were folding tables, and reclining seats. The handbrake was mounted underneath the dashboard, a mistake that was rectified in later models.

The performance was good for a big motor car; it would sweep five people up to 120mph (193kph) with little more than a murmur, and reach 60mph (96.5kph) in 10.2 seconds, and 100mph (161kph) in less than half a minute. I think the sheer size of it worried a lot of owners who never learned to appreciate how nimble it was, because the road-holding and handling for a car of its size was quite exceptional. It did, however, come in for some criticism. The manual gearbox was considered old-fashioned and not up to the rest of the car, while the powered steering was said to be too low-geared and lacking in feel, with which I agreed. It was also said the front seats lacked lateral support – it was much too easy for the driver to slide about; a criticism often levelled at American big cars, but not generally at Jaguars.

The whole package was priced at £2,392, which brought the usual gasps of disbelief, and the car did bring some cheer to a Motor Show which I recall was not one of the brightest – our proposed entry into the Common Market was in doubt, and the Rootes Group were struggling through an endless strike at their London body plant, which effectively put paid to this energetic family concern. These sort of strikes must have been very much in Sir William's mind – he always maintained that labour was his biggest problem – when he said that meeting orders for the new Jaguar cars in North America would 'represent the biggest challenge in our career, and will need every effort by both our management and men in order to meet it.' Happily, after the early teething problems already mentioned, they did.

## Variations on a Theme

In 1961 the V8-engined Daimler Majestic Major was

The Mk X was a very large motor car, but it seems quite at home in a London street.

put back into production; it was a car that attracted a lot of complimentary remarks, but not a lot of customers, which was not, perhaps, altogether surprising since it was a limousine and intended for the chauffeur-driven strata of society. It was being built alongside the glass fibre-bodied SP250 sports car, which found limited favour with the police as a patrol car, but in 1965 that was dropped, and so was the Majestic in 1967. This meant the end of the 'true' Daimlers, although the name did continue.

In 1963 a Daimler 240 was produced which was a combination of a Jaguar Mk II body, and a 2½-litre Daimler push-rod V8 engine, which had been used in the SP250 and gave 140bhp. It was equipped with a Borg Warner automatic transmission, cost £1,786 (£108 more than the equivalent Jaguar), produced a top speed of 110mph (177kph) and gave around 20mpg (32kpg). It brought the inevitable rude comments on badge engineering, but it found a devoted if limited niche in the market.

Then, to add to the line up, the Jaguar S-type saloon was announced in 1963, but not produced until the following year – a practice dear to Sir William's heart because, as a manipulator of men and markets, it gave his workforce a target to aim for, and the market something to look forward to as well. Unfortunately it took rather a long time to get the new S-type into large scale production, which prompted Sir William to remark that all rising costs had to be met by increased production efficiency. Clearly it was not happening at the rate he would have wished. At the time the S-type was heralded as 'the latest development of one of the world's most successful cars', and in his efforts to please every segment of his market, he had produced a saloon that was bigger than the Mk II, smaller than the Mk X, but owed everything to both. The shape

The S-type Jaguar was very slow getting into full production, which was a pity because I thought it a very attractive motor car.

A Mk X moderately disguised, being put through its paces in France.

The Jaguar S-type was an intermediate car, a Mk II with a Mk X independent rear suspension, a huge boot, twin tanks and styling changes. It was offered with either a 3.4-litre or 3.8-litre engine.

and the interior were more akin to the Mk II, but there was more head and leg room, while the exterior had been re-styled at the front end with bigger side lights, and wraparound indicators, and the rear end given a definite look of the Mk X which greatly added to the boot space, boosting it to 19cu ft.

It took on the independent rear suspension of the Mk X, and was offered with either a 3.4-litre or 3.8-litre engine, and prices were £1,669 and £1,758 respectively. I took one to the Belgian Grand Prix in 1964; it had synchromesh on all gears now, and the ride was a considerable improvement over the Mk II, and it so impressed the officials at Francorchamps they waved me into the paddock without enquiring about passes. Alas, those days have gone.

In the constant attempt to improve efficiency a new paint plant costing £350,000 was installed, and instead of the bodies being attached to their mechanical components fully painted, they now arrived with a first colour coat, and were finished once all the mechanical parts had been fitted, thus saving all the paint damage that could be inflicted while work was being done on the cars, as well as doing away with the rectification bay.

## Keeping the Pot Boiling

The Jaguar XJ model was still two years away, but Sir William believed that he had to keep the public on their toes; always wondering what Jaguar were going to do next, and do it without spending a fortune. There was a good deal of speculation about multi-cylinder engines in 1964, but when the 1965 model Mk X was announced it was powered by the 4.2-litre XK engine, which did nothing for the top speed, but improved the performance in the middle ranges. It was now equipped with a Marles Variamatic variable rate power-assisted steering system with three turns from lock to lock, which generally silenced the criticism of the

Sir William was capable of playing almost limitless variations on a theme, and as a result encouraging sales without massive expenditure – this is Jaguar Mk IX.

The dashboard of the Mk IX is singularly uncluttered by today's standards.

previous power-assisted system, and a Borg Warner Model 8 with two drive ranges. It also had the improved manual gearbox, better brakes and a new type of oil control ring which did much to improve the oil consumption. In view of criticism the front seats were provided with more lateral support. All this cost an extra £98.

Strikes were one of the principal activities at Jaguar in 1965, but time was still found to produce a limousine version of the Mk X, which boasted a cocktail cabinet, and folding tables, and an air-conditioning system made by Delaney Gallay Ltd, was now on offer for £275 10s. The Mk IIs were also given the new manual gearboxes. In July 1966 the announcement had been made that Jaguar Cars and the British Motor Corporation were to merge, but at the October Motor Show at Earls Court, Jaguar continued playing tunes on a theme, and produced the 420 G and the 420; two cars which may not have set the motoring world on fire, but helped to usher in the styling of the XJ range, and with their clean, eager-looking lines were attractive cars.

No one but Sir William thought that they could be produced in time for the show, but because of his intractable determination, and the efforts of his staff and that of Pressed Steel they were, and another miracle was added to his achievements.

In effect the 420 G was a Mk X with slim chrome strips down either side, a more pronounced central

The Jaguar 420 at Maxstoke Castle.

This interior shot epitomizes the special qualities of a Jaguar saloon.

slat down the radiator, and smaller front indicator units at the front. The 420 was a mixture of the 420 G and the S-type and created to bridge the gap between them; the 420 G being the front end, and the S-type the rear. It retained the 4.2-litre engine, but with twin SU HD8 carburettors instead of the triple arrangement used on the bigger 420 G. The 420 sold for £1,930 and the 420 G for £2,238, again exceptionally competitive prices for high-performance saloons. A limousine version was also produced under the new name of 420 G, which had a partition between the front and rear seats, and to add to the already formidable list of models a Daimler Sovereign was also introduced which was a 420 with a Daimler radiator, of which 5,700 were built.

In 1967 the Mk IIs became the 240s and the 340s, the 3.8-litre being dropped, but apart from the change of name there was not a great deal of difference between the two – the spotlights gave way to circular grilles and the heavy double bumpers were replaced by single slim ones. The interior was not quite traditional Jaguar, the leather seats gave way to Ambla for reasons of economy, but the 240 cost only £133 more than it had done ten years before.

The Daimler Limousine, which was very much one of Sir William's creations, was launched in 1968. It was a combination of Vanden Plas bodywork (Vanden Plas was now a subsidiary of British Motor Holdings) and a lengthened 420 G floor pan. It was nearly 19ft (5.8m) long and weighed over two tons dry. It was powered by a 4.2-litre XK engine which gave it all the performance required of such a vehicle, with an almost total absence of noise. When any comparable seven-seater cost well over ten thousand pounds, the Daimler Limousine sold for £3,824.

Its dimensions and price made it instantly popular with the funeral trade, but it also had its appeal in other directions, and its elegant lines – far superior to many one-off limousines – has kept it popular to this day.

## The Proof of the Pudding

In the following year the XJ6 was launched, and some slimming down of the model range had to take place, but had Sir William's proliferation plan worked? The answer must be that in 1968 the company reported that fifty-two per cent of production in the previous four years had been exported, sales had amounted to £56 million, and Jaguar was still a very profitable company, far more profitable than the British Motor Corporation of which it was now part under the name of British Motor Holdings. The merger was still new, but there had been attempts to rationalize the buying of parts, so that they could be bought more economically, but it had been discovered that Jaguar, small as it was in comparison to BMC, was buying many parts much more cheaply; a tribute to the presence of Arthur Whittaker who was to leave the company in 1968. There was also some attempt to merge sales points overseas, but in general Sir William was making full use of the autonomy given to him in his agreement with Sir George Harriman, and because he was respected – as well as being perhaps just a trifle feared by others in the motor industry – he still kept control until his retirement in 1972.

Major changes were on their way. In fact the indigenous British motor industry was in a dreadful state; it was producing far too many different models, most of which were completely uninspired, it lacked leadership, its operating format was dated, and it was short of money. As the opposition grew in size Sir William realized that he too must be part of the big battalions, which is why he merged with BMC. Other mergers were also being discussed, between Donald Stokes of the Leyland Group, which now owned Standard Triumph and Rover, and Sir George Harriman of British Motor Holdings, and both were being prodded with the best intentions, if not the greatest of knowledge, by the Industrial Reorganisation Corporation, and no less a person than the Prime Minister, Harold Wilson.

# 16
# Sir William's Ultimate Jaguar

1968 was a momentous year, not only for Sir William Lyons and Jaguar, but for the British motor industry. After much wrangling, and a considerable amount of acrimony the British Leyland Motor Corporation came into being in the spring, and at the Autumn Motor Show the Jaguar XJ6 was launched.

Clearly there was a need to gather the remnants of the British motor industry together to face the growing competition from abroad; a policy agreed by Sir William, but put at its kindest it was a mammoth merger of mergers, since all three companies involved (Leyland, BMC and Jaguar) had, within recent years, merged with other companies, and those concerned with its integration, and well-being, appeared incapable of steering this conglomeration in the right direction. However, while Sir William remained at the helm of Jaguar, his strength of character ensured that they had a good deal of autonomy.

Development work on the XJ6 had been progressing with varying degrees of intensity for several years, and it was Sir William's intention that this model, the last he was totally involved with, should be the culmination of his visions of a luxury car; quiet to the point of silence, graceful, and effortless to drive. And, of course, reasonably priced. With these qualities very much in mind Walter Hassan and his team had been developing the new V12 engine, but when the car first appeared it was powered by two engines, the well tried 4.2-litre and a new 2.8-litre version, an enlarged 2.4-litre engine, with a bore and stroke of 83x86mm (2,792cc), giving 180bhp, which was intended to appeal to more economically-minded owners at a time of rising fuel costs. (Excise duty on petrol soared to 22.5 pence a gallon in 1969.) This engine, however, was not particularly successful, experiencing piston failure, and was dropped in 1973.

The XJ6 weighed in at 32½cwt – less than current models – and an automatic version had a top speed of 120mph (193kph), and would accelerate to 100mph (161kph) in 30.4 seconds. Fuel consumption was around 17mpg (27kpg). It looked unmistakably Jaguar with its eager-to-go appearance and graceful lines, but its outstanding virtues were its quietness in all departments; its lack of road noise set a bench mark for all luxury cars, and was a great tribute to the painstaking work of Robert Knight and his modest team. I can recall talking to some Mercedes-Benz engineers shortly after the launch of the XJ6 who had been enormously impressed by the suspension and chassis of the car, and were even more staggered when they learned how many people were employed in Knight's department.

The XJ6 perpetuated the monocoque construction started in 1955, with a massively strong centre platform, a strong scuttle structure and a great deal of strength built into the lower half of the car. This resulted, as with the Mk X, in slim pillars, and an expanded area of glass. Regrettably the leaping Jaguar emblem disappeared for safety reasons. At the rear the E-type independent suspension was employed in a separate sub-frame, but at the front end there were considerable changes, and coil springs, wishbones and dampers with anti-dive characteristics which replaced the torsion bars. Rubber mounts were extensively used. Low profile radial tyres supplied by the ever faithful Dunlop were also used, and power-assisted rack and pinion steering was employed for the first time on a big saloon. Transmissions were four-speed manual with overdrive as an option, or a three-speed Borg Warner automatic. Braking was by servo-assisted Girling discs on all four wheels.

There were the usual eulogies after the announce-

The last E-type goes down the line in 1974, appropriately painted black. The price of the E-type new never exceeded £4,000.

ment, and with prices at £2,314 for the 4.2-litre manual, and £1,797 for a manual 2.8-litre, it was generally agreed that Jaguar had produced yet another winner, and after it had won the Car of the Year Award, some were moved to say that regardless of price it was a serious contender for the title 'Best Car in the World'. A far cry from the SS days, but thoughts that must have brought great joy to Sir William though, as usual, he refrained from displaying any excitement.

Production did not get off to a roaring start, and only around 150 of the new models were built a week in the early months, and there were the usual waiting lists of two years or even more on the home market, and the company's publicity department felt obliged to put out stories on the lines 'Don't shoot your dealer – he is doing his best'. But by the first half of 1970 shipments to the United States reached a record total of 3,536, and by the autumn of 1971– three years after it had been launched – production was up to 650 a week, and 50,000 cars had been built of which 28,000 had been exported. It may not have had the striking appeal of either the XK120 or the E-type, but it went on to be the company's most successful car.

Awarded the CBE for his efforts for Jaguar and the motor industry, William Mungo Heynes retired in 1969, after thirty-four years with the company. He had disagreed with Sir William on the V12 engine, believing that they should have gone ahead with the twin camshaft version, and his final months at Jaguar were tinged with sadness, but a long line of successful Jaguar engines and cars remain a tribute to one of the most unsung engineers in the British motor industry.

He was replaced by Lofty England, who became deputy chairman, and by Walter Hassan in the engineering department on engines, and Robert Knight in vehicle engineering. Walter Hassan, who had been made an OBE for his services to the motor industry stayed on at the company until 1972, when the V12 saloon was announced, and he was sixty-seven. It was, of course, very much his engine.

## Creation of the V12

From the broad prow of the XJ6 it was clear to the observant that there was plenty of room for the strongly rumoured V12 engine, and at the announcement of the XJ6 the company hinted that other engine

Sir William believed that the XJ6 was the best car he made, and it does personify the Jaguar mystique.

This is the LWB XJ6 Series II, which many Jaguar owners believe has not been visually improved to this day.

developments would be forthcoming in two or three years' time.

When Jaguar decided to withdraw from motor racing in 1956, it was considered at the time to be a temporary decision, and that eventually the company would return to motor racing and, hopefully, be as successful as they were in the 1950s. With this in mind Bill Heynes and his engineering department set about producing a 5-litre engine which would meet the prototype regulations, and in order to obtain the maximum potential power a 12-cylinder engine with a short stroke of 71mm was adopted to provide safe running at 8,000–8,500rpm. The first 60-degree engine was designed with twin-cam hemispherical cylinder heads, using Lucas fuel injection with individual air intakes to each cylinder, and with 10:1 compression ratio this gave 502bhp at 8,300rpm. With a bore of 87mm it had a capacity of 4,994cc.

This engine first ran in 1964 and two years later it was installed in the XJ13, a monocoque racer with a body designed by Malcom Sayer. The engine was mounted amidships, and despite its size the car had a magnificent profile. On tests at the Motor Industry Research Association (MIRA) near Nuneaton, it set a lap record for a British circuit of 161mph (259kph), and reached 175mph on the straight section, in the hands of David Hobbs. Unfortunately, driven by Norman Dewis it crashed on the same circuit and was badly damaged, but was subsequently rebuilt, and some years ago it made a guest appearance at Le Mans, its spiritual home. It is now in the Jaguar collection.

The need for a racing engine was receding as the relationship between racing sports cars and production sports cars receded, but Sir William was still determined to have a V12 engine, one which would carry his cars into the 1970s as the XK engine had in the 1950s, and Walter Hassan was given the brief that it must be smooth, powerful, quiet and economical to produce.

Walter was seeking extreme flexibility and near-silent operation, together with outstanding torque in the middle speed range, as well as adequate maximum power. Tests with a single cylinder engine showed that they could achieve what they wanted with greater certainty from a flat cylinder head and bowl in pistons,

Fortunate to be upright after four days at the Geneva motor show, we headed for home in great comfort in this recently announced 4.2-litre XJ6.

The XJ13 at the MIRA test track near Nuneaton, with test driver Norman Dewis at the wheel.

rather than from an hemispherical head. They also decided on a single overhead camshaft because it gave better power at low speeds, was less complicated, lighter and was cheaper to make.

By making the integral block and crankcase of alloy they were able to save 116lbs over the cast-iron six-cylinder, and the complete engine was only 80lbs heavier. It was cooled by two electric fans, and although fuel injection was tried Walter Hassan was satisfied with four dual-choke downdraught Zenith carburettors. Lucas-Opus transistorized ignition was used for the first time on a production car. Dimensions of the engine were 90x70mm (5,343cc), and it produced 272bhp. The most tiresome and time-consuming problem Walter Hassan and his team had with the new engine was meeting US emission control regulations, but this they achieved, and as mentioned, the first car to be fitted with the new V12 was the E-type in 1971.

In June the following year the V12 appeared in the car it was destined for, and the XJ12 went on sale at £3,725, undercutting all the opposition. It had a top speed of 146mph (235kph), and glided to 100mph (161kph) in an astonishing 19 seconds. Minor changes were made in that a mechanical fan replaced the electric ones on the E-type, the front suspension was beefed up to cope with the extra weight, and stainless steel guards were fitted beneath the bonnet to deal with high temperatures. The only gearbox offered was a Borg Warner Type 12.

The six-cylinder astonished most people by its silent operation, but the new V12 did meet the 'near silent operation' demanded by Sir William, and one had to look at the gauges to tell whether the engine was running.

When Sir William first heard the V12 running several years before it was announced he said, according to Walter Hassan: 'Yes, that's all right', and left. 'He was never delighted', added Walter.

In 1969 the fluted Daimler grille was introduced to the XJ6, and when the 420G went out of production in 1970 – a lot of models had been shed in a short time – the Jaguar range was all one shape, the XJ shape. Lofty England must have been thinking of his early days as an apprentice with Daimler when he introduced the Double-Six – a Daimler version of the V12. Again there were critics who scoffed at badge engineering, but it seemed to make marketing sense, and since over 70,000 have been made they must appeal to someone.

Sir William, in the centre, gave up the post of managing director in 1968, but remained chairman and chief executive. F.R.W. (Lofty) England and Robert W. Grice on the right became joint managing directors. It seemed a solemn occasion.

Sir William did not believe in chauffeurs, and drove himself up to his retirement.

## The Captains and the Kings Depart

In 1972, the jubilee year of the company, when he was well into his 71st year, Sir William decided to retire. A lot of people in BLMC must have heaved a sigh of relief, because without this erect, watchful, silver-haired figure about, Jaguar Cars would no longer be sacrosanct, and many were waiting to plunder the goose that was still laying the golden eggs.

His natural successor was Lofty England, but now, after many years service with the company, Lofty was sixty years of age, and he realized that if Jaguar were to retain any degree of autonomy his main task would be to find someone suitable to follow him. He did not have a happy introduction to the job of chairman and chief executive, for soon after his appointment an official strike was called which lasted for nearly three months, the longest in the company's history.

As explained previously Coventry had an historical association with piece work, a system that had worked reasonably well when cars were hand-built, but with mass production it produced many anomalies, and pay negotiations with scores of different groups of workers took an age, and were inflationary. The plan was to change over to a flat-rate pay scheme, but the workforce were reluctant to relinquish old practices which had seen their wages rise considerably, and after all the negotiating procedures had been exhausted, a strike was called. It had a devastating effect on production in 1972.

But the wheels that Sir William had set in motion continued to turn, and in the same year a long wheelbase Double-Six with an extra 4in (10cm) of wheelbase, vinyl roof and built-in air conditioning was introduced costing £5,439, to be followed by the XJ6L and the XJ12L. In the following year the Series 11 XJs were launched with reinforced bulkheads and doors, bumpers to conform to new US regulations, a different instrument layout, centralized door locking, and the ventilated disc brakes fitted to the V12 were now fitted to the Sixes.

The V12 was now only available on the long 112.8in (286.5cm) wheelbase, and in the relentless search for silence sound-absorbing material had been added to the footwells and transmission tunnels. When the

Sir William Lyons at the 50th anniversary celebrations of the company, staged in Blackpool.

These two cars mark the beginning and the end of Sir William's career as a designer and manufacturer, the two-seater Austin Seven Swallow and the Jaguar Sovereign.

Series 11 was released another new model was announced – the XJ Coupe: a two-door body of pillarless construction based on the short wheelbase. The doors were 8in (20cm) longer, and the electrically-operated windows would lower completely out of sight, giving the coupe a very sporting appearance. Devoid of central pillars the coupe was given torsional strength by increasing the thickness of the rear quarters, and introducing reinforcing beams inside the body.

It was, with its vinyl roof, a very attractive motor car, some said it was one of the most attractive made by Jaguar, but it carried the waiting list syndrome just a little too far; it was impossible to buy one. Because of torsional problems, which apart from anything else caused leaks in the windows, it did not go into production for two years. The severe car shortage caused by the summer strike was not helped by the introduction of a Vanden Plas landaulette on the Daimler chassis – only two were made.

For economy reasons – fuel costs were now soaring – the V12s were equipped with fuel injection in 1975, and the 3.4-litre engine was brought out of retirement, modified, and re-introduced to the four-door saloon range priced at £4,795. Inflation and a lack of effective management, were now being reflected in higher Jaguar prices.

The exclusivity of the coupe was ensured when it was decided to drop the short wheelbase in the cause of rationalization, and the coupe died, but not before a V12 version had been built which, with fuel injection was capable of 145mph (233kph) – not far short of the quickest two-seater E-type – and the coupe was, of course, a proper four-seater.

## A Glimpse of the Abyss

Jaguar's story at this particular time is totally interwoven with that of the British Leyland Motor Corporation and then with British Leyland Ltd, and its survival as a separate entity is little short of miraculous.

The survival of Jaguar Engineering, a jewel in the crown of the organization, was in no small measure due to an innings of incomparable tenacity by Robert Knight, who fended off everything that was hurled at him, and by implacable defensive batting, and astute captaincy, succeeded in bewildering the opposition until all thoughts of merging it with Austin-Morris, Rover, or anyone else, had faded. In doing so he, together with Peter Craig, the plant manager, and a few others, played a significant role in the survival of Jaguar as a whole.

This convoluted period of Jaguar's history is dealt with in great detail by Ken Clayton in his book *Jaguar: Rebirth of a Legend*, and to understand Jaguar's subsequent history it is necessary to have some knowledge of the horrors of the 1970s when they were literally teetering on the edge of the abyss.

From the post-war years when Nuffield and Austin merged to form the British Motor Corporation, they were many – often in high places – who were either Austin or Morris men, and who could never reconcile themselves to the fact that they were now in the same camp. They found it impossible to pull together. When

Walter Hassan says that the 4.2-litre XK engine was the best, and many people are of the opinion that the XJ6 with the 4.2-litre engine was the best car they have owned.

the conglomeration of conglomerations was formed into the British Leyland Motor Corporation, it was like introducing a South American United Nations division into the 51st Highland Division; resentment abounded, and internecine warfare was rampant.

It has already been pointed out that the line-up of vehicles in the popular mass production field was, to put it kindly, jaded, and these were being produced in scattered factories that were often old and inefficient, and renowned for their appalling labour relations. In 1974 23.8-million man hours had been lost in the Corporation, and a lot of the trouble could be attributed to the untidy nature of the company which had 170,000 employees in sixty different plants organized by eight divisions, in which there were seventeen different trade unions. Pierre Lefaucheux, an inspired man with the assistance of an inspired Government, put a shattered Regie Renault on the path to revitalization after the war, but he had the advantage of starting virtually from scratch.

Lord Stokes, who had the job of pulling the disparate groups of BLMC together, was an inspired salesman and marketing man of boundless energy, who gave everything unstintingly to the job, but he was not a production engineer, nor an economist, and he would admit that these were provinces in which he had no great interest. He had government backing of sorts, but it was inspired from a desire to keep them in government rather than anything else. What was needed was a strategy for the future, and the right people to implement it, but high fliers were not attracted to the Corporation, and the existing management were totally engrossed with the immediate problems of survival.

By the end of 1974 the Corporation was broke. But the Government could not let it sink since it had contributed £500 million in direct exports in 1974, and a million people would lose their jobs if it did.

Tony Benn, an instigator of BLMC, but now the Secretary of State for Industry, told the House of Commons that in response to the company's request for support the Government intended to introduce longer-term arrangements, including a measure of public ownership . . . and they also intended to appoint a high level team lead by Sir Don Ryder to advise on the company's situation and prospects.

## The Ryder Report

Sir Sydney Thomas Ryder, but known as Sir Don Ryder, was chairman and chief executive of Reed International, and had had a meteoric rise to success after editing *Financial Gazette*, a newspaper no longer with us. He subsequently became known to a wider public for his habit of arriving at his desk at a particularly ungodly hour in the morning. He was also an industrial adviser to the Government, and Chairman designate of the National Enterprise Board.

An abridged version of the Ryder Report appeared on 24 April 1975, and the conclusions ran to fifty-one paragraphs, including many that were anathema not only to Jaguar but many other groups as well. The solution to the labour disputes was management by consensus; in other words managers would no longer manage, but every move would be discussed until, one assumes, it was agreed by the trade unions.

Clearly Ryder was impressed by the Ford Motor Company and with good reason, because it was and is, an efficient organization, although Henry Ford II maintained that it was in dire straits when he took over in the 1940s . . . but then they always do. However, there was one enormous difference between Ford and BLMC: Ford had developed over a period of seventy years as one mainstream company, with a well-established structure and philosophy, and things were done 'by the book'.

The spirits of Sir Leonard Lord, Sir John Black, Lord Nuffield, Sir William Lyons, Maurice and Spencer Wilkes were still entrenched in the offices and production lines of the new Corporation, and turning it into a replica of the Ford Motor Company was an impossible task, particularly in the time available. Centralization was the theme, and integration was the means of implementing it. 'The creation of a single integrated car business as a separate profit centre within the Corporation would best serve the interests of BL in the future', it reported, and that sounded like the last rites for Jaguar.

Because of a lack of investment over many years the Report estimated that the cost of capital investment would be £1,264 million rising to £2,090 million when allowance was made for inflation. It was also estimated that £260 million, adjusted to £750 million for inflation, would be needed as working capital and this would have to come from the government since the Corporation was not expected to achieve a positive cash flow until 1981–82. They projected a dramatic rise in sales by the Corporation throughout the world; a scenario to which few outside the Ryder Committee would contribute.

Even the House of Commons' Expenditure Committee's trade and industry sub-committee was highly sceptical, and the chairman, Labour MP Albert Duffy, said that the Ryder Report had put forward recommendations on the basis of assumptions that could not withstand serious scrutiny. Unfortunately, the government did not think so, and appeared to swallow the Report hook, line and sinker, and the British Leyland Bill was published in May 1975, allowing the Government to buy the Corporation's shares at 10p each. It was a great opportunity missed, and the 1970s turned out to be the nadir of the British motor industry.

Having said that, Ryder had been given the impossible task of re-structuring the British motor industry in a few months, and if there was a genius who could have tackled such a herculean task he did not appear at the time.

Sir Don Ryder, later to become Lord Ryder, spent a brief time with the motor industry, but he had a searing effect on those with whom he came in contact. I know many people in the industry who had to deal with him, but I have yet to meet one who has a kind word to say for him . . . which is sad.

## The Cat's Nine Lives

Soon after the Ryder report Lord Stokes was made president – in other words he was pushed upstairs – of a new company, created out of BLMC called British Leyland Ltd, which had four divisions: Leyland Cars

The XJ13 about to show off its paces at the MIRA test track where, in the hands of David Hobbs, it set up a speed record for a British track of 161mph (259kph)

(including Jaguar), Leyland Truck and Bus, Leyland Special Products and Leyland International, and Alex Park became chief executive, and Derek Whittaker chief executive of Leyland Cars. Under a new title the monolith wallowed on under Alex Park, a nominee of Ryder.

All this had not happened without traumatic effects in Browns Lane. It was at Sir William's request that F.R.W. (Lofty) England took over as chairman and chief executive when he retired; he wanted a proper Jaguar man at the helm, but Sir William had held the reins of power so decisively for so long that no one had any real experience of running the company and, as explained earlier, Lofty England was keen to break in a successor. The opportunity to do so was not quite what he expected. In September 1973 Lord Stokes suggested to Lofty England that Geoffrey Robinson, a thirty-four year old who had been running a British Leyland subsidiary in Milan, Innocenti, should be brought into Jaguar as managing director. Robinson was a very intelligent young man with strong socialist leanings, boundless enthusiasm and a wholehearted belief in his destiny. You either liked or disliked Geoffrey Robinson and it is to his credit that most people liked him. At Cambridge he earned a BA degree in Russian and German, and at Yale he had been awarded an Economics MA degree. He also had, and probably still has, the ability to pick up languages almost incidentally.

He joined BLMC from the Industrial Reorganization Corporation and was financial controller for the Corporation at the age of thirty. It was clear that he and Lofty England would be uneasy partners. Whereas Lofty England envisaged that his successor would be gently introduced to the mysteries and mystique of Jaguar, Geoffrey Robinson saw himself as running the company from the moment he stepped through the managing director's door, and he wasted little time in making his mark. Bob Berry clearly found him a fascinating man, with a mind that was moving 'light years ahead', and while Robert Knight was of an entirely different temperament, he clearly had a soft spot for the enthusiastic Robinson.

Between 1969 and 1973 Jaguar had a cash flow of around £24 million, and according to Yorkshireman John Edwards, who became financial director, was making £10–£12 million a year in the early 1970s. To BLMC who were losing money hand over fist in most divisions this was the goose that could lay the golden egg; the obvious but not enlightened view was that Jaguar should increase production – double it if possible – and raise prices, and it would then become a 'nice little earner'. This view was flawed.

A point overlooked by Geoffrey Robinson was that an order book of five years could come down to five weeks with alarming alacrity. Sir William's policy was to create the impression that his cars were always in short supply. Even if there were half-a-dozen brand new cars sitting in the yard, the customer was told: 'We will do out best to find something suitable'. Dealers, knowing that their orders would never be met in full, over ordered, but it needed an old Jaguar hand to see through this bogus picture.

Lulled into believing that sales were no problem Robinson, having declared independence from the rest of the Corporation tackled the things he thought necessary to revitalize production and profits. With the exception of research and development virtually all the managers were fired, new ones brought in, and Robinson created an atmosphere in which the managers had control over their own domains. He agreed with the consensus approach to the trade unions, where most did not, and he was heavily criticized for having a 'too cosy' relationship with them. He decided to tackle the quality problem, and believing that a good deal of the trouble was caused by suppliers, brought in a new purchasing director in 1974. In that year Robinson increased production to 32,565, just twenty-four vehicles short of the record for the old Jaguar Company, and almost three thousand more than in the previous year.

However, the demands for increased production and better quality clashed, and according to Robert Knight the quality went down, not up – a view that was widely corroborated. Pressed to increase production Robinson envisaged not only a new paint plant, but a new factory to build car bodies. Lofty England decided that enough was enough, and retired to Austria in early 1974. From service department to chairman he had played a considerable part in the growth of the company, and was truly one of the last of the 'Old Brigade'.

## A Cog in the Wheel

Production had increased by about ten per cent, but Robinson announced an investment plan to increase production from 30,000 to 60,000 in under two years, a colossal undertaking in which the new paint plant was essential. If all had gone well it is doubtful if Robinson would have obtained all he asked for, but things did not go well; the Yom Kippur war, the explosion in oil prices, the drop in car sales, and BLMC broke. His plans were turned down, but believing he had been given a nod and a wink to go ahead on a long-term basis, the steel for the new plant was ordered, and duly arrived. It provided plenty of ammunition for his enemies, and he had quite a few, to ensure that he had little future with the Corporation. Robinson and his team at Jaguar took great pains to prepare their case for the Ryder Committee, which they believed conclusively demonstrated that the company should retain its autonomy. They hoped they would be able to put their presentation to Ryder and his team, but in the event little interest was shown in either them or their plans.

Geoffrey Robinson had always maintained that if Jaguar lost its autonomy he would leave, and when the management board was disbanded in the middle of the year he resigned.

The next two years were the toughest in the history of Jaguar Cars, because there was a concerted effort first to emasculate the company, and then to be rid of it completely. Jaguar were considered by the hierarchy to be the most integrated, determined and loyal faction within Leyland Cars, and if they were not to cause trouble they would have to be dispersed, and this they proceeded to do. All their power was taken away; sales, marketing, advertising, public relations, everything came under the umbrella of Leyland Cars with their headquarters near Coventry railway station.

Even the Jaguar factories were handed over to different divisions; Browns Lane became 'Leyland Cars, Large Car Assembly Plant' – quite a mouthful

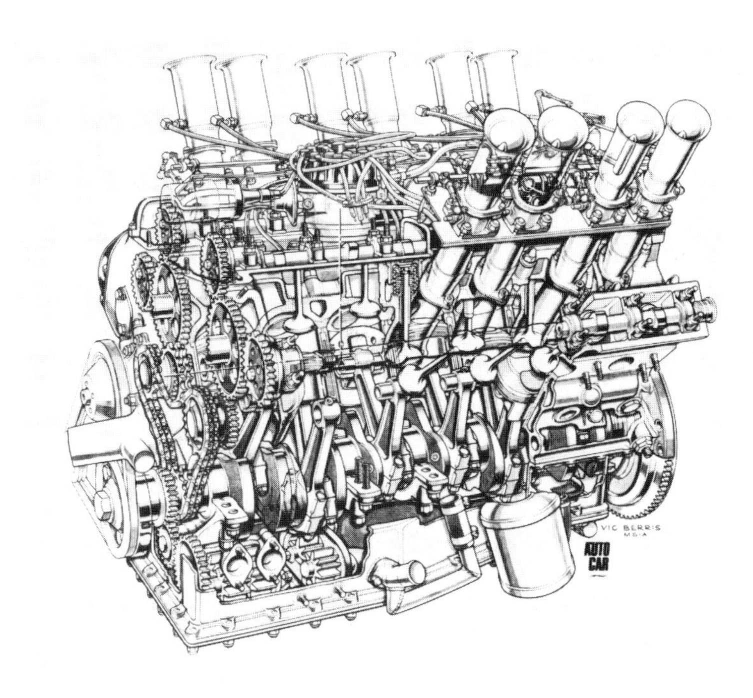


This cutaway drawing of the twin camshaft V12 engine gives some idea of its complexity. It produced over 500bhp but was considered too noisy for a road car.

for the girls on the telephone exchange – and the old Daimler factory at Radford became known as Radford Engine and Transmission Plant. Both were under separate management, and so liaison between the two became increasingly difficult.

The word was spread around that all the separate company names were to disappear, and everything would be called Leyland, that Jaguar would be slowly run down and all production transferred to the under-used Rover plant at Solihull, near Birmingham. Even the Jaguar stationery disappeared. A man from Cowley – it might as well have been Outer Mongolia – called Tony Thompson was put in charge of the Jaguar plant, which had now been reduced to a manufacturing unit.

Overrun as they had been by the occupying forces, one small detachment clung to its identity; the Engineering and Research Department. It should have come under the mantle of Spen King, the new engineering boss of Leyland Cars, but Robert Knight refused to hand over the reins of power, and went so far as to plead his case at the court of Sir Don Ryder, now boss of the National Enterprise Board, where he was told that not everything in the Ryder report was written in tablets of stone. Jaguar Engineering was not the apple of the eye of Leyland Cars, but at least it survived.

## The Show Goes On

An atmosphere where the question of survival was dominant was not ideal for launching a new car, but a car that was conceived in the early 1960s was launched to the press in September 1975, and to the public at the Motor Show in the following month. It was, of course, the XJS, a car that is still with us today. It was all rather confusing. First the new Jaguar was launched not by Jaguar at Browns Lane, but by Leyland Cars at Longbridge, and by a lot of people one did not associate with Jaguar. And the new XJS did not, as far as I and a lot of others were concerned, look like a Jaguar. The engineering had been done by Knight and Harry Munday, and the body had been designed, almost unbelievably, by Malcolm Sayer of D and E-type fame.

Robert Knight tells me that originally it was much wider, and bulkier than the production model, and a lot

There was plenty of space to stretch your legs in the long wheelbase XJ6.

of work was done to slim it down. Although Sir William was involved in the original concept, there appeared to be little of Sir William's inspiration in the end product. It also cost £8,900, and no one was asking 'Good Heavens, how do they do it at the price?' But it has got to be said that it still undercut the opposition.

It was built on a short chassis XJ, with the wheelbase shortened to 8ft 6in (2.59m), with the bulkhead and the engine compartment sides forming a rough triangle. The large doors were reinforced against lateral impact, the fuel tank spanned the rear suspension arch, forward of the luggage locker, and brakes were split circuit Girling discs. Adwest power steering, though higher-geared than on the E-type, was used, and the wheels were of die-cast alloy.

Power came from the V12 fitted with electronic fuel injection and horsepower was quoted at 285. There was a choice of a four-speed synchromesh or a Borg Warner 12 automatic transmission. In 1979 the Borg Warner was replaced by a smoother General Motors 400 automatic transmission, and although Harry Munday, who retired in 1980, had created a five-speed manual gearbox for the V12 – the six cylinders used the five-speed Rover gearbox for a short period – it was never produced because of that recurring problem of the time, a shortage of money. And the demand for manual gears on Jaguars as a whole was down to about fifteen per cent. To traditionalists the new Jaguar came as something of a shock, but it went like a traditional Jaguar; very quickly, and very quietly. It would reach 153mph (246kph), and had so much torque that a manual version could be driven from 0–140mph (0–225kph) in top gear, in little over a minute. Using the automatic gearbox it would get to 100mph (161kph) in 16.9 seconds, and to 140mph (225kph) in 45 seconds. Over 80mph (129kph) there was some wind noise, otherwise it was an exceptionally quiet car, and gave little impression of speed. And despite its size it was very nimble, and could be driven enthusiastically, and safely.

# 17
# A Return to the Track

Amidst all their problems BLMC and then Leyland Cars tentatively tipped their toes into the deep and treacherous waters of motor sport. Ford had discovered that success in motor sport could boost sales of production cars by a prodigious amount, and the temptation to have a go was considerable because the rewards of success could be very worthwhile. There were also a great many persuasive young, and not so young men around who were involved in motor sport, and who were totally convinced that if they were given a little financial backing they could bring fame and glory to their benefactors.

The Daily Mirror World Cup Rally to Mexico in 1970 attracted a number of 'works' entries from British and European manufacturers, and among those persuaded to compete were BLMC who entered a collection of Austin Maxis and Triumph 2500 Pis, apart from the many private entries and those with limited 'works' support. Prince Michael of Kent drove one of the Maxis, and their entries one way and another received a good deal of publicity, but the event was won by Hannu Mikkola and Gunnar Palme in a Ford Escort, and Lord Stokes decided that the cost effectiveness of rallying was disastrous, and the curtains were drawn on that episode.

A little later Triumph produced the Triumph Dolo-

The V12 Jaguar racing coupes looked purposeful enough, but they did have weight and braking problems among other things.

The V12 Coupe was used for racing because at the time Jaguar did not want to use the XJS, but the coupe needed more development time than it was allowed, and was not a success.

Bob Tullius did great things for Jaguar in the United States with his Virginia-based Group 44 team. This, believe it or not, is an E-type with which he was very successful.

mite Sprint, powered by a 16-valve four-cylinder single overhead camshaft engine which was a very lively performer. At that time there was still a lot to learn about casting aluminium, and the waterways on the Sprint engine used to block with unfortunate effects, but it was a problem that could be dealt with. Ralph Broad, an engine tuner, and engineer from Southam in Warwickshire, approached Triumph and told them that with the Triumph Dolomite he could win the RAC British Saloon Car Championship at little cost. With the aid of Andy Rouse and Tony Dron he did just that in 1974, and so when he approached Leyland Cars and suggested that he could win the European Touring Car Championship with an XJS, they paid attention.

Some alterations would need to be made to the rear seats, a matter of an inch or so, but Jaguar, who had just secured the identity of their engineering department, were not keen to hand over a car to an outsider. Harry Munday was told that Broad was getting 420bhp out of the V12, and he replied that he would eat his hat if it were true. He later went to Southam and there in the test bed the V12 was showing 420bhp, but Harry did not eat his hat. It was a bit rough, apparently, but later the engine was smoothed out, and one thing the car was never short of was power. But Broad did not get an XJS.

He later met Derek Whittaker at Leyland House in Marylebone Road, together with public relations man Simon Pearson, and a deal was arranged in which they would race XJ12 Coupes. There have always been grey areas in motor racing, and meeting rules of homologation is one of them. Some very well known racing saloons used aluminium bodies although the production models never saw a square inch of aluminium, and for some reason Ralph Broad was able to use a manual gearbox in the V12 Coupe although none had been seen in a production car. But he was not allowed dry sump lubrication until the following year.

The new cars, which were obviously Jaguar, despite their wide wheels and extended body work, only carried the name Leyland, because the idea of calling everything Leyland was then the dish of the day, but it looked quite ludicrous, and was not a happy omen. Neither was the launch at the new Inter Continental Hotel in London when the car was paraded before the press, and they were told how the new racing Jaguars would blow the all-conquering BMWs off the track. I

A Jaguar XJ12 used as a fire tender at Silverstone race circuit.

The influence of aerodynamicist Malcolm Sayer is very evident in this photograph of the Jaguar XK13.

The XJR–12 which competed in the IMSA series in the US in 1991.

recall that even some of the drivers such as Derek Bell, David Hodge, Steven Thompson and Andy Rouse were wincing slightly.

It takes time to develop a successful racing car, and while there was no doubt at all that the Jaguars were very quick, they also had some severe endemic problems – the wheels kept falling off; the loading caused by the big racing slicks was too much for the wheel assemblies, and hard cornering without dry sump lubrication was another problem. Another insurmountable problem was the weight of the cars, and the effect it had on the braking. In 1976 it competed in one race (the TT), and after problems with a flat tyre retired when a wheel came adrift. A full programme was attempted for 1977, but drive-shaft failure put Bell and Rouse out at the Salzburgring, another car finished well down at Brno, and at the Nurburgring Bell and Rouse actually finished second behind a BMW. They retired at Zandvoort, and at the TT they had no better luck when one car shed a wheel and Andy Rouse, after a great battle, had to retire when his car became undriveable.

Leyland decided to call it a day. It had cost about £270,000, and with a little more money and time they could probably have got the cars going well. There was not the will in Leyland Cars, and no doubt some concern over tax payers' funds, since the government now held ninety per cent of the shares.

## Success over the Water

In the United States Bob Tullius, who had cut his racing teeth on the likes of Triumph TR2s, was campaigning an XJS, which had six carburettors instead of fuel injection, dry sump lubrication, which eliminated oil surge, and like all his cars was particularly well prepared by a very efficient team. It was a very quick motor car, and he won the Trans-Am Drivers' Championship, and was narrowly beaten by Porsche in the Constructors' Championship. As Tom Walkinshaw went on to prove the XJS could win the European Touring Car Championship, perhaps it should have had a go in 1976.

# 18
# The Edwardes Era

At Leyland Cars the policy of integration was being pursued with vigour, and it stretched to the dealerships, where Trevor Taylor, who was then sales director for Leyland Cars was given the directive from the board, to 'create a single franchise under the Leyland Cars umbrella, and integrate Rover, Triumph, Austin, Morris, Jaguar, Daimler, Land Rover, Range Rover under a single franchise line.' It takes quite an effort to say it, to put it into effect was quite unrealistic. Trevor Taylor, a long serving member of the motor industry, realized that it did not make much sense, so instead a base line franchise was created – Austin-Morris.

Everyone had to sell them, and other franchises were bolted on. Jaguar was bolted on, of course, and it was estimated that they would need about 250 outlets for Jaguar. The rules then prevented a dealer from holding a Jaguar franchise, and nothing else. The rules were bent from time to time, and the Jaguar franchise was held as something of a carrot to dealers not making as big an effort as was hoped for with, say, Austin-Morris. People like Guy Salmon, a very successful Jaguar dealer at Thames Ditton, Surrey, had to sell Austin-Morris cars for a limited period, and looks back on it with unmitigated horror. Jaguars were not without problems, but he considered the other side of the

Despite the modifications for the American market which lost the E-type its spartan looks, it still remained a very attractive motor car.

There must be some compensations for doing development work on a Jaguar XJS in France.

G. Hampton hillclimbing with considerable enthusiasm in an XK140 in 1961.

This is a rather fine shot of a SWB Series II XJ6.

business a nightmare, and got rid of it as soon as he could.

Increasing the number of Jaguar dealers did not make for happy dealers, because the number of cars was being spread too thinly, and apart from the heavy investment in spares and specialist equipment, not a little poaching was going on between neighbouring dealers, which did not make for a brotherly environment.

## Marketing – A New Concept

While the managers were struggling to digest this new integration plan, and attempting to discover who was doing what and where, a new phenomena called marketing was introduced to Leyland Cars in the form of Cedric Scroggs from Cadbury. He was a very able man, with some intelligent ideas, but he was facing an uphill battle in the Midlands motor industry, which had, with few exceptions, been dominated by production engineers who believed that it was their job to make the cars, and the sales peoples' job to go out and sell them, and if it was good enough for Birmingham it was good enough for anybody. That was the thinking.

Sir Leonard Lord, as he was then, was a leading upholder of this philosophy, and a production engineer to his finger tips. On a visit to Longbridge a motoring journalist pointed out to him that the Japanese were fitting their family saloons with heaters as standard equipment. I recall his answer, delivered in a rich Midland's accent: 'If it gets cold, they should put their overcoat on like I do.' It was hard to sell marketing to men like that, and there were still plenty of them around. Jaguar's marketing had revolved around the instincts and experience of Sir William, and fortunately he had been right far more often than he had been wrong, but he would have looked very askance at a marketing department; just another way of spending money, and Cedric Scroggs had a hard time convincing them that he could help.

## Downhill All the Way

Morale throughout the company was extremely low

It was not always sunshine and light at Jaguar as this picket line of 1972 demonstrates.

and various attempts at convincing the workforce that there was a future for them at Browns Lane and Radford were singularly unsuccessful. The much vaunted employee participation scheme was not working, and industrial problems were growing. Scroggs said that attempts at communication were disastrous, and the results show that he was right. The quality of the cars produced was going downhill rapidly – a fact that a surprising number of people at Jaguar would not face up to – and the dealer network, if not in a shambles, was far from happy.

The picture was little better throughout Leyland Cars, or indeed British Leyland; it was a downhill struggle, and penury again appeared to be just a matter of time. Lord Ryder took it upon himself to visit various plants and exhort the managers and trade union officials to greater efforts, but all it did was upset the existing management and cause yet further problems.

This unhealthy atmosphere was a potent breeding ground for Leyland Cars' sickly industrial relations, and in 1977 the Toolmakers, the aristocrats of the industry's workforce, claimed that they had slipped behind in the pay league, and demanded separate negotiating rights. Pay negotiations were already a complex nightmare swallowing months of management time, and a further complication was the last thing they needed. It was turned down, and the Toolmakers did not receive any support from the Amalgamated Union of Engineering Workers who also refused to recognize the Toolroom Committee.

By February 1977, more than 3,000 workers in eleven different plants were on strike, and 40,000 assembly workers were laid off, and Leyland Cars took another step towards oblivion. Eric Varley, who was then Secretary of State for Industry, froze all funds, and the board said that they would not ask for more money until the strike had ended, and they added that since the Toolroom men were on unofficial strike they would be sacked unless they returned to work; a threat that appeared to work since the Toolroom men returned without gaining anything. Leyland Cars had, however, lost more than a month's production.

Although the government had vetoed the massive redundancies they had been told were necessary if British Leyland was to operate efficiently and profitably, and had bent over backwards to promote industrial relations campaigns of conciliation, nothing was

The XJ6 Coupe was a very attractive car, and much sought after because few were made.

This Swiss-registered XJ6 was equipped with wire wheels, which makes it look different, but not better.

working quite as they expected. With the strike over Eric Varley asked the National Enterprise Board for another assessment of British Leyland's future. He was given another rosy picture which, amazingly, he accepted. But changes were afoot, and the first of these happened when Lord Ryder resigned as chairman of the NEB, and was replaced by Leslie Murphy. The dictatorial approach to BL adopted by Lord Ryder, who had treated his fellow board members as cyphers, was over. Before leaving Lord Ryder had asked Sir Richard Dobson to become chairman of British Leyland; Sir Richard had been chairman of BAT Industries and a fellow board member of the NEB. His tenure was quite brief because at a private dinner party he made, so it is said, a jocular reference to 'wogs'. Unfortunately for Sir Richard a fellow diner made a tape recording of his remarks, and passed them on to the press, and as a result Sir Richard resigned.

Michael Edwardes, soon to become Sir Michael, was brought up in South Africa, and had had an extremely successful career with Chloride, restructuring companies within the group, and by the age of thirty-nine he had joined the main board. Conscious of his small stature – he would never stand next to anyone who was tall if he could possibly avoid it – he had the right sort of aggressive and incisive mind that was required to stop the downward spiral.

## Stopping the Rot

Edwardes had been a member of the NEB, but under Ryder had not been able to make any worthwhile contributions, although when Murphy took over things were different. In his book, *Back from the Brink* he says that post-Ryder it did not take long for the NEB members' views on Leyland to emerge, and they realized that changes at the top were essential if the company was to survive.

'Most of us saw that even with board and manage-

The Jaguar Sovereign V12 still retains the old body style, since it is claimed that shoe horning the 'big lump' into the new XJ6 body shape is not on.

The Daimler marque is not exported to Germany any longer since it was decided there might be some confusion with Daimler-Benz, makers of the Mercedes-Benz.

ment changes the Ryder plan could not be executed successfully; the first thing to do was to establish a team at British Leyland who would face up to and define the more limited objectives which were clearly needed', he wrote. Murphy's problems were appalling, because for every second that was wasted BL's financial troubles grew worse; no more money was available from the government, at least for the time being, and if the banks were to be persuaded to help, they would have to be convinced that the leadership was right.

Michael Edwardes was persuaded to take the job, was seconded from Chloride, and on 1 November 1977 took up his appointment as chairman. Before accepting the post he had, however, made it abundantly clear that he was to be the boss. He spent the first three months planning what he was going to do, and then went into action. In the public mind he is remembered for his successful confrontations with Red Robbo, the trade union leader at Longbridge, but important though this was, it is for his re-organization of the group that he should be remembered, because he took a diametrically-opposed view to Ryder, and once again it was all change, but as far as Jaguar was concerned it did give them some limited autonomy.

Michael Edwardes brought in two people to help; one was Ray Horrocks, a former Ford man then with the Eaton Group, and William Pratt Thompson, an American who had been deputy managing director of an electrical components company called Bowthorpe Holdings. Both Edwardes and Horrocks did not believe that the Ford approach would work with British Leyland Cars, and that the organization should be split into separate companies, and on 3 February 1978, Edwardes announced to dealers at the Wembley Conference Centre that the car division would be split into Austin-Morris, Jaguar-Rover-Triumph (JRT), and BL Components. According to David Boole, now director of Communications and Public Affairs for Jaguar Cars, and then a new member of Jaguar's public relations

Robert Knight, as director of engineering in the days of BL played a decisive role in keeping Jaguar's engineering department intact. He is also a brilliant chassis engineer.

staff, there was a great deal of debate about JRT before it was finally implemented, and John Egan was offered the job of running it, but turned it down believing the amalgamation would not work – he was right.

Edwardes had an idea to set up one engineering group for JRT and invited Robert Knight to see him in London with this in mind, but having once rescued Jaguar Engineering from obliteration, Knight was not happy to see the same thing happen again, and pleaded for time before giving a reply not only on the engineering issue, but the prospects for JRT as a whole. The result must have pleased Edwardes because shortly afterwards Knight was made managing director of Jaguar. But as he later pointed out, 'I was called managing director of an organization that could neither buy anything nor sell anything.'

The finances of JRT were muddled to say the least, and in the convoluted accountancy system of BLMC and British Leyland, no one appears to be quite sure how much any company was making, but it does appear to be well authenticated that Jaguar was making money up until 1978, and that a good deal of it was going over the garden wall in the direction of Austin-Morris. In the event it seemed that JRT made a pre-tax profit of around £6 million in 1978, with Land Rover doing well, Jaguar breaking even, and Rover and Triumph between them losing about £40 million. JRT was not going to be the money-spinner it was thought to be.

For Jaguar there were other problems. A new paint shop at Castle Bromwich had come into operation in the late 1970s, and in 1978 the XJ6 Series III models were to go through this £18 million plant with a new technique using TPA, or acrylic paint. It caused a great many problems, and reduced production to a trickle – in 1979 production was down to 14,861, the lowest for twenty-two years. The company was also planning their replacement for the XJ6, known at the

The V12 engine in the Jaguar XJS looks a bit like Battersea Power Station. There is certainly little room to spare.

A youthful, and exuberant Geoffrey Robinson, with a rather older, and somewhat wary F. R. W. (Lofty) England.

Italian coachbuilder Pinin Farina made some small but significant improvements to the XJ6, but when he designs a complete body it becomes an attractive Italian car, not a Jaguar.

Exhaust gas emission testing became a matter of paramount importance if cars were to be exported to America.

time as the XJ40, and a new engine, the AJ6, to replace the ageing XK series. This involved Pratt Thompson in a battle, and demonstrated to a somewhat jaded and cynical workforce, that the boss of JRT was on their side. Before they could go ahead with the new engine they had to get approval from the BL board, and they could not see why the Rover V8 engine could not do the job quite effectively, and certainly more economically, than producing a new and complicated, aluminium, 24-valve six-cylinder engine.

The theory at the time was that Jaguar must have a much more economical engine, with fuel costs constantly rising, and even the Americans turning their backs on gas guzzlers. Pratt Thompson made the point very forcibly that Jaguar's American customers, and they were the majority of the overseas customers, were not going to be very keen on buying a Jaguar powered by a Buick engine, because that is from where the Rover V8 had emanated. Pratt Thompson won that battle, and Jaguar were given the go-ahead for the new engine, but he had problems in other directions, and could achieve little more independence for Jaguar, whose overseas sales were controlled by BL International, and whose home sales were still not directly under their thumb.

The Series III models had been face-lifted by Pinin Farina, and the subtle changes to the roof height, bumpers, flush-fitting door handles, made it perhaps the most attractive of the XJ6 models. Mechanically it had Lucas-Bosch L-Jetronic fuel injection, and a Rover 5-speed manual gearbox, but mechanically it was not dramatically different from its predecessors. It produced a catalogue of electrical and tyre problems, and some fuel injection problems, and Jaguar and the suppliers were busy blaming each other for the troubles – certainly not all the blame could be laid at one door. Extensive engineering programmes were launched to eliminate the problems, and these, together with the work being done on the new engine and the XJ40 meant that Jaguar engineering was at full stretch.

## Yet Another Change

After sixteen months it was becoming clear that JRT was not going to work as envisaged, and the arrival of a Conservative government in 1979 changed attitudes about the future, and the size of the company. Because Triumph was producing an ageing range of cars in an ageing Canley factory, and a lot of money had been poured into Solihull, the home of Rover, the prospects for the company that had produced a very successful range of TR sports cars looked very bleak, and it was clearly going to follow MG at Abingdon, and be closed down. It was also clear that in the long term the Conservative government were determined on privatization, selling off each company one by one, so Edwardes had another change of plan, and Austin-Morris and Rover-Triumph were merged with Ray Horrocks established as the new boss, and Pratt Thompson, who had made a valiant effort for Jaguar, was moved to BL International.

Jaguar, which was considered an early prospect for privatization was left on its own, and Percy Plant was installed as caretaker until a new boss for the company could be found. Unfortunately, Percy Plant had the reputation of being the harbinger of doom; the man who came to plants before they were to be shut down, and that sent shivers through Browns Lane. Another move that did not help to restore confidence at Jaguar was a new sales and marketing organization for all the car companies called BL Europe and Overseas, which rejoiced in the initials BLEO, and the ebullient Tony Ball was its chairman. Little by little Jaguar had been moving towards establishing their own sales and marketing organization, but BLEO effectively put an end to that – for the time being at least.

Jaguar's future was on a razor's edge, not because Percy Plant had been installed, but because it was losing money at an alarming rate, and someone had to be found who could save the company . . . it was as simple as that.

# 19
# John Egan to the Rescue

John Leopold Egan, was forty years old and corporate parts director for Massey-Ferguson when he was approached by Ray Horrocks to take on the Jaguar job. Since leaving Imperial College, London, he had enjoyed a successful career, but his ambitions were far from fulfilled and his mind was ranging over the industrial horizons; an overseas job where he would not be taxed out of existence, had appealed strongly to his robust capitalist thinking.

If Margaret Thatcher had not been Prime Minister, and a Conservative party in power, it is almost certain that he would not have taken the job. He was an admirer of Margaret Thatcher, and a firm believer in what she was attempting to achieve. He also admired the energetic way in which Sir Michael Edwardes had tackled the industrial problems of Leyland.

Having worked for BL for five years, and taken part in the development of Unipart he knew about the group's problems in general and Jaguar's problems in particular, although the depth of the Jaguar malaise was still to be something of a shock.

John Egan was determined to make his mark, but his determination was, and is, leavened by a Celtic romanticism, and this certainly played its part in his decision to join Jaguar. 'As a boy in Coventry I had always admired Jaguar cars, and I was particularly impressed with the looks of the Series III, and thought it could and should succeed. Also, I thought "what are all these people in Coventry going to do if it does go under, is it going to be yet another tombstone in the industrial graveyard".' Such metaphors trip easily from his tongue.

'I had no illusions about the difficulties; I knew it was going to be an all-consuming job, and I always maintained that there was no more than a 50–50 chance of success, but I decided to have a go.'

Sir John Egan, who grabbed the colours when all around him was despair and defeat, and lead Jaguar out of the abyss.

1 April 1980 might not have seemed a propitious date to start a new and demanding job, and when he drove through the gates of Browns Lane, as managing director of Jaguar Cars Holdings, and chairman of Jaguar Cars Ltd, the factory was on strike and the production lines at a standstill. 'I could visualize myself as the first chairman of a car manufacturing plant that never built a motor car', he recalls.

**Sir John Egan**

Sir John is very much a man's man; as much at home in a rugby club changing room as he is in the board room, and I could think of few better companions for an evening out. When he walks into a room his personality fills it, and you are aware that this man of medium height, whose challenging eyes shine intensely from a face worn by years of hard decisions is a very special person. His intensity and enthusiasm create an aura of adventure, and it is clear who will lead the way.

It was these qualities, perhaps more than any academic ones, which were essential to the salvation of Jaguar. It needed a hero to grab the colours, steady the troops, then lead them back to the heights of self esteem. Sir John filled that roll admirably. A keen military historian, one of his most admired commanders is the Russian General Kutuzov, who kept a demoralized Russian army in being after the battle of Borodino, and eventually drove the Napoleonic armies out of Russia.

Sir John believes that operating a business today is a form of warfare, and there is a lot to be learned from the great military commanders.

Like them he has learned to take hard decisions, such as reducing the workforce by a third and, playing the part of the modern manager with consummate ease, he points out that it was just something that had to be done. But you know it hurt.

A number of people at Jaguar who went through the last decade would now say that if they had known what it was going to entail they would have had second thoughts. Even so they did not achieve all they set out to achieve but, as Sir John points out elsewhere, they did all that 'flesh and blood could do'. And it took its toll.

Lady Egan once told me that at the height of his plans to save the company, Sir John could talk about nothing else but Jaguar; it was all-consuming. She could understand why: 'If he was going to be successful it had to be his life for that particular period'. There is little doubt that it was, he was successful, and he kept Jaguar alive.

John Leopold Egan, was born in Rawtenstall, Lancashire, on 7 November 1939, and was introduced to the motor industry early in life because his father was a Ford dealer. The family moved to Coventry, and Sir John went to Bablake school – although he has never lost a slight Lancashire burr – and London University where he graduated in petroleum engineering. From 1962 to 1966 he worked as an engineer for Shell International, mostly in the Middle East.

By now his ambitious nature was in full bloom, and the young John Egan was looking for the path that would lead to the top, and he realized that an engineering degree was not sufficient – to get to the top you had to know about business. So in 1966 he spent two years at the London Business School, where he gained a MSc degree in Business Studies.

It was in 1968 that he started his career in the motor industry, joining General Motors as general manager of the AC-Delco Replacement Parts Operation, and he then had his first sortie with British Leyland, when he became managing director of Unipart. Another leg up the ladder came in 1976 when he was appointed Corporate Parts Director of Massey Ferguson. It was from this job that Sir John joined Jaguar Cars Ltd, as chairman in 1980. He bowed to the inevitable in 1989, and sold Jaguar for a very good price, as a going concern, to the Ford Motor Company, and stayed on as non-executive chairman until he retired from Jaguar on 30 June 1990.

Now Sir John is chief executive of BAA plc in London, but still living in Warwick with his wife and two daughters, and one gets the impression that he finds his facet of the aeronautical world a little less demanding than the motor industry.

Sir John managed the re-privatization of Jaguar, he was knighted in 1986, and saw Jaguar win Le Mans in 1988 for the first time for thirty-one years. Other awards were literally heaped on him during his time at Jaguar. Such a golden figure attracts critics as surely as honey attracts bees, and there are plenty who say that he was not a motor engineer, that he made insufficient use of his engineers, that his priorities were wrong, and all he was doing was preparing Jaguar for sale.

He freely admits that when he came to Jaguar he had never run a motor manufacturing plant; that he did make mistakes, and eventually – which is important – he did realize that Jaguar would have great difficulty surviving on its own. But the name is a monument to him, and the country, the employees and not least the shareholders should be eternally grateful that Ray Horrocks nominated him for the job, and that he accepted. In those confused and depressing days in the late 1970s Jaguar could have so easily slipped out of sight – he saved it.

The strike was part of the re-structuring plan put together by Sir Michael Edwardes in the previous year, with the aim of returning management powers to managers, improving labour mobility, and revising annual pay awards and grading structures. It was the question of grading that upset the Jaguar workers who firmly believed that building a complicated luxury car such as the Jaguar, demanded more skill than was required to build, for instance, a Metro, and although Ray Horrocks, who was chairman of Jaguar Cars Holdings, agreed to some degree with this thinking, they were in no position to restructure the gradings of the company – they were too concerned with keeping it alive.

When John Egan joined Jaguar it was losing £47 million on a turnover of £150 million, only 14,000 cars had been sold, which was the lowest figure for twenty years, and those 14,000 cars were produced by 9,210 employees – less than 1.5 cars per employee. The quality was poor, and to back up this accusation the independent research organization J.D. Power in the United States said that only twenty per cent of Jaguar owners in the US were satisfied with their cars thirty-five days after delivery, a truly damning statistic. Added to that BL were threatening that if the company was not turned around quickly it would be closed, and there was no doubt in anyone's mind that they meant it.

Inflation had risen to twenty-two per cent, petrol prices had soared from 84p a gallon to 134p in a year – not good for a company making thirsty motor cars – and in America, Jaguar's biggest export market, the dollar was slipping dramatically against the pound sterling, which for Jaguar meant a severe drop in profitability.

For an amateur car manufacturer, for that is how John Egan described himself – 'I had been in the parts business, but I had never been in the car manufacturing side of the industry' – it must have been a daunting prospect. But John Egan is not easily deterred, and like a terrier, once he gets his teeth into a problem, he will not let go.

## Last Chance

The first thing to tackle was the strike, because unless that was sorted out, there would have been nothing else to sort out; Jaguar would have closed. John Egan met the trade unions involved. 'The grading system

Sir John Egan and his team shortly after he took over at Jaguar in 1980.

The XJS HE was announced in 1981 and equipped with the 'May' cylinder head for increased efficiency and lower fuel consumption.

was at the heart of the problem, and they were saying that they had a very difficult job because very often the bodies and the parts did not fit – which I subsequently learned was often true – but there was no way we could change the grading system, and I just had to tough it out. The thing I did offer was to say "I was new, that I would not have been hired unless they thought there was some future for Jaguar Cars, and I was going to do my very best to make the company survive and work for independence." And I began to realize that I was their last chance, because I knew beyond doubt that if they did not go back to work soon the place would be shut down.'

It was a close run thing. In the end John Egan was to spend the whole weekend arguing his case. Eventually he was backed up by the shop stewards and officials of the trade unions who, he says, fulfilled their obligations. In the end, by a very narrow margin, they voted to return to work. At least they could breathe again. But the situation was still desperate.

The recently commissioned paint plant at Castle Bromwich was still not working properly, so 'we had bodies coming in unpainted and we had to get down and paint them in Jaguar's own paint plant that was forty, maybe fifty years old. The quality was appalling and none of our customers appeared to be satisfied, and there were people everywhere. Can you imagine it? We were making 14,000 cars with almost the same number of people as subsequently made 50,000.'

Sometimes ignorance is bliss and it worked with John Egan whose knowledge of car manufacturing plants was minimal. At the time he was unsure whether the manufacturing facilities at Browns Lane were archaic or not. 'I did not dare go to our competitors such as Mercedes-Benz or BMW, because I thought I might be frightened by what I saw, so I assumed, or had to assume that my job was to make things better, and not to become too concerned with the facilities.'

'We got down to it in the first weeks, and started with quality as the number one objective, and told everyone that we were going to do our best to improve things, but in those early days our efforts were very hit and miss, because we had to do things very quickly, and the problem seemed so big that we simply put in task forces to work on each problem', he says. Later through market research they established that compared to their principal competitors Mercedes-Benz and BMW, Jaguar had three times as many faults, and through their warranty claims they could identify what those problems were. 'In those early days we sometimes got it wrong because the warranty only covered a year, but when we introduced a three-year warranty in the US, we realized that some of our fixes had not worked over a longer period', he added. 'So we had to do some hard work, and re-fixing.'

Sir John is quite adamant that they made enormous improvements to the quality of the cars, and when the Series III went out of production they had about a third of the faults they started with, and in 1986 they had climbed to third place in J. D. Power's reliability league. 'Although our efforts might have seemed amateurish, they did work', he says.

It was Sir John who decided that the launch of the XJ40 would have to be delayed because the first priority was to improve quality, and there were just not enough engineers around to do both jobs at the same time. Naturally, a great deal of effort was made with the suppliers. Without the industrial clout of the giant motor makers, there is a limit to what hectoring can achieve, and a more subtle approach was to institute the Supplier of the Year Contest, an annual event which fostered a desire among suppliers to improve standards.

It was not only essential that improvements in quality should be made, but equally important that they should be seen to have been made, and in this department David Boole and his public affairs department did well.

However, Sir John was fully aware that quality is not a bolt-on business, it has to be built into the car from the word go, and this is why his first major capital expenditure was on a new engineering and research centre at Whitley on the outskirts of Coventry. 'We had a whole lot of Nissen huts and lean-to sheds for our engineering department, and it was amazing that we were able to design anything. Our design studio was so small that you could only take one step back to look at anything, and if you wanted to have a proper look at a clay model you had to take it outside to see it properly'; he adds.

'When we built Whitley it gave us the opportunity to design and develop proper componentry, and to test it, something we had never enjoyed before.' As the quality improved so did the sales, and Sir John is categoric that it was as simple as that. And the sales did improve, dramatically, and so did the profits. At the end of 1981 they were showing a month-by-month profit and by the end of 1982 they recorded a £15 million profit – not a lot, but a move in the right direction.

## Gathering in the Reins

It was part of the deal when John Egan took over that he would be in charge; that he would have control over all manufacturing, marketing and so on. He didn't; not to start with. Ray Horrocks would not hand over the paint plant until it was working properly, and Tony Ball at BLEO hung on to sales and marketing because it was thought to be more economic that way. They had not taken into account the determination of the new chairman, and before long Egan had taken control of the paint shop; the sales and marketing took a little longer. After a good deal of acrimony between Egan and Ball – both were fighting for what they thought was right – Egan got that aspect of the company under his wing in 1982.

He had a lot of balls in the air at the same time, since apart from improvements in quality and productivity, and reining in the departments still not under his control, it was essential that he developed a new spirit within the company, and with the workforce in particular, but this was not helped by the fact that in the first two years a third of the workforce was made redundant. As Sir John now points out, it was not calculated to improve morale, but other efforts were made with such things as the 'Hearts and Minds' programme which initially centred around social events aimed at showing what Jaguar was about, and introducing people from various factories to each other. It worked extremely well. The workforce were also kept abreast of what was happening to the company; how the survival plan was working, and quality circles were created so that information moved up as well as down. A great deal of effort was put into these pro-

The most expensive car in the range, the XJS Convertible.

grammes, although Sir John now maintains that no conscious effort was made to boost morale; they were simply urging everyone to do their best, and an improvement in morale was a corollary of that effort. Employees were also encouraged to go on courses, not necessarily related to their own jobs, and a magnificent social centre was built at Browns Lane.

'The workforce was really flattened, and they had lost faith, and when I look back now I think that perhaps I should have done things slightly differently, and put more effort into a training structure, but we did get things moving', he adds.

It was also true that for many years Jaguar had had an outstanding leader in Sir William Lyons who, if not an approachable figure, was well known around the factory, and was always seen to be in charge. The remote, hands-off approach of BLMC and then BL clearly did not suit Jaguar, and they were glad to have someone, just a little larger than life, running the show. Again, David Boole did a good job in promoting the image.

## Revitalizing the Dealer Network

After quality and productivity one of John Egan's first onslaughts was on the dealerships, and to do this he hired two first-class managers; Neil Johnson who came from Land Rover to take over sales and marketing, and Roger Putnam, who left Lotus to become sales operations director. Ably abetted by Egan they waded into the dealerships with a will in 1982, and the results were quite dramatic. The 'Old Boy' network had virtually disappeared, and there was no longer one law for the big companies and another for the smaller ones. The eager Roger Putnam had some very positive ideas and often expressed them rather bluntly; a mode of address that many of the great and the good were unused to.

At the time Jaguar had about 300 dealers in the United Kingdom, selling an average eighteen cars each, and both Johnson and Putnam thought this ridiculous. John Egan was also appalled at the standard of many Jaguar dealers, having visited some who did not even have a demonstration car, or had charged the customer for fuel when he was taken for a demonstration run. 'It was', says Sir John, 'unbelievable'. Neil Johnson told a gathering of the all-powerful BL dealer council meeting that he intended to reduce the numer of Jaguar dealers, and 'rip through' those who were Jaguar dealers in name only. It was not riotously received since many depended on Jaguar for almost half of their business. Later, at another meeting he spelt out how many dealers he expected to have in eighteen months' time, a mere 150, and probably less in due course. In those days the principle was the more dealers the merrier, and to improve sales by cutting the number of dealers was a new, and unpleasant idea.

It was decided that any dealer selling fewer than twenty-five cars a year would have to go, and so would many others whose standards were deemed to be beyond redemption. It would be foolish to suggest that all Jaguar dealers were hopeless, but John Egan was insistent that they all had to improve, a policy that was fully supported by his lieutenants. Whatever happened the dealerships had to be in fighting order by the time the XJ40 was launched in 1986.

It was at this time that the franchise development fund was created, a means of persuading the dealers to improve standards by using a cash bonus. Jaguar dealers were given a 17.5 per cent discount off list price, and this was their profit margin. However, to sell cars some dealers had been discounting them, and this had debased the value of Jaguars and slashed their re-sale value – which was already low enough. To

The cabriolet was the first Jaguar into which the new 3.6-litre AJ6 engine was fitted.

encourage dealers not to discount their cars the franchise development fund was instituted under which their margins would be cut, but those who met minimum standards in their dealerships, in regard to sales, training, presentation, decor etc, would receive a cash payment. They were persuaded that none of the money saved by cutting their margins would be retained by Jaguar Cars and, amazingly, they accepted the scheme, and it went into effect in early 1983.

Some of the bigger groups, while voting for the idea, believed that in reality it would not affect them, and a word on the telephone to the right chap would sort everything out. They received a very rude shock.

Henly's played a major role in the development of Jaguar Cars before and after the war, and at one time had nearly forty Jaguar outlets, but at the time of the new deal it was taken over by the Hawley Group, and according to the dealership agreement Jaguar had the right to withdraw the franchise if there was a change of ownership. Much to the astonishment of the new owners they were left with three Jaguar dealerships.

Used cars also came under the watchful eye of Roger Putnam, who maintained that most Jaguar dealers were almost giving their used cars away, and not selling them. Instead of trying to sell them on their own sites many were hiving them off to the trade, and Putnam believed that in doing so they were losing a profit opportunity, and robbing Jaguar of the control of used-car prices. So he introduced a used-car programme, and it soon became an inherent part of every Jaguar dealership. So did a salesman's club, which encouraged serious sales training, incentive programmes and grants, but operated under the genteel appellation of the Jaguar Foundation.

By now 8,000 cars were being sold by 110 dealers in the UK instead of the recent 5,000 through 300, and the result was a smaller, wealthier, and more efficient dealer set up. 'Considering that we had no Jaguar dealers to start with, they were all BL dealers, and we had to convert them into Jaguar dealers, the effort we put into our dealer development programme was enormous, and I believe it was very successful', says Sir John. 'Equally our straight-forward sales and marketing programmes were very successful, and our advertising was consistently of a high standard', he adds, and these facets of the business were important to him, because for the first time for a decade they were under Jaguar's control.

## Cutting the Fuel Bills

According to David Boole, in the first twelve months after John Egan's arrival at Jaguar, they did not make one XJS model; there were so many floating about unsold that they did not need to. Indeed, the sales and marketing people at BLEO were suggesting that the company should cut their losses and stop production of the XJS and concentrate on the saloons. Fortunately John Egan did not take that advice.

For the first time, possibly in their history, the Americans were becoming concerned about the cost of fuel, and fuel consumption, and the V12 was seriously considered as a non-starter in the US market. But for several years a cylinder-head for the V12 had been under development by Michael May, to be known as the HE cylinder-head, which not only increased power but reduced fuel consumption by up to twenty per cent, and this was just what was required to change the image of the V12 in both the saloon and the XJS.

Normally a manufacturer does not make a big fuss over an engine modification, but on this occasion David Boole persuaded John Egan that since they had little else to announce in the way of new models, they should make the most of the new HE head, or 'fireball' combustion chamber, and it must be said that Jaguar were the first to put it into volume production.

The new engines got a good 'press', and at about the same time prices of Jaguars were reduced by an average of 3.2 per cent. 'By now we had improved quality sufficiently for customers to put their trust in the cars; they were happy with them . . . I think it was as simple as that. And as people saw other people buying them they started to buy, and that coupled with the reduction in prices, and the new HE models gave sales the boost we so badly needed. I think that June 1981 was the turning point', adds Sir John. The policy of BL had been to load as much on the price of Jaguar as they thought the market would stand, and although Jaguars were to remain very competitive compared to the opposition, they were never to regain the incredible 'value for money' price tags of pre- and immediate post-war years. Quite simply the motor industry had become far too complicated with the introduction of safety and emission control legislation, and for the luxury car market complicated and expensive mechanical systems had become a must.

In the following year Neil Johnson surprised everyone by suggesting that they should introduce a Sovereign model to the Jaguar range, a name that had in the past been associated with Daimler. Worried that under BL the Jaguar interior had been made to look as much like an Austin as was possible, and that a Sovereign version would add another model to their range, he had one built in the experimental shop, and took the board to a surprise viewing. John Egan liked it. The Vanden Plas range was dropped because BL had been using the name on everything from an Austin 1100, somewhat tarnishing the mystique, and the name Daimler was dropped in West Germany, to avoid confusion with Daimler-Benz. The only time I ever took a Daimler to Germany the population looked on the fluted radiator unknowingly, and appeared bewildered by the name Daimler. But it was no doubt a good move.

For many years the replacement for the XK engine had been under consideration, and a lot of work had been done by Robert Knight, who had taken early retirement when John Egan was appointed, despite the latter's keenness for him to stay on. Knight had been made managing director by Sir Michael, and had played a major role in holding Jaguar together, so it was perhaps understandable, although regrettable, that he should decide to go. He had seen attempts with a V8, which had never worked properly because of secondary out-of-balance forces, a half of a V12 planned to be mounted at an angle, but that was not powerful enough.

Jim Randle had now become the boss of engineering, and Trevor Crisp was his engine man, and they were told that not only must they build a suitably powerful and quiet engine, it must also be economical. They were influenced to some degree by the 24-valve V12 competition engine, which never competed, and by the HE head on the V12, and it was decided that two versions of AJ6 would be produced; one would be a 24-valve twin overhead camshaft unit with a bore and stroke of 91×92mm, giving a capacity of 3,590cc. It produced 225bhp at 5,300rpm, a reasonable if not outstanding power output. Extensive use was made of alloy to reduce the weight by twenty-five per cent compared to the XK, but it was well known that providing the silence and smooth running from an aluminium block was much more difficult than from a cast-iron one, becaue of the reduced rigidity. The new engine was criticized in road tests as being less smooth than the XK 4.2-litre, but I thought the difference was extremely marginal. The second unit employing the May's head was to be an economic version.

We went down to the West Country to drive the new 3.6-litre AJ6-engined XJSC, a cabriolet, and the first soft top Jaguar since the E-type in 1975. The new engine was also fitted to the coupe supplementing the V12, and they were priced at £19,250 for the coupe, and £20,756 for the cabriolet. Both were fitted with a West German Getrag five-speed gearbox, which worked exceptionally well, and both models would top the 140mph (225kph) mark, the coupe, naturally, being slightly quicker than the soft top. The AJ6 engine was, of course, intended for the new XJ40 saloon, but following Jaguar practice it was given a development run in a sporting car. By now sales of the XJS were increasing and by 1984 had reached 6,070. In mid-1985 a V12 version of the cabriolet was introduced costing £26,995 (the E-type in 1961 cost £2,098), and this, with a Lucas-Bosch Digital Electronic fuel injection system would not only reach 150mph (241kph), but give a fuel consumption of 15–16mpg (24–25kpg).

## Happy Days are Here Again

By 1982 Jaguar had delivered a total of 21,340 cars, as opposed to 13,812 in the previous year, and by 1983 that figure had leapt to 27,331, and in the following year it reached a record total of 33,355, of which 25,798 went abroad – over 19,000 to North America. By 1986 sales of over 24,000 were recorded in the US, a truly amazing achievement for a company that was on the verge of closing down just six years before. Not only were Jaguar selling a lot of motor cars in the US they were making a lot of money selling them, because through the early eighties the pound sterling fell against the US dollar.

Trevor Crisp, a former Jaguar apprentice, who is now their engine man, and who was very much responsible for the development of the AJ6 range of engines.

'I do not think it contributed to our sales', says Sir John, 'but it certainly helped our profitability, and we were able to put that to good use on capital expenditure because, do not forget, nothing had been spent at Jaguar for fifteen or twenty years, and then it was often on second-hand equipment.' This was a reference to the production line which Sir William bought second-hand. Incidentally, Sir William was able to observe the re-vitalization of his old company. He was a great admirer of Sir John – their Lancashire backgrounds may have helped – and on 4 September 1982 he celebrated his 81st birthday and the Diamond Jubilee of the company. He also lived long enough to see the company he created back in private hands.

In his eighty-fourth year he died peacefully at his home Wappenbury Hall, on 8 February 1985. Sir William had made no secret of the fact that he thought the Ryder Report was totally wrong in submerging Jaguar, and it was good that he should have seen the company he created and nurtured, prospering again.

## The US Market

Sir William, as mentioned earlier, was very wary of the US market, and would never allow it to take too big a share of production; he was convinced that it was far too fickle. But Sir John says that if you are going to be in the luxury car market you have to be in the US in a big way because it is far and away the biggest market, and often America had taken over fifty per cent of Jaguar production. By the end of the 1970s BL had bought the distribution network in the US for about £7 million – cheap to what they would have had to pay ten years later – and everything was under one roof at Leonia, New Jersey, with Graham Whitehead, a former BMC man, as boss. He later did a first-class job with Michael Dale, reorganizing the dealerships in the US, as did John Mackie in Canada.

But when John Egan joined Jaguar, sales in the US were down to around 3,000 a year, through 240 dealers, most of whom spent a good deal of their time complaining ineffectively about quality. Another of his many tasks was to convince them that there was a future with Jaguar; not an easy job. But as a student of military history Sir John knows how to rally the troops, and he did so to great effect on this occasion.

In the summer of 1981 the American dealers were called over to a conference, shown round the factory, and given a glimpse of the new XJ40, which for them was six years away. John Egan was confident that he could turn the American market round, and that he

The Alpes Maritimes is a delightful setting for the XJs V12 Convertible.

would need the dealers, but he had little more than his personality, and the wonderful props of Warwick Castle and the band of the Grenadier Guards, to persuade them. There was also a lot of loyalty to Jaguar Cars, and he traded on it outrageously. John Egan told them that he wanted them to take 9,000 cars in the following year, a suggestion that was not met too enthusiastically at first, but by the time the band of the Grenadier Guards marched in there was not a dry eye in the house, and everyone was chanting 'nine thousand'. In fact, in 1982 the US dealers sold 10,400 cars. In the US in 1989–90, Jaguar sales were slightly down, but because of the strength of the pound, Jaguar's profits from the US were dramatically down, and contributed in no small measure to their losses.

## European Sales

Although many British manufacturers had launched sales campaigns in West Germany, including Jaguar, none had been successful, and most of them petered out. More money is spent on luxury cars in Germany than in any other European country, and John Egan realized that no real attempt had been made to exploit the market, and in early 1983 Jaguar, in conjunction with Emil Frey AG of Zurich, their importer since before the war, set up a jointly-owned company called Jaguar Deutschland GMBH; the first really professional organization they had had in Germany. In 1982 sales in Germany amounted to a derisory 845, but by 1985 they had struggled to 2,350 and now they are running at around 5,000 a year, which may not seem many, but is around ten per cent of Germany's luxury car market. As Lars Schmidt, boss of the company, once explained to me: 'The Germans are chauvanistic people, like most others, and they do not believe that anyone can build cars that are technically better than those produced in Germany, but the Jaguar has gracefulness, style, and an exclusivity.'

## Selling Overseas

Export sales had been effectively removed from Jaguar Cars in the period when BLMC were in control, and from 1981 onwards with the aid of Neil Johnson and John Morgan, who had been Jaguar export sales director in the 1960s, and was now director in charge of European exports, they got down to revitalizing their sales abroad. This was achieved very effectively in the US, but since the days when Madame Joska Bourgeois ruled supreme over a large slice of the continent, the European distributors had gone through turbulent times, with policy changes coming almost as frequently as management changes in the Midlands.

John Morgan, whose latest appointment had been with BL in Japan, returned to play a great part in re-establishing confidence in Jaguar on the continent. Not only was he a very considerable linguist, but he combined a wealth of knowledge and experience with inexhaustible charm and courtesy. Apart from the new German company, a formidable Frenchman both in bulk and ability called Christian Vilaseca, led Jaguar France from 1985, and in 1990 the two Italian companies, which operated in the north and the south, as most things do in that country, were joined together.

Proof of the pudding was that sales in Europe rose from 2,391 in 1974 to 3,995 in 1984, and then to 8,199 in 1989 – not astronomic figures, but a very considerable improvement after a very late start. Sir John Egan was as aware as anyone of the problems of having all his eggs in the North American basket, and worked hard at spreading the load, but breaking into new markets with a luxury car is an exericse delicately balanced between vision, outlay and profitability. However, Jaguar recently moved into Greece to complete their coverage of the European market, then into Chile, and in 1990 moved into South Korea, and started a joint venture company in Taiwan. They are also considering Thailand and Brazil, but Ford, who have an international sales network denied to a small company like Jaguar Cars, will also have their ideas on where Jaguars can be sold at a profit.

# 20
# Privatization

Privatization was not something someone dreamed up in the 1980s; it had been on the cards since the 1970s, and had gained momentum with the arrival of Mrs Thatcher at 10 Downing Street. Sir John says that it was referred to in obscure ways, but he always visualized Jaguar as an independent company, and the pressure from the Government steadily increased.

In 1982, and during the following three years Jaguar paid £102.6 million back to BL, as the decks were cleared for privatization. It was announced that in 1983 on a turnover of £472.6 million, Jaguar would have pre-tax profits of around £50 million, and then low and behold in early 1984 it was indicated that profits for the first six months would be in excess of £40 million.

The question now was not whether it would be privatized, but when. There were arguments that the new XJ40 should be launched before privatization, and others arguing the precise opposite, but by late 1983 the merchant banks, Cooper and Lybrand, and Hill Samuel had moved in, and the process of privatization had started. The first offer for sale document gave BL a twenty-five per cent stake in Jaguar – Ray Horrocks thought this necessary to keep predators at bay – but although it was accepted by the Department of Trade and Industry it was turned down in the Cabinet, on the insistence, so it is generally believed, of Margaret Thatcher, who wanted no half measures.

The government's answer to unwelcome predators was the Golden Share, referred to officially as the 'special share', held by the Secretary of State for Trade and Industry, which would allow him to block any attempted take-over or voluntary liquidation of the company. Apart from that it had no special benefits. For Jaguar it was welcomed as a protection until it expired on 31 December 1990. Work started on a new offer for sale, and since Jaguar were now to be divorced from BL the two Edwards, Ken and John, Company Secretary and Finance Director, respectively, were involved in burning a lot of midnight oil as a hundred and one contracts were torn up and replaced.

## A New Chairman

By May 1984 the structure of the new private company was becoming clearer. John Egan would remain as chairman and managing director of Jaguar Cars Ltd, and chairman of Jaguar Cars Inc, which looked after the US, but there would also be a new company – Jaguar PLC – and for this they needed a new chairman because BL were totally against Ray Horrocks continuing after flotation. So he was given the job of finding his own successor, someone who would appeal to the City, the Board, the Department of Trade and Industry, and not least to John Egan. Hamish Orr-Ewing, who had been involved with marketing the Ford Cortina, had worked for BLMC for a few years and was then chairman of Rank Xerox, appeared to fill all the requirements and was duly appointed.

At the same time Edward Bond joined the board. He had been finance director of the Beecham Group, and while no one underrated the abilities of John Edwards, it was felt that Bond would carry more weight with that mystical body, the City, with whom they were now becoming very much involved. The offer for sale was issued immediately it was ready, and the sale was scheduled for July but the BL board kept finding reasons to delay the sale, and the final date for applications was 3 August, when the price was fixed at 165p a share, which was 10 to 15p below what the analysts had been forecasting.

Sir William and Lady Lyons at the 50th anniversary Exhibition in Blackpool enjoy a chat about the Austin Swallow, the first car he made.

Hidden among the reports of the Los Angeles Olympic Games in the day's newspapers was a motor racing story stating that at the 24-hours race at Francorchamps near Spa in Belgium, a stocky Scotsman called Tom Walkinshaw had won the 24-hour race, leading home a team of three Jaguar XJS cars. It seemed that at long last Jaguar was back on a winning streak. The punters thought so.

At Barclays Bank, in London's Farringdon Street, where share applications had to be lodged it was more like Twickenham than a financial institution as hundreds struggled to buy shares. It is said that the rush to buy had been very enthusiastic some fifty years earlier when thirty-three years old William Lyons had floated SS Cars Ltd, but then he was starting something, now Jaguar were trying to regain their identity, and it looked as though everything was going their way. Certainly it seemed a good opportunity to make some money. Privatization brought each Jaguar employee a windfall, in the shape of an allocation of shares. They had to hold on to them for four years, but now, apart from their jobs, they also had a financial stake in the company.

Three days later it was announced that 320,000 valid applications had been made, and that the offer had been oversubscribed 8.3 times. The flotation had brought well over £2 billion into the coffers of BL. On the other hand practically everything that Jaguar possessed was written down to nothing. 'We had very little in the way of assets', comments Sir John. But hope springs eternal, and the full enormity of what they were attempting to achieve, had not really sunk in.

## Latest in the Line

Robert Knight was a firm supporter of the idea that design and development engineers should work together, a philosophy born of the fact that he had suffered a great deal from the absence of such cooperation. The accepted idea was that the designers would design a motor car, and then hand it over to the 'manufacturing chappies' who would get down to building it.

Naturally, this caused a number of problems, not the least of which was ease and cost of production. Some of Sir William's body lines were breathtakingly

Two stablemates, but forty-seven years between them. The 1935 SS1 saloon and the 1982 XJ6.

attractive, but they were diabolical to produce, and needed a lot of lead loading to reach the right effect, and this, of course, was the antithesis of economic mass production. When the XJ40 was first discussed Sir William was still around, and in 1972 Lofty England and Robert Knight were talking about plans for a car with an XJ6 floorpan, a V12 engine, and in addition one half of a V12 laid on its side, as power units. As mentioned BL were later to suggest that the Rover V8 engine should be used, but by then the front end had been made so narrow that neither a V8, nor a V12, would fit. However, Robert Knight still maintains that he could get the V12 into a current XJ6 without much trouble.

But with the same factory and the same facilities it seemed that the new XJ40 would have to be built in the traditional ways. In one direction, however, things were changing. Sir William, against the common practice, had insisted that his design models were built in metal, but the models for the XJ40 were produced in the traditional clay, and quite a number were built, because over the years a considerable array of people had a hand in its development.

The original plan was to introduce it in 1977, but the first models were rejected by Lord Stokes and John Barber of BL as being too much akin to the current XJ6. Then Geoffrey Robinson, influenced by his time in Italy, brought in designers Bertone and Guigiaro, and although he left after the Ryder Report, the impact of the Italian designers lingered for some time.

Rosemary Massey was the driver of this XK150 competing in the 200-mile relay at Silverstone in July 1959. Find yourself a set of numbers and some sticky tape and off you went motor racing. Well, almost.

Another version of a Jaguar-powered single seater, driven by G. Parker in the Cheltenham MC Sprint in 1962.

The Jaguar XK engine powered several racing sports cars and the odd single seater. The HWM Jaguar was one, and this shows Rivers Fletcher with his sons Peter and Jeremy, and Dennis Ibbotson.

A Jaguar six-cylinder show engine.

A major move in its development had come in the spring of 1977 when Leyland Cars product planning produced a Pre-Concept Proposal LC40, which was an analysis of Jaguar's current market position, and an indictment of their poor quality. It also outlined what the new model should be all about: an all-new car with evolutionary styling, radical engineering and production techniques, minute attention to detail and an extended development period.

Serious thought was being given to improved production techniques, and because of the threatened US corporate fuel consumption legislation – which was implemented – it called for fuel consumption saving by loss of weight, and the use of six rather than twelve-cylinder engines. Laudable as those objectives were, it was difficult to save weight as more luxurious equipment was demanded by the customer, and more safety and emission control equipment was required by various authorities. For instance the number of electric motors needed on a luxury car was now almost enough to operate a production line.

Throughout those dreadful days in the 1970s Robert Knight had kept the new model alive, along with everything else, and when John Egan arrived in 1980 he too urged it on. He also launched the intensive attack on the quality of the Series III, by September 1980 the prototype schedules had been issued, and early the next year the BL board had approved the £74.4 million expenditure on the XJ40, and two months later so had the Department of Trade and Industry.

By now Jim Randle, a former Rover apprentice, but a long serving engineer with Jaguar was, since the early retirement of Knight, director of engineering, and it was appropriate that he should be in charge of the development of the XJ40, since the basic engineering, and to a large degree the styling, had been his responsibility.

## Getting It All Together

It was very fortuitous that the Series III was selling well, and the company was making money as they faced up to the production of the new model. As Sir John now points out: 'We were faced with the problem of replacing virtually everything that the company

The XJS 3.6-litre Cabriolet in 1983 was the first Jaguar with a soft top since the last E-type in 1975.

A back view of the Series III Sovereign V12 is the one familiar to most of us.

owned, so we always realized that unless we had very benign circumstances surrounding us we were facing an almost impossible task of replacing everything, or virtually everything, as well as putting a new model programme together to compete with the best car companies in the world, because no one could argue that Mercedes-Benz and BMW are not two of the best car companies, and now there are two others in the luxury car market – Nissan and Toyota'.

Because the Series III was selling so well, particularly in the US where 16,000 were sold in 1984, the need to launch the XJ40 was not so pressing, and Jaguar had the luxury of some serious re-thinks. The original launch date of 1983 was put back, and it was put back a second and a third time before it was eventually shown to the public at the Paris Motor Show in 1986.

Because the XJ40 does not look very different from the XJ6 it is easy to forget that it is different in virtually every respect, from the AJ6 engine (Advanced Jaguar Six) to the number of body panels, and building a completely new car was an enormous undertaking, particularly for a company that only months ago was in danger of closing, and was still short of cash. With very few exceptions most new cars launched since the war had had either new bodies or new engines, but rarely both. Production boss Mike Beasley introduced new production techniques – robots were introduced, and the body was lowered on to the engine, instead of the other way round – and when he was promoted his successor from Ford, Derek Waeland, while somewhat amazed at the lack of new manufacturing facilities, continued the good work. Slowly, it was clawing its way into a new manufacturing era.

Joe Greenwell, now in the public relations department, but then in sales and marketing set up a series of clinics for the XJ40, in which current and prospective customers were invited to inspect the car, and offer their opinions on styling, the interior decor and so on. These were held in 1984 in New York, Sandown Park, Surrey, and to a lesser degree in Germany. I believe that it could be said with considerable accuracy that the interior of German cars gave the impression of a very efficient office, while the interior of the Jaguar was of a comfortable sitting room. However, Jaguar's competition came mainly from Germany, and their cars were selling well, so the new Jaguar was given an interior similar to theirs; rather cold and clinical.

It was not what Jaguar owners wanted. They loved their walnut veneer, their leather; the traditional features of a quality British car. John Egan had been very concerned about the interior, long after he was satisfied with the exterior, and these clinics confirmed his fears. The interior returned to traditional Jaguar furnishings. These delays to the launch gave the engineers opportunities to test the car they had never been afforded before, and a test base was set up in Phoenix, Arizona, where the cars covered 1.5 million miles of mountain and desert roads. Tests were also carried out in Australia, Canada and on the Nardo circuit north of Rome, as well as at home. Total mileage was said to be about 5.5 million, and no Jaguar had been so thoroughly tested before.

The Jaguar Sovereign in appropriate surroundings.

May people have modified Jaguars, and this is one man's dream . . . the Bucknall-Jaguar.

A slightly modified E-type.

The Italians are very clever at body design, but somehow they never end up looking like a Jaguar.

## Chairman and Managing Director

Changes were also taking place in the hierarchy. Hamish Orr-Ewing had doubts on whether it was sensible that Jaguar should have so many eggs in the American basket – a perpetual concern of Sir William Lyons – and he was also concerned that Jaguar was, in effect, a one-model manufacturer, which was true. He thought it would be wise if they broadened their base. Sir John now maintains that Orr-Ewing never did tell them – the board – what he wanted to do, and the basic issue was that they had to have a full board of directors both executive and non-executive working in harmony, and not pulling in different directions.

'The major bone of contention was that we were beginning to be told by other people that there were plans and we did not know anything about them. The board decided that he was not being very helpful and he retired', says Sir John. And so did Ray Horrocks who had been abroad and absent from the board meeting when the vote was taken. John Egan was now chairman and managing director of Jaguar PLC, and as President Harry Truman observed: 'The buck stops here'.

It is conservatively estimated that the cost of the development of the XJ40 was around £200 million, and it was stretching the finances of a minnow like Jaguar Cars to the limit to support that programme. John Egan, through Jim Randle and his engineering team, were also developing the XJ41, a sports car with a twin turbocharged straight-six engine, of which more later, and they were well aware of the need for a new medium-sized successor to the Mk II, but today Sir John estimates that this would have cost anything up to £500 million, and that sort of money was simply not available. The US was a large slice of their exports – some American dealers looked upon the US as Jaguar's home market – but what were Jaguar to do; turn down the opportunity to make much needed profits?

One thing that had not been decided in the lead-up to the launch was the name of the new car, since XJ40 was only the code name. Much to the joy of the Americans, and conservatives elsewhere, it was decided to

The Jaguar V12 engine was used in the power boat *Miss Windermere V*.

The interior of the V12 Convertible is a tribute to the upholsterer's art.

stick with the now well-respected name of XJ6, and it was this car that the press of Europe flocked to Dunkeld on Tayside to see in the autumn of 1986. Although not a panel was identical to that in the Series III the car did not look as different as I, and some others, expected. The main changes had been made for production reasons, and not for the sake of appearance, but it seemed that under the mantle of evolution something a little more positive could have been done to distinguish between the new car and the Series III.

The AJ6 engine which had been conceived by Harry Munday, developed by Trevor Crisp, and launched in the XJS three years earlier, had been considerably refined. For continental markets where there was a penalty on engines over 3-litres, and for those who the company believed would want a more economical engine, a 2.9-litre unit with two valves per cylinder and a single overhead camshaft was also on offer. Germany produced the gearboxes, a five-speed manual by Getrag, and a four-speed automatic by the giant transmission, suspension and powered steering manufacturer ZF. The front suspension was similar to that of the Series III, but an entirely new rear suspension, the work of Jim Randle, was introduced which not only gave an exceptionally good ride and road-holding, but also reduced axle and road noise even further than on the very acceptable Series III. The interior was traditional Jaguar, but the speedometer and rev counter had been reduced in size; a mistake that was later rectified.

The route chosen for test drives by journalists was over some very demanding highland roads, many of which had appalling surfaces, and clearly demonstrated the confidence Jaguar had in the suspension of their new car. As a means of getting from one place to another, the Jaguar had always been a smooth, comfortable, and effortless means of transport. In achieving those qualities the torque of the engine, particularly at the lower end, played a significant role. The new 3.6-litre engine lacked a little of the torque of the bigger 4.2-litre unit, and although the performance figures were very similar, it did not 'feel' as

The XJS V12 Cabriolet had a short life, and was succeeded by the convertible.

though it was moving off so effortlessly, and a lot of Jaguar driving is in the mind.

A positive attraction of the new XJ6 models was their pricing: the 2.9-litre cost £16,495 and the 3.6-litre £18,495, which made them competitively priced in the luxury car market. And on paper the 3.6-litre version could hold its own with the previous model having a top speed of 137mph (220kph), a 0–60mph (0–96.5kph) time of 7.4 seconds, and a fuel consumption of 20.7mpg (33.3kpg). As mentioned, it just made a little more fuss getting about its business at the lower end of the engine revolutions. The 2.9-litre had a top speed of 112mph (180kph), and a 0–60mph (0–96.5kph) time of 10.7 seconds, but a fuel consumption figure that was very little better than that of the 3.6-litre version. For a Jaguar it felt under-powered, and as the sales figures show – it sold just a little over 14,000 in five years – it was not a particularly popular model. Attitudes had changed since the days of the 1½-litre SS saloon; the vast majority of people who bought a big Jaguar in the 1980s wanted the performance they expect from the name, and were prepared to pay the extra to achieve it.

Most of all, however, after the biggest test programme that any Jaguar car had enjoyed, it was inexcusable that the new XJ6 suffered, initially, from a few niggling problems with the brakes and the electrics.

# 21
# The Road Back to Le Mans

'The image of the company is like putting money in the bank, but we had been spending money for a number of years, and I thought it was about time that we started to put some money back in the bank.' With those words Sir John Egan explains his decision to return to motor racing.

'We always knew that the key to our success was to sell more cars in North America, and we felt it was important to go back into motor racing, and the first programme we had in the US was racing S-types in the Trans-Am, and even though we got into the programme very late in the year we almost won the first year we were at it. But my real long term plan was Le Mans; I believed that was the way to go.' More than thirty years before Sir William Lyons had the same convictions – Le Mans was the race that mattered.

'I did not know a lot about motor racing, but I felt that if we could get into the IMSA Series in the States that would be the right thing for our sales promotion, and from that car we could possibly build a Le Mans winner. My estimation having seen Group 44 (the American team lead by Bob Tullius) race twice at Le Mans was that they were never going to win it.

'In the meantime Tom Walkinshaw had come to me and said that the XJS looked absolutely super for Group A racing in Europe, so we came to a deal where we gave him a great deal of help, and we paid him mostly by results – but Tom did a lot of winning – and I began to see that he was putting together an extremely professional racing organization, and I believed that Tom could do a better job at Le Mans than Group 44. So we then switched to one programme with him', says Sir John. 'Although it took three attempts at Le Mans before we won, you could see from the start that here was a team with the potential to win and, of course, we won the World Championship in 1987, a year before winning at Le Mans. And because we were good at merchandising, we were able to go and find sponsors who paid most of the cost of the racing programme, so I think we were able to put something together which supported the image of the company at relatively little cost', he adds.

These relatively brief comments are the bare bones of Jaguar's racing revival, but they cover a lot of territory and a number of personalities. One was former racing driver Guy Edwards, who was smart enough to turn sponsorship into a successful, full-time business, and it was Guy Edwards who persuaded the tobacco company Gallahers to support the Jaguar racing team, and without that there would have been no racing.

Bob Tullius, who I first met at the Earls Court Motor Show in the 1960s when he was racing Triumphs, could only have flourished in the US, because he managed to combine an enthusiastic amateur outlook, with an intensely polished, professional organization, and while winning Le Mans may have been beyond him, he did a lot for the image of the British motor industry, racing Triumphs of various sorts, and E-types, before demonstrating that the XJS had considerable potential as a racer.

Tom Walkinshaw, son of a market gardener from near Edinburgh, was a successful saloon car racer, and a very successful businessman, whose TWR team (Tom Walkinshaw Racing) based at Kidlington, Oxfordshire, had prepared a couple of Jaguar XJSs for racing in Australia in 1982. From this he saw the potential of the car in the new European Touring Car Championship, and in half a season's racing collected four wins. Officially supported by Jaguar in the following season he was beaten in the Championship by just one win by a large contingent of BMWs but in 1984

**Tom Walkinshaw**

Tom Walkinshaw, the stocky Scotsman who masterminded Jaguar's victories at Le Mans, and Group C racing in general, was not only a successful saloon car driver himself, he is now one of the most dynamic businessmen in the country.

Although he had no formal training as an engineer he started a modest development engineering company, catering for competition cars, at the age of twenty-eight, in 1976. At the last count he had twenty-two companies – he sometimes has to check the exact number with an aide – ranging from a farm, horticultural equipment to a string of car dealerships, and he passed the multi-millionaire stage sometime ago. He used to thunder about the countryside in a powerful Mercedes-Benz or a much modified Jaguar, but it became too time consuming, so when he is not in his private jet he uses his own helicopter.

One lunchtime at Silverstone I noticed he sat down chatting for over half an hour. Except for official meetings I had never seen him immobile for so long. The son of a market gardener from near Edinburgh, he has the figure of a shortened Rocky Marciano, and a reputation for toughness not short of that accorded the American boxer. Throughout his life he has fervently believed that 'there are no prizes for coming second'.

He believes in putting a hundred per cent effort into everything he does, takes infinite pains over details, and expects everyone who has anything to do with him, let alone those who work for him, to do the same. Being in charge, working, doing the job properly is all important; being popular has a very low rating. You feel that Tom Walkinshaw never switches off, indeed he told me that after a few days' holiday he got bored, and returned to work, but if you are not wasting his time he is a charming man to talk to, and he does care about the people who work for him; proof of the pudding is that many have been with him for years.

Although he attended a business school – 'which did not teach me much' – he had an ambition to be a racing driver, and if grit, determination and ability were all that were required to reach the top in Grand Prix racing he would have rocketed to stardom. Regrettably you also need money in one form or another, or a great deal of luck. At the age of twenty-one as Scottish Formula Ford Champion, he crossed the Border to try his luck, and got as far as a 'works' drive with two Formula 11 teams, but the canny Scot realized that saloon car racing could be a more practical way to success, and for three years he worked for Ford, not only driving, but assisting in the development of their cars.

He changed to BMW, starting his own company at the same time, and two years later he had moved to Kidlington, in Oxfordshire, from where he still operates, and changed the name of his company to TWR. He prepared sixteen BMWs for a racing series, and his business started to take off. So did his racing career. It is said that no one else can drive a car set up for Tom Walkinshaw. For instance, the brakes are set so hard that you need legs like a shire-horse, to get them to work at all, but Tom went on to win two Spa 24-Hour races, four Tourist Trophies, the Silverstone 1000 Kms and the Bathurst (Australian) 1000 Kms, and in 1984, driving a Jaguar XJS prepared by TWR, he became European Touring Car Champion. He also won many other races and championships in between.

When he took on Jaguar's Group C racing in Europe and the IMSA series in the US he stopped racing himself, on the grounds that while racing saloons was restful and relaxing after running his businesses through the week – it takes all sorts to make a world – Group C needed 100 per cent involvement. Tom Walkinshaw discovered – possibly confirming his own thoughts – that creating a successful engine is much more difficult than developing one that is already successful, albeit in a different field. In 1991 the plan is to use the 3.5-litre lightweight Ford V8, that had been used successfully by Benetton in Grand Prix racing, and was being further developed during the winter. It should be a competitive engine, and if it is I am quite confident that Tom Walkinshaw is up to organizing the rest.

with a three-car team they led the twelve-race series from beginning to end, and Tom Walkinshaw was the champion driver. In the Series they won the 24-hour race at Francorchamps, the first 24-hour that Jaguar had won for twenty-seven years.

In June 1985 Tom Walkinshaw took one of the racing XJSs to the Millbrook race track in Bedfordshire, and lapped at 174.2mph (280.3kph) which, unofficially, must be the fastest lap for any British circuit.

## Birth of an All-Out Racer

In 1982 the Lee Dykstra designed V12 mid-engined prototype, had been built by Group 44 at their Virginia headquarters, with the object of competing in the American IMSA Championship, and eventually Le Mans. Now called the XJR–5 it had a one-two win at the Miami 'Grand Prix' in 1984, but otherwise it was only moderately successful, being ostensibly slower than the best of the opposition. It came to Le Mans,

From top left this was the Le Mans team in 1986: Derek Warwick, Eddie Cheever (USA), Jean-Louis Schlesser (France), Gianfranco Brancatelli (Italy), Brian Redman, and Hurley Heywood (USA).

with no hope of winning on its first outing, but hoping to learn. By breakfast on Sunday morning they were lying sixth and seventh, an honourable performance, but then one car went out with damage caused by a deflating tyre, and the second car retired with a faulty gearbox, something that was to cause problems for a few years. At Le Mans the following year it was quite clear that the Group 44 cars did not have the pace of the Porsches, and it was too much to hope that a battery of Porsches would all fade away. As usual most of them kept going – the first three cars past the flag were Porsches – and the best that Group 44 could manage was 13th place with a car that was only operating on eleven cylinders. The second car had retired with a broken driveshaft during the night, and it was a very disappointed Group 44 team that left Le Mans, never to return. They continued, however, to race successfully in the United States.

Although TWR were not officially given the go-ahead by the Jaguar board until February 1985, designer Tony Southgate, who had created a number of Grand Prix cars, was already hard at work producing the

Martin Brundle, who was the World Champion Sports Car driver.

Although the racing Jaguars kept a similarity, the 1986 model was very different in detail from its successors.

Norfolk driver Martin Brundle drove the Jaguar superbly, and here he is at the wheel of the XJR–9 which won the World Sports•Car Championship.

These drawings show the dramatic difference between the XJR–6 used for circuit racing and the Le Mans car.

XJR–6. Walkinshaw had made an appraisal of the XJR–5 and decided that it was too far off the pace to be developed into a winner. Something of a dreamer, and a man who treasured his freedom, Tony Southgate had produced a car built of composite honeycomb and kevlar – which was extremely strong and light – and incorporated the latest ground effect principles. The V12 engine was placed as far forward as possible to concentrate the weight in the centre of the car. It was a fully stressed member and linked to a March/Hewland gearbox. To maintain the ground effect, by reducing the escape of air from the chassis venturi tunnels the rear wheels had detachable spats, a feature which has lasted until the 1990 models.

The engine man at TWR was a New Zealander called Allan Scott, who had learned his trade the hard way, and who first came to Walkinshaw's notice for his ability to squeeze that little extra out of Mazda rotary engines. He refers with affection to the V12 as the 'Big Lump', and it soon became an integral part of his life. It was a good engine to start with, and although it did produce problems with, for instance cylinder-head gaskets, it was rarely the cause of failure. When fuel regulations came into force, the trick was to get the maximum power for the lowest fuel consumption and Allan Scott proved very adept at doing so with the V12.

When TWR took two Jaguar XJR–6s to Mosport in Canada for their first outing in August 1985, the engines were increased in capacity to 6.2-litres, and were developing 650bhp. Norfolk driver Martin Brundle, then in his early twenties, surprised everyone by taking the lead in a daring, and dramatic manoeuvre at the beginning of the race, a feat which caused even Hans Joachim Stuck, to blink. But the Porsches regained the lead by the simple expedient of turning up

The XJR–40, and the racing Jaguar make a fine pair.

the boost on the turbochargers, and when wheel bearings put the Brundle/Mike Thackwell car out, they took over the second car and finished third – not bad at all for their first outing. They did reasonably well for the remainder of the season collecting fifteen points in the championship.

The following year the cars turned out in their new Silk Cut livery of mauve and white, with the engines boosted to 6.5-litres and almost 700bhp. The drivers now were Derek Warwick (who rejoined the team for 1991), Eddie Cheever, Jean-Louis Schlesser and Gianfranco Brancatelli. After a poor start at Monza Derek Warwick and Eddie Cheever won the 1,000km race at Silverstone beating the Porsche of Stuck and Derek Bell by two laps – the first World Sportscar Championship win for Jaguar for twenty-nine years.

## Knighthood

In the Queen's Sixtieth Birthday Honours in June, John Egan was made a Knight Commander of the British

The 1988 Le Mans winning car which was driven by Jan Lammers, Johnny Dumfries and Andy Wallace.

Jaguar had not won Le Mans since a D-type of Ecurie Ecosse won in 1957, but the XJR–9s of 1988 made up for everything.

They did not finish 1–2–3 in 1988, but they took the flag in line astern behind the winning car to tumultuous applause from the huge British contingent of spectators.

The star of the 1988 motor show at the NEC Birmingham, the Jaguar XJ220.

Empire, for his outstanding contribution to the British motor industry; in other words for keeping Jaguar alive. So we greeted him for the first time as Sir John when he arrived at Le Mans, for he was now becoming a dedicated racing enthusiast. Like Sir William Lyons before him Sir John was in motor racing to win, and make the company more successful, and his visits to the Sarthe circuit were stressful occasions. I used to comfort him by saying that it had taken most manufacturers three attempts to win the race, but he still described the Le Mans 24-Hour Race as 'refined torture'. In 1986 neither his knighthood nor the third Queen's Award for Export Achievement did the trick at the demanding French circuit.

Low drag bodywork was fitted so the most could be made of the Mulsanne Straight, but the ground effect gave the drivers a very hard and tiring ride, and it was decided to put three in each of the three cars entered. The first car to go went after three hours with fuel pressure problems while lying third, and the second Brancatelli/Percy/Hahne car gave Win Percy a nasty turn when the drive shaft broke while he was flat out in fifth. The Warwick/Cheever/Schlesser car, was lying second after sixteen hours when a rear tyre burst at 220mph (354kph) on the Mulsanne Straight, causing no end of damage to the suspension and bodywork. But the engines went like a dream.

The XJR–8 was produced for the 1987 season, and scores of modifications were made to the design, including the re-alignment of the V12 engine, so that the drive-shafts were not at such an acute angle, and wear would be reduced on the constant velocity joints. The season got off to a cracking start with wins at Jarama and Jerez in Spain, another at Monza and a 1–2 victory at Silverstone – indeed Jaguar won eight out of the ten races in the Series to become World Champions for the first time, and Brazilian Raul Boesel became the Driver's Champion. We all went to Le Mans in June with high hopes. And when I say we, I mean about 50,000 British visitors, because Jaguar had attracted the biggest British contingent ever seen at Le Mans. Again it was a bitter disappointment.

For the first time the teams had to use commercial petrol and this caused a number of piston failures among the Porsches, inflaming the hopes of Jaguar, but the first car to go was Win Percy's when he had a burst tyre on the Mulsanne and the car careered down the circuit on its side for more than two hundred yards. The imperturbable Percy, having telephoned his wife to say he was fit and well, if a little shaken, stayed to watch the rest of the race. That was the first blow, and then Martin Brundle burst a cylinder head on Sunday morning, and spirits were flagging. The final blow came when Eddie Cheever, well behind, lost some gears, and despite a superb effort could only manage fifth place. Derek Bell and Han Stuck won the race in a works Porsche, and they were followed by two other Porsches. At Silverstone that year it was announced that Tom Walkinshaw was going to lead not only the Silk Cut Jaguar team, but an IMSA team, sponsored by Castrol, in the US.

## Victory at Le Mans

The importance of winning cannot be over estimated with people like Sir John and Tom Walkinshaw, which is one reason why they formed such a successful partnership. Sir John puts his views of the subject of winning very succinctly: 'If you come second you are the first of the losers'. Tom Walkinshaw, a man not given to casual observations, adds: 'Winning sure as hell beats getting beaten'. So when they started the American season by winning the Daytona 24-Hour Race in convincing style it was a huge boost for morale and taken as a hopeful omen for that other 24-hour race across the Atlantic.

The Swiss-based Sauber team, with an enormous amount of backing from that colossus of the motor industry Daimler-Benz, had entered two cars powered by 5-litre twin turbocharged engines, which were considerably more powerful than the normally-aspirated Jaguar engine, and more powerful than the turbocharged Porsches. In the past Sauber had had problems with reliability, but now they had the vast technical resources of Mercedes-Benz behind them, and those of us who had seen Mercedes-Benz in action in the past, both in racing and rallying, were apprehensive.

But our fears came to nothing because in testing Mercedes blew a tyre, could find no reason for it, and with the horrors of 1955 still in their minds decided to retire. So Jaguar had to beat their old adversary Porsche, plus the growing, if still unreliable might of Japan represented by Nissan, Toyota and Mazda. Jaguar arrived at Le Mans looking like an offshoot of the Sixth Armoured Division, with five Jaguar XJR–9 LMs, assorted transporters, trucks and caravans, plus scores of mechanics, technicians and administrators. Nothing was forgotten, the party even included a doctor and a physiotherapist, and slices of cucumber which during rest periods at night were placed on the driver's eyes for their soothing effect.

When his car retired Martin Brundle joined car No 3 which won the 1990 Le Mans 24-Hour Race.

The windswept press stand high above the circuit is still occupied by many who would have difficulty reading a newspaper let alone writing for one, but now in this new electronic age another press centre has been built on the pit side of the track, ablaze with computerized results, and television screens, while rows of telephones and fax machines ensure an almost instant contact with the outside world. The days of two-hour waits for a call to England, and pencilled notes on the back of l'Equipe have long since gone. The humble but hospitable caravans of Champion, BP and Dunlop have also disappeared, and giant companies have hospitality suites to match their status, hired at horrendous cost from the organizing club. Now it is smoother, slicker and more detached. The mega-money needed to compete successfully at Le Mans has turned it into a massive business venture, but fortunately the spectators now flocking back to Le Mans either do not know or do not care.

## A Close Run Thing

Jan Lammers, a faithful Jaguar driver, Johnny Dumfries and Andy Wallace were the drivers of the winning Jaguar, which crossed the line just ninety seconds ahead of the Porsche driven by Hans Stuck, Derek Bell and Klaus Ludwig, that had harried them throughout the twenty-four hours. A second Jaguar finished 4th and a third in 16th place, but half an hour before the race finished Walkinshaw told the drivers by radio telephone to get into a one–two–three formation, and that is how they crossed the line for their first victory on the famous Sarthe circuit for thirty-one years, and they were given a tumultuous welcome by the thousands of Union Flag-waving Britons who spilled on to the track. It was a very emotional moment. It was particularly so for Sir John, the man who had said on two occasions, 'We'll be back'. And now his persistence had been rewarded, and the warm-hearted man inside the efficient modern manager came to the forefront, and he was close to tears. Tom Walkinshaw had never beamed so broadly in all his life, and somewhere Gallahers who had paid up patiently, must have been delighted.

It was good to see that one of the first to congratulate Jaguar was the team manager of the Porsche team, Peter Falk.

# 22
# Off the Boil

After the euphoria of 1988, Jaguar racing came down to earth with a bump. It had become clear that the 'big lump' was nearing the end of its days in anything but 24-hour races. In both the United States where a turbocharged Nissan entered by Electramotive had won eight races, and in Europe where the twin turbocharged Sauber Mercedes V8, though not so successful, was showing enormous promise, it was clear that the Jaguar team needed another power unit. TWR decided to build a twin turbocharged V6 engine with a 3-litre capacity for IMSA in the US, and 3.5-litre for Group C in the rest of the world. It was decided that the first priority was for IMSA, and that is where the V6 first appeared, but not surprisingly it lagged behind the well developed Nissan V8. Allan Scott had produced the V6 within a year, from a block loosely related to the V6 engine that was rallied by BL, and some help from a Swiss engineering firm. He had one racing in just over twelve months which was good – although a number of successful racing engines had been built in that time. Allan Scott had achieved great success with the V12, but that was a good engine to start with, and repeating that success from scratch against the financial and technical might of both Mercedes-Benz and Nissan proved an insurmountable uphill struggle.

While TWR wrestled with the new V6, the V12 XJR–9 which was still competing in Group C, received less attention, and like all thoroughbreds it suffered. The Sauber Mercedes-Benz cars were now appearing in the traditional German silver livery, and no one was making any pretence about it being a private team; the Sauber pits were swarming with Mercedes-Benz engineers and technicians, and my goodness it showed.

The Jaguars had been disappointing in the races up to Le Mans, but on their traditional territory it was hoped that their fortunes would change – no one more fervently than Sir John. Because of internecine warfare between the organizers, the Automobile Club de l'Quest, and FISA, over television rights, the race did not count for the World Championship, but this did not affect the crowd which was about fifteen per cent up on the previous year. Once again a contingent of about 50,000 travelled from Britain.

## A Promising Start

The Silk Cut Jaguar team arrived with four XJR–9LMs, and the Sauber Mercedes team with three C9s. On the Wednesday and Thursday qualifying sessions the Mercedes were very quick, and Jean-Louis Schlesser set up the fastest time with a record breaking lap of 155.234mph (249.818kph), reaching almost 250mph (402kph) on the 3.6-mile Mulsanne Straight. In 1953 the winning Jaguar C-types were reaching 160mph (257kph) on the same stretch of road, although the surface was not quite so good in those days.

The Mercedes C9 of Jochen Mass had suffered problems with the specially prepared fifth gear during the qualifying period, news which soon buzzed around the pits and brought some comfort not only to the Jaguar team, but to the many Porsches as well. For the sake of reliability the Sauber team decided to replace all the fifth gears with a shorter, but well-tried one, which made a marked difference to their top speed during the race. The Mulsanne Straight is famous, and it is very quick – many drivers have told me that in a good car it is one of the few places where it is possible to relax, look at the instruments, and talk

The V12 engine was used for Le Mans in 1990, and this is the winning XJR–12 still capable of topping 200mph (322kph) despite the two chicanes in the Mulsanne Straight.

on the radio. It is easily forgotten that on many other stretches of the circuit, the cars are approaching 200mph (322kph), and there is not a moment to relax. Few fatal accidents have occurred on the Mulsanne.

Two Mercedes lined up side-by-side on the front of the grid, followed by two Jaguars, with the other two Jaguars on the third and fourth row. It looked promising. Hindsight brings wisdom, but those of us who had seen Mercedes return to rallying, to Grand Prix racing and to Le Mans in the 1950s were wary. By the second lap Jaguar were in the lead clearly the fastest cars on the circuit now that Mercedes had changed their fifth gear.

But troubles had already started for Jaguar. At the end of the first lap Jan Lammers came into the pits, and he was followed by Frenchman Alain Ferte, both of whom had had warning lights activated indicating that tyre temperatures were too high. In fact they were both false alarms, but the stops put them well back. On the fifth lap Danish driver John Nielsen was hit in the rear by Julian Bailey's Nissan while lying second, and he had to pit stop for body repairs and attention to the exhaust system. All eyes, and hopes at Jaguar were on American Davy Jones who was still in the lead. When Irishman Derek Daly took over after four hours there was no competitor in sight, then trouble on the Mulsanne. Suddenly, and inexplicably he could not get into any gear. By moving the actual selector on the gearbox Daly managed to find one gear and limped back to the pits. Fifteen laps down he rejoined the race only to drop a valve three hours later. Now a Porsche was in the lead but it too came into the pits with a water leak early on Sunday, and the Lammers/Tambay/Gilbert-Scott car which had been progressing, albeit somewhat erratically, took over the lead at almost 1.30am, and the British contingent, who never appear to sleep, went wild with excitement.

But, ominously, Sauber Mercedes cars were now lying second and third, and if they were suffering from transmission problems it was not apparent. The order was Jaguar, Sauber, Sauber, Jaguar, Jaguar. Soon after 4am the Ferte car was in the pits losing seventy minutes with a broken third gear, and an hour later the Nielsen car retired with valve gear problems. Now it all depended on one car, but when Patrick Tambay came into the pits for a driver change at 6am he reported to Jan Lammers that the car was 'just fantastic'.

A few minutes later and it was back in the pits requiring a new gearbox, an operation that took a remarkable fifty-two minutes, but barring a miracle it put them out of contention. The two leading Sauber Mercedes swapped the lead according to pit stops, until an hour before the finish when the Kenneth Acheson's car jammed in fifth year. Despite almost burning out the clutch on rejoining the race he managed to continue and Jochen Mass led the Sauber Mercedes to victory, followed by the Sauber of Baldi/Acheson/Brancatelli, the Porsche of Wollek/Stuck, and the first Jaguar XJR–9LM of Lammers/Tambay/Gilbert-Scott. The third Sauber finished fifth and the remaining Jaguar was eighth.

## A Fine Farewell

The 1990 Le Mans race was to be the last official appearance of Sir John Egan at the race, and for Sir John, who had put so much into the Jaguar racing programme, to leave on a high note was something he dreamed of, but hardly dare mention. He had officially retired, and Ford was now in charge, and this was reflected by the appearance of Bill Hayden at Le Mans as the new chairman and chief executive. Once again there had been a rumpus between the race organizers and FISA, and the result was that two chicanes were inserted in the Mulsanne Straight, and again it did not

The XJR–11 powered by a 3.5-litre turbocharged engine was used in all the Championship races with the exception of Le Mans in 1990, but was totally out-powered by the Mercedes-Benz.

The 1990 Silk Cut Jaguar team which tried very hard but unsuccessfully to retain the World Championship, from top left, clockwise: Martin Brundle, Alain Ferte (France), Andy Wallace and Jan Lammers (Netherlands).

count for the World Championship. Because of the latter Mercedes-Benz, who were now in command at Sauber, decided that they would not compete, which was a considerable disappointment because they were clearly the team to beat.

However, this could have escaped your notice if you had taken all the pre-race ballyhoo produced by Nissan at face value. They were out to give the impression that they were the team to beat. Jaguar turned up with four V12 XJR–12s, in the usual Silk Cut livery, shod with Goodyear tyres, a team of 130 and fortified by a 1–2 victory at the Daytona 24-Hour Race.

The race did not start well for Nissan. Forty-nine cars set off on the pace lap but only forty-eight took part in the race; Kenneth Acheson's Nissan came to a halt with no brakes and a seized crown wheel a quarter of a mile from the pits. This left four Nissans and four Jaguars and the Brun Porsche to dominate a race in which the lead changed thirty-one times. The Nissans took the lead to start with while the Jaguars occupied fourth to seventh place in a solid phalanx of mauve and white. The Brun Porsche 926C refused to go away and was right up among the leaders.

The *cognoscenti* were, however, confident that the Nissans would not last, and one had already been delayed by a loose wheel, and then Brancatelli was involved in a heavy brush with a Toyota at the Dunlop Curves which required a new nose and wheel. Shortly after midnight the Nissan field was reduced by one when Blundell retired with a broken gear selector rod. The lead was now being contested with great vigour by Geoff Brabham in a Nissan, Martin Brundle in the No. 1 Jaguar, Nielsen in the No. 3 and the remarkable No. 16 Porsche.

In the early hours of Sunday it was the Brabham Nissan gradually pulling away from the Nielsen Jaguar, but then two factors conspired to bring the Jaguar back into contention. First the Nissan's brakes began to fade, and the pace car came out following a serious crash by the Mussato team Lancia, allowing the No. 3 car to refuel while the pace car was out. It soon caught the ailing Nissan, but then a series of events caused a few tremors in the Jaguar pits. The No. 4 Michel Ferte Jaguar arrived in the pits at 4.30am with a broken radiator. Twenty minutes later Nielsen had to have a new nose section. At 5am Austrian Franz Konrad went off on one of the Mulsanne chicanes and was temporarily stuck in the gravel, and just before 7am Martin Brundle came into the pits with a badly overheating engine which proved terminal. But No. 3 was still in the lead, and Tom Walkinshaw had deliberately kept the third driver, Elio Salazar out of the driving seat just in case he wanted to replace him with Brundle. He did, and the sad Chilean was given a drive in the Ferte No. 4 car which was in eleventh place but eventually dropped out with engine failure. Just before 8am the leading Jaguar lost fourth gear, and was rapidly losing its brakes. Nissan's hopes were raised, but not for long. A ruptured fuel cell put the Brabham car out later in the morning. American Price Cobb, shattered by his night time efforts retired from the No. 3 car and it was left to Nielsen and Brundle to nurse the Jaguar to the finish line, because behind them, waiting to pounce, was the Porsche, now being driven by only two of the three team drivers; Oscar Larrauri having retired, ill and exhausted. Regrettably for them he was the fastest of the three.

Just before midday the leading Jaguar came into the pits reporting an overheating engine. Adding water made the problem worse, and in the next two pit stops the crew used an air hose to blow out bits of rubber that had been blocking the radiator. It worked, and now the Jaguar, almost brakeless and still without fourth gear, was keeping the Porsche at arm's length. The Joest Porsche which had held third place retired with a broken exhaust and Jan Lammers and Andy Wallace in the No. 2 car took over third place.

The Union Jack and Jaguar flags were out all round the circuit when, with fifteen minutes to go the Brun Porsche was seen crawling down the Mulsanne Straight with smoke pouring from the engine cover. If it could have managed just another three miles it would have finished second, but its race was over, and into second place stepped the Jan Lammer's Jaguar. First and second at both the major 24-hour races in the world; a fitting racing farewell to Sir John.

## Mercedes Dominate

At the Nurburgring towards the end of the 1990 World Sports Car Prototype Championship that genial German racing driver Jochen Mass, told me this about the Mercedes-Benz sports car: 'It is just about the best car I have ever driven . . . anyone could drive it quickly, it does exactly what you want it to do; the chassis and the engine are just about perfect'.

Since Jochen had been one of the drivers throughout the season, and taking into account his natural modesty, it clearly was a superb motor car, as its record proved. There was simply nothing to touch it, and by the Donington race it had walked home with the World Championship for the second year in succession. One can only speculate what would have happened if it had raced at Le Mans.

The V6-engined Jaguar had raced for the first time at Brands Hatch in the autumn of 1989 in the World Sports Car Championship, but as far as fuel consumption and performance were concerned it was, as they say in motor racing, off the pace. In 1990 it was equipped with a Bosch electronic engine management system and, like the V12 at Le Mans, with Goodyear tyres, but neither of these, nor other modifications made to the engine during the winter, could overcome its inherent weaknesses.

The TWR team tried hard, and certainly no drivers in sports car racing try harder, or have more talent, than Martin Brundle and Jan Lammers. They could not cope with Mercedes-Benz, but they did keep the rest of the field at bay – for most of the time.

## In-House Racing

In the 1950s Jaguar developed their own racing cars and their own engines which were, of course, modified production engines. Would it have been impossible to do the same in the 1980s? The racing cars had long since lost any relationship to road cars, although the V12 engine was still in use right up to 1991. Sir John says that he would have liked to have kept the racing in-house, but had decided against it because of lack of resources.

'Our engineering staff was minute compared to that of Mercedes-Benz or Nissan, and they were fully stretched developing new models and coping with the problems of the Series III. It would have been great, but it just wasn't on', he said, ruefully.

There are those who disagree, and one of them is Walter Hassan, who maintains that Jaguar had far fewer engineers in the days when they ran their own competition department, than they have today. It seems that Parkinson's Law applies to motor racing as it does to so many other things; it needs more and more people to achieve the same results.

# 23
# For Sale

On the face of it 1988 was a glorious year for Jaguar Cars; their sales were running at a record level, the reception afforded the new XJ6 had been approving, if not ecstatic, they were making money, and they had just won the Le Mans 24-Hour Race for the first time for thirty-one years. No one would have thought that Sir John Egan had anything more than the day-to-day worries of administering a successful car company.

Yet in 1988 Sir John had decided that 'it was going to be difficult to remain independent. We were going to do badly by our shareholders'.

'By the spring of 1989' says David Boole, 'he knew he would have to sell the business'.

At the same time, four thousand miles away, Donald E. Petersen, chairman of the Ford Motor Company, in Detroit, Michigan, had decided that his company was going to buy Jaguar Cars. He was not the first to have such thoughts. In the early 1980s Ford made their first approach to Jaguar, suggesting that it should act as an importer of Jaguar cars into both Germany and the United States. The liaison did not last long and was centred around the European deal. Ford wanted an up-market name, and suggested that they should sell Jaguars, called either Daimler or Lanchester – a name owned by Jaguar – through their distributors in Germany. It sounded as though it might have possibilities because Jaguar lacked a good dealer set up in Germany, the biggest luxury car market in Europe.

Neil Johnson looked at the Ford distributorships in

The heart of Jaguar operations was the Browns Lane factory which was a Daimler shadow factory during the war.

The cost of the Jaguar is making it much more of a rarity in police colours, but there are still a number about.

Germany, and although he conceded that they were excellent for selling Fords, he did not think they would be ideal outlets for selling luxury cars. Ford also did a lot of research on the names Daimler and Lanchester, and they both rang all the wrong bells, and the fleeting relationship fell through – for the time being.

Next to pay court to Jaguar were the makers of Bavarian beauties BMW, and it must have been love at first sight for an extraordinary degree of openness and trust was shown by both companies, who happily gave details of each others still top-secret models; Jaguar the XJ40, and BMW the Series 7. Jim Randle, who was very much involved, thought it was a most remarkable relationship, and possibly unprecedented. BMW were exploring the possibility of taking a controlling stake in Jaguar, and collaborating on a new small Jaguar, possible based on the floorpan of the successful BMW 5 Series – everyone appreciated the need for a modern successor to the Mark II.

The Jaguar management decided that they had pulled themselves round sufficiently to keep on trying, and not hand over the glory to Bavaria, so negotiations stopped without any official proposals being made. Then there was an approach from Daimler-Benz, who normally speak only to God, but this again did not develop into an official proposal, and quietly faded away.

## Serious Bids

The next approaches came from across the Atlantic in 1988, and they were serious – both Ford and General Motors wanted the Jaguar name. In the luxury market they were already up against Mercedes-Benz and BMW, but they knew that the Japanese were to launch luxury models, and having witnessed what the Japanese had achieved at the lower end of the market they were keen to add to their armoury. Ford had the Lincoln, but it was tarred by the Ford brush in the minds of most luxury car buyers, and General Motors had allowed the Cadillac to vegetate to such a point that even in the United States its magic was badly tarnished.

At first General Motors wanted a partial stake in Jaguar, while Ford were making an offer to buy right

The 2.9-litre version of the XJ6 did have a limited following, but was generally considered under-powered for a Jaguar.

The XJS V12 Coupe has a top speed of 150mph (241kph) and a 0–60mph (96.5kph) time of 7.7 seconds.

from the start. When it became clear to GM that they too would have to make an outright offer if they were to keep Ford out, the bargaining started, with Sir John and the Jaguar board determined to get the best price possible. When Ford offered £1.6 billion late in 1989 – about five times the book value of Jaguar Cars – General Motors dropped out, and along with Aston Martin the Coventry company became a part of the Ford empire.

In between, Nicolas Ridley, Secretary of State for Trade and Industry, having given Sir John about twenty minutes notice, announced in the House of Commons that the Government were to waive the Golden Share agreement. At that point it was academic.

Sir John is convinced that they sold the company well, and did their duty by the shareholders. He was also under no illusion that he was ever going to stay there once Ford owned the company. With such a colossal investment Ford wanted a Ford man in charge, and Bill Hayden, who had been Vice President, Manufacturing Ford of Europe, was put in charge. It was indicative of how Ford assessed their priorities. Ford is a very tribal organization, and with very few exceptions the people who get to the very top are nurtured and conditioned by the company, and Bill Hayden is a good example. In the European hierarchy of the Ford Motor Company he occupied a very elevated position, being responsible not only for the four major manufacturing plants in Britain, but for those in Germany, Spain and Belgium as well as the transmission plant in Bordeaux, France.

It was sad that shortly after taking over at Browns Lane he had to undergo a heart by-pass operation, but happily he is recovering well.

## The Reason Why

If all was going so well in 1988, why was Sir John convinced by early the next year that Jaguar would have to be sold to survive? 'We did make mistakes, but if we had not made any mistakes, we would still have been bought by Ford . . . there was an inevitability about it', he says.

Ultimately it was a question of size. An example is Mercedes-Benz, part of the giant Daimler-Benz or-

Olivers Mount at Scarborough was the scene of many motor cycle races, and this motor cyclist looks all set for a burn up with the Jaguar XK120. No crash helmets of course.

The XJS V12 Convertible is not just a very pretty car, it also has a top speed of 150mph (241kph), and while priced at £41,200 at the beginning of 1991, it compared favourably with the opposition.

ganization of Germany which, quite clearly, was one of Jaguar's principle competitors in the luxury car market. By comparison Jaguar was a minnow. In 1989 Jaguar made 48,139 cars (51,939 in its peak year of 1988), but in the same year Mercedes-Benz made 542,000 motor cars. Even in the British market Mercedes outsells Jaguar two to one. And apart from their many other engineering interests Daimler-Benz is also the biggest producer of heavy trucks and buses in Europe; a formidable company.

Yet as Sir John points out it takes just as much engineering effort to produce competitive cars in relatively small numbers, as it does to produce them in quantity. Because of their reliance on the United States market – and they had to sell there – there was an underlying instability caused by the fluctuations of the pound sterling to the dollar compounded by the fact that UK inflation was uncompetitive for the later years of the 1980s. And because of their size they never had the buying clout with component manufacturers enjoyed by their bigger competitors. The importance of this cannot be over estimated in the cost effectiveness of a company, because in the late 1980s Jaguar pruned their suppliers drastically, yet they still had over 500 major ones in 1990. It was just another example of how they were operating in the major league without the benefits of other major league players.

## Fears for the Future

Toyota and Nissan were already established in the luxury car market at the end of the 1980s, with the prospect of other Japanese manufacturers to follow, and the portents were that life would become increasingly difficult for luxury car makers.

Sir John had no doubts that luxury cars would have to become much more fuel efficient, with higher standards being set in the US, and these would have to be matched by engines that had much improved exhaust gas emissions operating, possibly, on alternative fuels. There was also a general tendency for governments to increase the tax on luxury products. Jaguar were as aware as anyone of the hazards of operating

James N. Randle, became director of engineering on the retirement of Robert Knight, and was responsible for the engineering of the new XJ6, and XJ220. He is now director of vehicle and concept engineering, and an insatiable amateur flyer.

with virtually only one model, but the cost of producing a new small Jaguar was now estimated at £500 million. In 1955 when the 2.4-litre Jaguar was produced, the first with an integral body, Sir William Lyons was horrified to learn that tooling for the new body would cost £1 million.

It has already been said that when Sir William left he bequeathed to his successors a production line he had bought second-hand, and factories that were suffering from a lack of investment. In the years that followed under the mantle of BLMC and then BL the profits made by Jaguar were funnelled to the volume car side which was considered to have the more urgent needs. Longbridge, the home of the Austin, had long been deprived of investment too, and for the first time in the late 1970s and early 1980s millions were spent bringing it up to date. Only in the 1980s was any sizeable investment made in Jaguar Cars, but these left a lot to be desired at a time when the rest of the motor industry was well into the age of robotics and other advanced manufacturing techniques.

In the opinion of Sir John the requirements to remain competitive were beyond the resources of a small company. 'I think we achieved all that flesh and blood was capable of achieving, and for a small number of years people did things which were far beyond what anyone could have expected of them'.

'In 1980 Jaguar was literally on the verge of closing down, but by a supreme effort we did show them that a little company could make its way', he adds. Flesh and blood saved the company from extinction, and in another era it might have been sufficient to propel it into a new lease of life, but to survive in the 1990s more than human spirit is required, for this is the age of mega-money and the corporate body; endless in its ramifications, and monstrous in its might. With plodding diligence these giant corporations have sucked every desirable minnow into their computerized corporate being.

Jaguar just happened to be the last.

# 24
# A Few Modifications

In the later years of the development of the new XJ6 it was considered that fuel consumption would be of paramount importance. This attitude gained weight when even the profligate US market had a temporary twinge of conscience, no doubt encouraged by the fact that gasoline had reached the alarming price of a dollar a gallon, and it was decided that the thirsty V12 had had its day. This attitude soon changed when it became known that both Mercedes-Benz and BMW were to produce multi-cylinder engines, and while the US officially encouraged economy, the enthusiasm of the car buyer waned somewhat as gasoline prices began to drop.

As we know the V12 engine would not fit into the new XJ6, so adherents to the big engine were offered it in the old XJ6 body, and a new modified body with all the mechanical changes necessary, was planned for 1992, though whether it will come to fruition remains to be seen. It was not the most economical arrangement having two production lines, and it was also untidy in that the V12 was unable to take advantage of the new gearboxes or the improved interior.

Despite several assurances that its demise was imminent, in some distant corner of Browns Lane production of the Limousine, using the old 4.2-litre engine, continued at least until the end of 1990, much

The most noticeable difference between the old and the new XJ6 is at the back end, which is illustrated in the Sovereign 3.6-litre.

A 3.6-litre Jaguar XJ6 with left-hand drive, somewhere in the German mountains.

The Daimler 3.6-litre with its distinctive headlamps and different wheel trims.

to the joy of up-market car hire companies, and undertakers in general.

In the meantime Jim Randle and his team were working on a replacement for the E-type which was codenamed the XJ41, and was envisaged as having either a coupe/targa, or convertible body, made partly of aluminium. A 4-litre AJ6 engine equipped with twin turbochargers was said to give 350bhp, 160mph (257kph), and a 0–100 mph (0–161kph) figure of 12 seconds. Three prototypes were built with four-wheel drive – essential for 350bhp – and a considerable amount of test work was done on the cars, but their gestation period was lengthy, again due to a shortage of cash, but Sir John told me: 'although they would not be class leaders in performance, they would be good looking enough to sell'.

When Ford took over in late 1989 their initial assessment was that they were too heavy, and would be too costly to make, and there was little enthusiasm to put them into production, but modified versions, so rumour has it, might eventually see the light of day. But the talents of Randle and his team were fermenting away, and one result was to burst into view at the 1988 International Motor Show at Birmingham, producing some of the greatest crowds ever seen around a Motor Show stand, but more of that later.

## More New Models

In April 1988 the most expensive Jaguar ever made was launched to the world's press – appropriately enough – in the South of France. It was the £36,000 Jaguar XJS V12 Convertible, equipped with a power-operated hood, with parts supplied by Happich of Germany assembled in Britain, and with the most sumptuous interior; all Connolly leather and walnut veneer. Although it has a top speed of 150mph (241kph), and handles extremely well its spiritual home is the Corniche, Florida or the fleshpots of California, where it should be seen, suitably adorned, purring from one exotic place to another. German Jochen Mass, who

The Jaguar XJ6 3.6-litre with the four-eyed look. Despite the 24-valve head the 3.6-litre did lack a little torque at the bottom end.

When Jaguar increased the engine size to 4-litres in the XJ6 in September 1989, the effortless acceleration associated with a Jaguar was back in place.

When the 4-litre car was introduced other modifications were made to the instrument layout, including a bigger speedometer and rev-counter. With electrically-operated seats this Daimler version has all the mod cons.

races for Mercedes-Benz, but lives in the South of France, was a recent customer, which says something for its elegance and performance, compared to the opposition. By 1990 the price had gone up to £41,200.

It was in the same year that JaguarSport Limited was formed, a joint venture company between Jaguar Cars and TWR. Following their successful co-operation in motor racing it seemed a natural development. Although its primary role was to manufacture vehicles with sporting connotations it also played, and still does, a key role in the development and application of 'leading edge' technology on behalf of Jaguar Cars. The added image they create for Jaguar is another bonus. The backbone of their production as they moved into the 1990s was the 4-litre XJR saloon, and the 6-litre XJRS coupe, both based on production cars, but transformed in their performance by sophisticated engine improvements, modified suspension and aerodynamic additions, but as we will see they have also gone in for the supercar business, something that appealed to the romantic in Sir John Egan.

## Show Stopper

Every show, whether it is a motor show or a musical needs a star, and Jaguar provided one at the 1988 Motor Show in Birmingham, that must have added considerably to the attendance figures. It was the XJ220, a truly remarkable two-seater coupe that was the personification of the accolade 'supercar'. Yet it had been built by Jim Randle and his team almost in their spare time, and they certainly worked like trojans in the run up to the show to get it there on time. When it was installed on the Jaguar stand it had not turned a wheel in anger. But the reception the car received must have made it all seem worthwhile to Randle and

In September 1990 the XJ6 3.2-litre Jaguar was introduced and the 2.9-litre was dropped. A sports pack, offering a stiffer suspension was an optional extra.

The dashboard layout of the XJ6 3.2-litre is very similar to the 4-litre, but the Getrag five-speed manual gearbox suits the characteristics of the 3.2-litre engine particularly well.

The engine compartment for the 3.2-litre unit.

Like the V12 Jaguar saloon the Daimler Double-Six retains the old body shape.

his team. For the exercise the engine was a four-valve version of the V12, of which Jaguar knew a great deal, mounted amidships, or thereabouts. It was increased to 6-litres, had four-wheel drive, and the calculated top speed was 220mph (354kph).

Some months later it was announced that a road-going version of the car was to be built by JaguarSport at a new factory in Banbury, to be powered by a modestly de-tuned turbocharged V6 engine which Silk Cut Jaguar had used in Group C racing, and those plans are going ahead on schedule, and the car should be launched in the spring of 1992. The price quoted when the car was announced was almost £300,000 but it will have gone up considerably by 1992. At the end of 1990 JaguarSport also announced another supercar, the XJR–15, but this was intended purely for racing. In November Tom Walkinshaw, and Bill Hayden, the new chairman of Jaguar Cars, announced a million-dollar Intercontinental Challenge, which would be competed for at three Grand Prix – Monaco, Silverstone and Spa – and would be open to the owners of thirty new XJR–15s, which would be theirs for the outlay of a modest £500,000. This small fortune, it must be said, covered the preparation of the cars, and their transport to the circuits. The offer was snapped up immediately, and TWR promised that a maximum of fifty cars would be built. When the Challenge was completed the owners would be able to race them as they wished, or even convert them for road use, but that, of course, was not the intention.

It made the pricing of the Convertible look positively cheap, but the new XJR–15 was, in the view of many, the most beautiful Jaguar ever made. It was based on project R9R; a concept car developed by JaguarSport as a means of testing the application of carbon composite materials and plastics in high-performance vehicles. Mechanically it was based on the 1988 Le Mans winning V12 powered XJR–9 racing car.

The XJR–15 was developed from these two vehicles; the 6-litre engine was de-tuned to give 450bhp, and driven through a six-speed gearbox, and according to gearing could provide a top speed of 185mph (297kph). Despite its neat appearance it weighed about 150kgs more than the pukka Group C racing version, but with the appropriate engine some private entrant might possibly enter an XJR–15 in Group C.

## New Venture

Since 1986 Jaguar had decided that they wanted their own body-making facilities, and several avenues were explored. It was decided that to build their own plant would be uneconomic, so they looked for a partner, and in 1988 it was announced that Jaguar PLC and GKN were to form a joint venture company, and invest £40 million in a plant to supply all major body pressings for the Jaguar range. The new company was called Venture Pressings, and a factory belonging to GKN at Telford in Shropshire was refurbished to do the job: a move which attracted little publicity, but which was of historic importance to the Coventry company. In November 1990 Venture Pressings started operations building body panels for the XJS, and in the following year they were eventually supplying all the body panels for the Coventry company.

For the first time since 1931 when William Lyons made his first SS1 motor car, the company was in charge of its own body-building facilities. For most of its life Jaguar Cars had been dependent on Pressed Steel for its bodies, and this was one of the reasons, it

Again, a rear view is appropriate for a Series III Daimler Double Six – I normally see them disappearing into the distance.

This is the Jaguar Sovereign with either the 3.2-litre or 4-litre engine equipped with the Sports Pack option.

will be recalled, why Sir William Lyons decided to join the British Motor Corporation. To be dependent on other people for body supplies can be a harrowing business, and once a company gets above a certain size it is also uneconomic, and inconvenient. To be in charge of your own body supplies brings practical self-sufficiency a major step nearer. It was a shrewd move by Sir John, and one which Sir William would have applauded, because he never managed it himself.

## Big is Best

Feedback from almost every quarter showed that while customers were not complaining outrageously about the performance of the 3.6-litre engine, there was that desire for more and smoother power at the bottom end, and in September 1989 the 4-litre AJ6 engine was introduced, along with a number of minor modifications to the dashboard.

Top speed increased modestly to 140mph (225kph), and the 0–60mph (0–96.5kph) time was reduced in the lighter XJ6 4-litre to 7.1 seconds, but again it was not the figures that really mattered, it was the way those figures were achieved, and the 4-litre returned to Jaguar the reputation for effortless performance for which it was renowned. In September 1989 the 4-litre cost £25,200, and the Sovereign version which had everything, cost £32,500. The 2.9-litre now cost £21,200.

In September 1990 the 2.9-litre engine was replaced by a much more powerful (200bhp) 24-valve, 3.2-litre catalyst only engine, which gave a considerable increase in performance over the previous model, accelerating from 0–60mph (0–96.5kph) in 8.5 seconds and reaching a maximum of 132mph (212kph). The new engine had very different characteristics from either the 4-litre or the one it superseded; it was more sporting, revved more freely, and literally begged to be driven hard. Maximum power was reached at 5,250rpm, and maximum torque at 4,000rpm. It was particularly suited to the five-speed manual gearbox, and would have appealed, in my view, to a younger owner than the 4-litre version. The weight of the new car was nearly 35½cwt, which appears to be standard for a modern Jaguar.

As if to emphasize that the company had the younger owner in mind with the 3.2-litre version, they also announced in September that they would be offering a sports handling pack, for all XJ6 saloons. The handling pack involved changes to the suspension to stiffen the ride, a bigger front anti-roll bar, changed damper settings, less assistance with the power steering, reduced ride height and 8in×16in forged alloy wheels, with low profile tyres.

These changes give the car a much tauter feel, more direct steering, and virtually rid the car of any body roll. The road-holding of the standard Jaguar is extremely good in my view, but there is a degree of body roll which can deter some drivers on twisting roads. With the sports handling pack it goes round corners like a Mini but it is a less relaxing car to drive.

Prices of the sports handling pack varied with each model and for the XJ6 cost £2,900; for the Sovereign £2,100 and for the Daimler £1,600.

The 1991 range included other changes with a new custom-designed audio unit offering compact disc, tape and radio facilities, plus the Radio Data System, four new exterior colours, while seating on the XJ6 models was changed from all-cloth, to a combination of cloth and leather.

With hindsight the 3.6-litre and 2.9-litre AJ6 engines were a mistake, but like many they were inspired by the best of intentions. The extra cost of producing the new engines came at a most unfortunate time, because in 1989 Jaguar lost money for the first time for ten years. A loss of £49 million was mainly attributable to the strength of the pound against the dollar. Although sales in the United States were slightly down on the previous year they were still very good, but the profit on those sales was down dramatically. Jaguar made strenuous efforts to increase sales elsewhere, but because the dollar remained weak against the pound, and the US was still their biggest export market by far, it was certain that 1990 would show another considerable loss.

The next few years were certainly going to be very difficult. Having survived the very real threat of closure, another herculean effort would be required to turn Jaguar into a genuinely twentieth-century company, and this onerous task was the responsibility of Bill Hayden.

# 25
# Ford and the Future

In their grand strategy the Ford Motor Company decided that they needed Jaguar Cars at least two years before they became the new owners in late 1989. Amazingly, the giant American manufacturers had been shaken by the vigour of the Japanese manufacturers' onslaught on their markets both at home and worldwide, and Ford, lacking a quality name, could see the potential of Jaguar in a battle with, initially, Nissan and Toyota in the luxury car market. Although it was a minnow in the world's motoring pool, it defied its size with a name that was instantly recognizable.

Its acquisition for a staggering £1.6 billion was a very long-term investment, but in the years to come it may be judged a very shrewd and cheap one.

The appointment of William J. Hayden as chief executive and then chairman, was indicative of where the Ford Motor Company assessed Jaguar's problems to be. Bill Hayden's principle qualifications are his achievements. In a demanding organization such as the Ford Motor Company they are formidable. Educated at Romford Technical College, he gained his initial business experience with stockbroking and insurance companies in London, and joined the Ford Motor Company aged twenty-one in 1950 in the Cost Accounting Department of Briggs Motor Bodies Ltd, at Dagenham.

His promotion was nothing short of meteoric, and gave him a wide knowledge and broad experience of financial affairs as a controller – and few companies keep a tighter control of financial affairs than the Ford Motor Company – before moving on to senior manufacturing management in 1966. Again his promotion was rapid. He started as an assistant manager, trans-

The XJS V12 Coupe before its face lift.

William J. Hayden became chairman and chief executive of Jaguar Cars in 1990, and as one of the top production engineers in the world has the job of turning Jaguar into a competitive unit. He spent forty years with the Ford Motor Company, and left as vice president manufacturing, Ford of Europe.

mission and chassis division, and before joining Jaguar had risen to be Vice President, Manufacturing group, Ford of Europe, and in the Ford pecking order in Europe you do not get much higher.

## The Immediate Task

As a man who is totally dedicated and has made enormous efforts in his life to reach his present position, he is not unnaturally a firm believer in those virtues. I recall him talking about the Ford Halewood plant on Merseyside, and remarking that if the workforce would only put half as much effort into building cars as they did into Liverpool Football Club it would be the finest motor manufacturing plant in the world.

Before Ford had taken over Jaguar he told me that they knew it was under-achieving compared to everyone else, and from a labour relations and trade union standpoint it was still operating in the 1960s. Investment had been poor, and what had been spent, had not been spent wisely. Also, the basic disciplines were lacking, something that clearly shocked his Ford-trained mind, and what was worse 'they had done nothing to tighten them up'. From his chairman's office he noticed one minor breach of the disciplines which he soon put right, and that was that the buses which took some of the workforce home were often full long before 4.30pm, the hour when manufacturing was supposed to stop.

As a more important example he points to the XJ41 sports car which he said was over weight, over cost, and very late. 'It was never going to achieve the objects set for it, and it had been in that situation for three years', he says. Getting things right was not simply a question of throwing money at the problem, as had been suggested, indeed no decisions had been taken on further investment – Bill Hayden came round to his favourite theme, that it was dedication, and not necessarily money that was going to solve their immediate problems.

The wages and working arrangements agreed with the unions had been a quantum leap forward, and should produce the efficiency they wanted, but it had to hold, and if they were going to compete with the Japanese – and that was what it was all about – everything they did they had to do well, because for the moment they could not compete with them technically.

He was clearly concerned that manufacturing standards and quality had to improve. They had, he said, some beautiful cars, but everyone had to do their job as competently as they could; the execution had to be beyond reproach, and this was a problem they had to address. It was of the utmost importance that customers had complete confidence in their present range of cars before the company moved on to anything new, and that was his first priority.

## Staying On

The Jaguar factory facilities at Browns Lane and

The 'Lyon's line' is still very evident in the Daimler 4-litre, and is shown off to good effect against the background of Eastnor Castle.

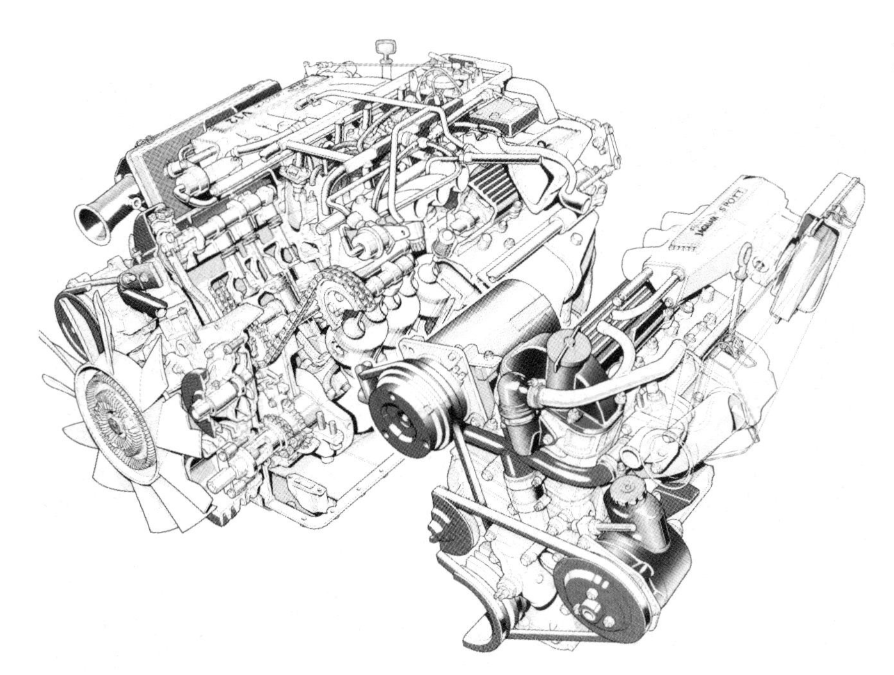

An exploded view of the XJR–S 6-litre engine, which is still incredibly quiet.

The three models in the 3.2-litre range, the Sovereign to the left, the XJ6 on the right and behind them the 3.2-litre Sport.

Radford were capable of producing 150,000 cars a year, of this he had no doubts, and with the hard-nosed approach of a manufacturing man he points out that if it is not producing the number of cars it is capable of producing it is not efficient. They could survive in their present location for the next ten years, but they had to make it viable – otherwise it was back to the drawing board, with all the horrors that would entail.

The engineering department had grown considerably but because of the lack of discipline it had not been giving value for money, and that had to change – he was confident that it would. They also had the benefit of the resources of the Ford Motor Company whose spending on research and development was more than the revenue of Jaguar. Ford was also their banker – very tough bankers he was quick to point out – but a comfort to have behind you.

This would all help in their future programmes, and for the tackling of such problems as emission controls and improved fuel consumption: 'We can dip into their knowledge'. The Ford Motor Company, as one of the big players in the motor manufacturing business, enjoys a considerable amount of clout with suppliers – there are 500 major ones at Jaguar – a privilege denied to Jaguar when it was a small independent manufacturer. When I spoke to Bill Hayden he was not to be drawn on their future model programme, although he agreed that a smaller Jaguar would be, as he put it, 'great'.

## The Future

Speaking at the end of 1990, Bill Hayden stressed that they were 'having a very rough time at the moment',

The XJR–15s had their own series to compete in this year, but they would not be competitive in Group C without a lot more power. They could be turned into a road car.

Tom Walkinshaw is building a limited number of these XJR–15 super cars, powered by a V12 unit mounted behind the driver.

and there were no early prospects of a dramatic improvement and, although he made no mention of it, a second consecutive loss was inevitable. But Hayden was optimistic about the future. 'If you are in the motor industry, particularly at a time like this you have got to be', he observed with a wry smile. It was going to require a lot of hard work on the part of everyone, but as a man who had tackled major problems before, he was confident they would make it.

Saloon bar chat about a Ford-Jaguar are, of course, nonsense. Ford have not spent a fortune, and geared themselves to this considerable enterprise simply to build another Ford; they realize as clearly as anyone that the special qualities of Jaguar – quietness, driving pleasure and distinctive lines – must be maintained. John Grant, another former Ford man who is now deputy chairman, told me that they must also achieve that other memorable feature of Jaguar – outstanding value for money.

However, the next four or five years are going to be difficult, and a lot of tough decisions will have to be made. A face-lifted XJS was announced in the spring of 1991 which should extend the life of the model which very nearly died more than ten years ago. The next major priority will be a replacement for the XJ6, which is likely to be produced in the middle of the decade. This model is the backbone of their range, and on it depends the success of the company. Then a new 'small' Jaguar saloon, and a sports car should appear, with a new range of engines.

The new engine range being contemplated is a V6, V8 and V12. These are, of course, some way off, but essential if Jaguar is to compete technically with the opposition, which has always been good, but is becoming more formidable with every year.

Sir John Egan was pleased that the Ford Motor Company became the new owners of Jaguar, and I have a feeling that Sir William Lyons who started it all in 1922 would have been pleased too. They know they have bought a beautiful motor car, and a very special place in motoring history. I do not believe they are going to ride roughshod over the old regime, and with their massive knowledge of manufacturing techniques, and vast technical resources, they will harness the innate knowledge and experience that exists in Browns Lane and Radford, and produce some magnificent successors to a glorious range of Jaguars. I wish them well.

# Index

Page numbers in *italics* refer to illustrations.